AMERICA LOVES COOKIES!

And you're going to love each and every one of these 460 delicious, time-tested cookie delights ranging from simple, old-time favorites, like sugar cookies and Frosted Ginger Creams, to stunning party creations like Jeweled Meringues.

With special sections on foolproof hints for making great cookies, how to pack cookies for mailing to family and friends, and recipes for every type of cookie, here is a cookbook to delight cookie-loving kids of all ages.

**FARM JOURNAL'S
HOMEMADE COOKIES**
The Food Editors of *Farm Journal*
Edited by Nell B. Nichols

Also by Farm Journal
Published by Ballantine Books:

FARM JOURNAL'S COUNTRY COOKBOOK

FARM JOURNAL'S COMPLETE PIE COOKBOOK

By the
Food Editors of <u>Farm</u> <u>Journal</u>

HOMEMADE COOKIES

Edited by Nell B. Nichols
<u>*Farm Journal*</u> *Field Food Editor*

BALLANTINE BOOKS • NEW YORK

Library of Congress Catalog Card Number: 79-15791

ISBN 0-345-29783-0

This edition published by arrangement with Doubleday & Co., Inc.

Manufactured in the United States of America

First Ballantine Books Edition: December 1981

Contents

Choice Homemade Cookies
from Countryside America

GOLDEN BROWN cookies, warm and fragrant from the oven—could anything taste better? And what arouses greater enthusiasm—watch the children head for the cookie jar when they return home from school. Notice how your husband lingers in the kitchen if the spicy aroma of cookies, spread on cooling racks, greets him. Doesn't he take seconds—and sometimes thirds?

Don't you yourself recall your mother's wonderful date bars or whatever was her specialty? Maybe your own son, as a serviceman, appreciated your boxes of cookies . . . "love from home." Eating homemade cookies is happiness that builds memories to treasure.

This cookbook contains superior recipes representing all types of cookies; among them are sure to be some you associate with your childhood. We include the best cookies published in FARM JOURNAL through the past twenty years—many of them from country kitchens. But we also feature original Test Kitchen recipes that never before appeared in print.

First in this book you will find recipes for the Big Six traditional cookies—bar, drop, rolled, refrigerator, molded and pressed cookies. The way you handle the dough determines the family to which a cookie belongs —whether you bake it in a pan and cut the cookies with a knife; whether you shape it into rolls and refrigerate them to bake later; roll the dough out thin and use a cutter to form shapes; drop it from a spoon right onto the baking sheet; shape it into balls with your hands; or squirt it from a cookie press.

Newest among the traditionals are the refrigerator

cookies, known as icebox cookies before electric refrigerators became commonplace. These are special for women who want to bake thin, crisp cookies without bothering with rolling pin and cookie cutters. It's so much easier, they insist, just to slice dough and bake it.

When Europeans came to America from overseas to establish homes in a new world, the women brought along their treasured cookie recipes, sometimes written down, sometimes memorized. We include some of these old-time specialties, adapting them to the ingredients and appliances and tools we have and to flavors we like. Some of these first colonists made room in their crowded baggage for sandbakelser molds and hand-carved springerle boards or rolling pins. Those who could not bring either the board or rolling pin to use for making these picture cookies improvised by pressing butter molds or glass dishes with cut designs on the rolled cookie dough. You will find in this book up-to-date recipes for Sandbakelser and Springerle and other cookies that originated in many lands. Italy, for example, produced Florentines—rich, melt-in-the mouth, chocolate-covered cookies flavored with candied orange peel and almonds.

Americans made their own cookie discoveries. Chocolate chip cookies are the classic example. Developed by a Massachusetts home economist who cut up chocolate and added it to her cookie dough when she found her raisin box empty, the cookies caught on at once and skyrocketed to popularity across the country. This book offers you a variety of recipes for this kind of cookie. Try our Cape Cod Chocolate Chip Cookies (molded), Soft Chocolate Chippers (drop) and Chocolate Chip Bars to see which kind you and your family like best.

Cry Baby Cookies, molasses-flavored drop cookies that contain such good things as coconut, nuts, raisins, rate tops with navy men. The first recipes for these cookies are believed to have evolved in kitchens of Maryland's Eastern Shore. Bake them when you want a big batch of cookies to please men. The recipe makes about 9½ dozen cookies, but you can freeze part of the dough to bake later if you like.

Jumbo Sugar Cookies are another all-American

treat. The sugar-cinnamon top scents the kitchen delightfully while they bake. One of our home economists who tested this recipe baked a batch and took them to a P.T.A. food sale. They sold fast at 10¢ each! These big cookies are first cousins of Snickerdoodles, an early American, but you handle the dough differently and the ingredients vary somewhat. You'll find recipes for both in our book.

Meringue cookies, or kisses, have been special-occasion treats for generations, the favorite way to use leftover egg whites that accumulated in kitchens where lots of baking was done. You'll be surprised how many appetizing ways this cookbook gives for flavoring meringue cookies and making them distinctive.

Many of our native cookies, once enjoyed, disappeared along with the special need for them. Boom Cookies are an example. They were giant size—about 5″ in diameter—molasses/coffee-flavored cookies, which hungry lumberjacks joyfully ate at the Boom in Minnesota, a sorting station when logs were floated down the St. Croix River. Gone is the cook shack, the circumstance and the cookies, but our Soft Molasses Cookies in smaller sizes have the same taste provided by molasses, spices and instant coffee powder. It is one recipe of many in this cookbook for molasses cookies.

Christmas and cookies go together, although every season has its cookies. Certainly women bake more cookies for the holidays than at any other time. One reason is the visiting that goes on around the country-side during Yuletide. The traditional refreshments for open houses consist of Christmas cookies with coffee, wine or a fruit drink. In the Bethlehem, Pennsylvania, area, this visiting is called "putzing." It's when a family welcomes neighbors and friends who come to see their crèche under the Christmas tree. The "putz" is the crèche and the name comes from *putzen,* which to Germans means to decorate.

There are many reasons for Christmas cookies other than sharing the treats with visiting friends. They make ideal gifts from the home kitchen to neighbors, shut-ins, business associates and other friends. There also are gift boxes to mail, children home from school eager to feast on Mother's cookies. Cookies are an important

3

part, too, of refreshments served at parties given by clubs and organizations. And in many homes, Christmas cookies help decorate the gala tree.

Cookies such as White Christmas and brown Spiced Christmas Cookies and Pepper Nuts—the kind grandmothers of Swiss and German descent used to keep in their apron pockets to reward grandchildren for good behavior—still are baked at Christmastime (see Index for the recipes). We give suggestions for decorating these and many other cookies, though all are good plain also. It's the opinion of women who contributed their choice recipes, that the trims justify what they cost in time and effort.

You'll observe recipes in this book that call for frostings, white and tinted to top or coat the cookies and sometimes to put them together in pairs for sandwiches. This dress-up helps both their appearance and disappearance!

You'll find many recipes that call for fillings. In fact, all of the traditional cookie types lend themselves to fillings. One of the favorite types is the bar cookie in which the filling bakes between two layers of dough, sometimes in a jelly roll pan. Some women lament that cookies go so fast, even though they want them to appeal and please. Mothers sometimes have to hide cookies to save them for serving at some special occasion. One mother stores some of her cookies in empty rolled oat boxes because the children never think of looking there for cookies.

To make cookie baking pleasant and memorable, enlist the help of the family, especially with Christmas cookies. You may prefer to bake the cookies and let the children help decorate them—gingerbread boys and animals for Christmas, for instance. Or dream up your own ways to stimulate their interest. We give recipes for making farmyard cookie animals (see Cocoa Cookie Barn), a cookie family, as well as recipe, patterns and directions for making a Christmas gingerbread church. This makes a great Christmas centerpiece and the children will love to help.

In fact, we have included a special section for junior cooks with cookie recipes in their language and with extra how-to detail.

Important as traditional cookies are in our collection, we include many other newer types. Cookie confections have many loyal boosters. These are the easy-to-make cookies that children like to fix for their friends, and also to eat. But homemakers as well like to make cookies that are little work and taste really good. Some of them are no-bake cookies, and several of them require brief *cooking* in a saucepan!

Cookie confections are close kin to candies. You often make them with ready-to-eat cereals or with rolled oats, crackers or vanilla wafers substituting for flour. Many ingredient goodies contribute to their popularity—raisins, marshmallows, chocolate pieces, coconut, nuts.

One of our new cookie triumphs is what we call the pie-bar dessert cookie. It's a cross between a bar cookie and a piece of pie. These luscious cookies that taste like pie salve the calorie-counter's conscience.

Since many women today must stretch time, this book offers quick ways to speedily glamorize packaged store cookies you can keep in your cupboard. The recipes show you how to add homemade touches to cookies you buy.

Today's appliances have speeded up and simplified cookie making. The electric mixer can be used to mix all or part of the dough (see "How to Bake Good Cookies Every Time"). It especially excels for quickly and easily creaming the fat and sugar until light and fluffy, and for thoroughly blending in the eggs and flavoring. The freezer enables women to keep baked cookies or the dough for baking cookies on hand for months.

Most of the recipes in this cookbook are for use in homes located in areas with an altitude under 5,000 feet. But because families living in the mountain states also like homemade cookies, we include the Colorado Basic Cookie Mix for high altitude baking. The basic mix can be used for a wide variety of excellent cookies.

We also give you the recipes for two other popular basic mixes (for altitudes under 5,000 feet): Cookie Starter and Eight-in-One Sugar Cookies. And you'll find many excellent basic recipes with several variations.

For your convenience, we have selected and listed

5

for you cookies appropriate for mailing; to serve at women's luncheon and tea parties; to sell at bazaars; to pack in lunchboxes; to offer at coffee parties; for children to bake; we also list cookies of foreign origin and Christmas specialities.

No one knows where cookies originated, but their name comes from the Dutch word *koekje,* which gets a mention in this old, anonymous American jingle:

> "The British call it biscuit
> And it's *koekje* to the Dutch
> But no matter what you call it
> All cookies please us much."

How to Bake Good Cookies Every Time

YOU WILL bake wonderful cookies with the recipes in this cookbook if you follow them carefully. To assure you the greatest satisfaction with your results, we pass on some of the points we watch in our Test Kitchens.

COOKIE INGREDIENTS

Flour—Use all-purpose flour in our recipes unless otherwise specified. If a recipe calls for sifted flour, spoon it lightly into measuring cup and level off with straight edge of knife or spatula. Some busy women skip the sifting (we don't recommend) and instead stir the flour in the canister or other container to incorporate air. If you then spoon it lightly into measuring cup and level it, you sometimes get approximately the same amount as in sifting, but *often you get a little more*. Avoid tapping the cup filled with flour; this packs it.

Fats—The fats called for in this book are butter, regular margarine (in sticks), lard, shortening (it comes in 1- to 3-lb. cans) and salad oil (vegetable). Soft, tub-type margarines are whipped and so contain air and less fat than regular margarine. Use the fat the recipe calls for with one exception: You can substitute shortening for half of the butter listed. For instance, instead of using 1 c. butter, you can use ½ c. each of butter and of shortening.

Many women prefer to use butter in refrigerator cookies because it gets very hard when chilled; the dough slices neatly and evenly. Regular margarine also gives satisfactory results if you freeze the dough or chill it until very cold before slicing.

Pack solid fats firmly in measuring cup and level off. Bring them to room temperature before you start to combine and mix ingredients.

Sugar—Use granulated white sugar (cane or beet) unless otherwise specified. When a recipe calls for brown sugar, use light brown unless dark is designated. Superfine sugar is very fine granulated sugar. Confectioners sugar (called powdered sugar in many areas) should be free of lumps before measuring. Some recipes call for sifted confectioners sugar.

Molasses—Use light molasses unless recipe calls for the dark. You can use either type, but the dark has deeper color and stronger flavor. The light comes from the first boiling of sugar cane, the dark from the second boiling.

Eggs—Recipes in this cookbook were tested with medium to large eggs. If you have small eggs, break two of them into a ¼-cup measure. A medium egg measures about ¼ cup. You can measure the correct amount for the recipe you are using. Since eggs are often the only liquid in cookies, the size used affects the results.

Milk and Cream—When your recipe calls for sweetened condensed milk, read the label on the can to make sure that's what you have. Evaporated milk and sweetened condensed milk both come in cans; they *cannot* be used interchangeably. Recipes calling for buttermilk were tested with commercial cultured type. You can substitute evaporated milk for fresh milk if you mix it with an equal amount of water. A few recipes list packaged instant dry milk powder as an ingredient.

In case you do not have sour milk, measure 1 tsp. vinegar or fresh lemon juice into a ¼-cup measure. Fill with milk and let stand several minutes; then stir and use. (For 1 c. sour milk, use 1 tblsp. vinegar or fresh lemon juice in a 1-cup measure.)

Cream in the recipes is either heavy or whipping (30 to 35% butterfat), coffee or light (18 to 20% butterfat), dairy half-and-half (10 to 12% butterfat) or dairy sour (commercial with 20% butterfat). Do not substitute one kind for another. Our recipes use commercial dairy sour cream.

Chocolate—Recipes in this book may call for one of four kinds of chocolate: unsweetened, semisweet, sweet cooking and no-melt unsweetened chocolate in envelopes. Use the designated type. You can substitute unsweetened chocolate squares for no-melt chocolate when recipe directs it may be done. Melt the squares in a heavy bowl set in a pan of hot, not boiling water, or put the chocolate in the top of a double boiler over hot water. You also can melt it in a small pan over very low heat, stirring constantly, but do watch closely, for chocolate scorches easily. Cool melted chocolate before adding it to other ingredients. Many recipes use chocolate pieces: semisweet, semisweet mint-flavored chocolate and milk chocolate—all have different flavors. Women quite commonly refer to these chocolate pieces as chocolate chips.

If you do not have unsweetened chocolate when ready to bake cookies, you can use 3 tblsp. unsweetened cocoa and 1 tblsp. butter for 1 square unsweetened chocolate. When a recipe calls for cocoa, use the unsweetened.

Peanut Butter—Unless a recipe designates crunchy peanut butter, we used smooth peanut butter in testing.

Rolled Oats—Use either the quick-cooking or regular kind as specified.

Raisins—Seedless raisins, from grapes without seeds, are designated in most recipes, although a few call for seeded raisins, from grapes with seeds that are removed, as the first choice.

Food Color—There are two kinds, liquid and paste. You can use the type you prefer. We found in our testing that the paste gives especially vivid colors, but use it sparingly. Liquid food colors are more widely available. Add them drop by drop until you get the shade you desire. It is easy to mix these colors. For instance, 3 drops of red and 2 of yellow food color make orange.

Decorating Sugars and Candies—Packaged coarse sugar in glistening white and many colors is widely available. Among the other favored cookie decorations are silver, gold and colored dragées, tiny candies of one or many colors and chocolate shot (jimmies).

9

Nuts—Store nuts in refrigerator or freezer if they are to be kept several days or weeks before use. To chop nuts, spread on wooden board. Hold top of sharp knife close to surface of board with one hand, then move knife handle up and down, and around in a semicircle with other hand so blade contacts uncut nuts. Nut choppers do a good job, too, and so does the electric blender. Chop nuts very fine if recipe calls for grated nuts, or put them through food chopper or chop in blender. When a recipe lists ½ c. nuts (or other measurement), we usually used pecans or walnuts.

UTENSILS AND TOOLS

The tools and utensils you use can simplify cookie baking and contribute to good results. It is especially important to use the pan sizes designated in recipes. Here are the utensils and tools that were especially helpful to some economists perfecting these cookie recipes in our Test Kitchens:

Graduated measuring cups
Measuring cups for liquid
Mixing bowls
Electric mixer (portable or stationary)
Wooden spoon
Small spatula for spreading frosting
Measuring spoons
Double boiler
Rolling pin
Stockinet cover for rolling pin
Pastry cloth
Cookie cutters
Baking sheets—two or more, at least 2″ shorter and narrower than the oven. Shiny baking sheets are best for delicate browning. If you have only one baking sheet, use an inverted baking pan for a second one. Or cut heavy-duty aluminum foil to fit your baking sheet. Arrange cookie dough on it while one batch bakes. When the cookies are done, remove them and transfer the foil with the cookies for baking to the hot baking sheet. Put in the oven at once.
Baking pans of standard sizes—8 and 9″ square, 13 × 9 × 2″ and 15½ × 10½ × 1″ jelly roll pan

Broad spatula for removing cookies from baking sheets
Wire cooling racks
Timer
Cookie press

MIXING COOKIES THE RIGHT WAY

Every recipe in this cookbook gives precise directions for mixing the dough, but here are a few general pointers:
Bring ingredients to room temperature before you combine and mix them. This is especially important with solid fats.
Use the electric mixer at medium speed for creaming fats (beating them until light), for creaming together fats and sugar and to blend in eggs and flavorings. You can beat these foods until light and fluffy by hand with a wooden spoon, but we used the electric mixer extensively in testing recipes. Either add the dry ingredients with the electric mixer at low speed, or mix them in with a wooden spoon.
If the cookie dough seems too soft, chill it an hour longer. As it becomes firm enough to handle easily, work with a small amount at a time, leaving the remainder in the refrigerator until you are ready for it. If the dough still seems too soft after chilling, bake a test cookie. If it spreads too much, work 1 to 2 tblsp. flour into the dough.

Here are some of the reasons why your cookie dough is sometimes a trifle too soft: skimpy flour measurement; flour stored in humid place; too generous fat measurement; melted or very soft fat instead of fat at room temperature; large eggs instead of medium size; mixing dough in a very warm kitchen.
When the dough seems too dry, bake a test cookie. If it is dry and crumbly, work 1 to 2 tblsp. soft butter or cream into dough with your hands.

Here are some of the reasons why cookie dough sometimes is a trifle too dry: flour stored in place with low humidity; too generous flour measurement; skimpy fat measurement; soft tub-type margarine instead of regular kind; skimpy liquid measurement; cold fat,

11

such as butter taken directly from refrigerator; small eggs instead of medium size.

Flour has remarkable ability to absorb moisture from the air and to release moisture when stored in a dry place. There is a slight variation in the amount of moisture, due to atmospheric conditions, it can take up in a recipe.

COOKIE BAKING POINTERS

Be sure to heat oven to the correct temperature before putting cookies in to bake. When you bake one batch at a time, place baking sheet on rack in center of oven. If baking two batches at the same time, divide the oven into thirds with racks. Use cool baking sheets for all bakings; cookies spread too much on warm sheets.

Notice whether the recipe calls for a greased baking sheet. If it does, rub the surface lightly with unsalted fat, such as shortening. Some doughs are rich enough that cookies will not stick to ungreased baking sheets and pans. (Ungreased sheets or pans are easier to wash.)

Check cookies for doneness at end of the shortest baking time given in the recipe. When only one baking time is given, test 2 minutes before it ends. Try to avoid overbaking—it makes cookies dry. (Tests for doneness for the different cookie types are given with the recipes.)

Use a timer.

Remove cookies from baking sheet with wide spatula at once, unless recipe specifies otherwise. When left on baking sheet even a few minutes, they continue to cook. Some recipes direct leaving cookies on baking sheet briefly before removing them. These cookies are fragile and easily broken when hot.

Spread cookies in a single layer on cooling racks. When cooling bar cookies in pan, set it on rack. You cut most bar cookies when cool or at least partly cool. Use a sharp knife.

When a frosting appears with a recipe, it makes enough to frost that amount of cookies unless noted otherwise. So when using the frosting for another cookie, use your judgment about whether it will be enough, too much, or whether you'll have to double the recipe.

HOW TO STORE COOKIES

Once your cookies are baked and thoroughly cooled, store them correctly and in a cool place if possible. This helps them to retain appetizing freshness. Here's the way to do it:

Crisp Cookies—Store in container with loose-fitting lid. If they soften despite your care, spread them on a baking sheet before serving and heat them 3 to 5 minutes in a slow oven (300°).

Soft Cookies—Store them in a container with a tight-fitting lid. If they seem to dry out, add a piece of apple, orange or bread, but replace fruit or bread frequently. You can freshen soft cookies. Before serving, put them in a casserole, cover and heat 8 to 10 minutes in a slow oven (300°).

Bar Cookies—It often is convenient to store them in the pan in which they baked. Lay a piece of plastic wrap over top of cookies; then cover pan with its lid or with foil.

HOW TO FREEZE COOKIES
AND COOKIE DOUGH

You can freeze either baked cookies or cookie dough for 9 months to a year. Space in the freezer may determine whether you freeze them baked or unbaked in dough form. Frozen dough frequently takes up less space than baked cookies. Since frosted cookies freeze less satisfactorily than unfrosted, most women prefer to add the frosting shortly before serving them. This gives them a fresh taste. Here's the way to freeze cookies and cookie dough:

Baked Cookies—Layer thoroughly cooled cookies in a rigid container, such as a sturdy box, lined with plastic wrap or aluminum foil. Separate the layers and top with plastic wrap, which clings to them and keeps out the air, or with aluminum foil in which you can seal cookies. Seal foil lining and top covering. Close box, label and freeze. Let cookies thaw unwrapped in package 10 to 15 minutes before serving.

Cookie Dough—Put dough for *drop* cookies in frozen food containers and cover tightly. Or wrap in plastic wrap sealed with freezer tape, or in aluminum foil. Place the wrapped dough, when frozen, in a plastic bag. When ready to bake, thaw dough just enough so that you can drop it from a spoon.

Pack and freeze *molded* cookie dough like drop cookie dough. When ready to bake, thaw dough just enough so that you can shape it.

Arrange cutout dough for *rolled* cookies in layers in a sturdy box lined with plastic wrap or aluminum foil. Separate layers with plastic wrap or with foil you can seal as for drop cookies. Cover tightly, seal and label. Or spread cookie cutouts on a baking sheet and freeze; then package in the same way. The frozen cutouts are rigid and easier to pack. Put frozen cutouts on baking sheet and bake; no need to thaw.

Shape *refrigerator* cookie dough in rolls of the desired size, wrap tightly in plastic wrap and seal ends with tape, or wrap in aluminum foil. When ready to bake remove from freezer, let thaw just enough so that you can slice the rolls with a sharp knife. You can thaw them in refrigerator for 1 hour and slice.

Freeze dough for *bar* cookies in the pan in which you will bake it. Cover dough with plastic wrap, then with pan lid or foil.

How to Pack Cookies
for Mailing

ONCE YOU'VE baked and cooled good cookies, you may get the desire to share some of them with members of your family who are away from home or with friends who live too far away for you to take your prizes to them. You can mail them successfully. No homemade gift travels more extensively than cookies. And no food tastes better to the recipient. If you want your cookies to reach their destination in tiptop condition, follow these rules, which we have tested:

Choose the right cookie for mailing (see Index for suggestions). Soft drop, bar and fruit cookies travel well, while thin, crisp cookies (refrigerator and rolled types) are likely to crumble.

Select a strong packing box; a pasteboard box is not strong enough. Line the box with plastic wrap or aluminum foil.

Have plenty of filler on hand to use between layers of wrapped cookies. You can use shredded or crushed tissue paper, waxed paper or aluminum foil. Popped corn sometimes is used, but occasionally it molds, especially in overseas shipments.

Wrap each cookie separately, or two cookies, back to back, in plastic wrap; fasten with tape.

Place a layer of filler on bottom of box for a cushion. Arrange wrapped cookies close together in neat rows to fill box with some of the filler between each layer. If sending more than one kind of cookie, put the heaviest ones in the bottom of the box.

Spread layer of filler on top. Then lay folded paper

napkins or towels on top. Enclose your gift card. Close the box. It should be so full that you have to exert light pressure to close it. Tape box shut. (It's a good idea to write on top the name and address of the person to whom you are mailing the cookies.)

Wrap box with heavy wrapping paper and tie securely. Stick on the clearly addressed label.

Mark the box "FRAGILE—HANDLE WITH CARE," and "PERISHABLE." If you are sending the package overseas, send it by air parcel post if you can.

Bar Cookies

BROWNIES, RICH, moist and fudge-like, top the list of bar cookies. But there are many wonderful-tasting competitors, for the bar cookie family is large. All the cookies you make by spreading dough in a pan and cutting it, after baking, into bars, squares, diamonds and other shapes are generally called "bar cookies."

When women across country send us their favorite cookie recipes, the brownie contributions come in great numbers. Some of them appear on the following pages. They may sound alike but each is different. Try them and find out which you, your family and friends like best—Candy-Top Brownies that make you think they're baked fudge, less sweet California Chocolate Brownies so luscious when topped with whipped cream peaks and frozen, Brownies for a Crowd baked in a jelly roll pan, handsome Two-Tone Brownies and other varieties.

Compare them with the other bars you make from recipes in this section—elegant Cheesecake Squares that melt in the mouth; gently spiced Chocolate/Orange Bars; English Tea Squares with strawberry jam filling. The homemaker who shares the recipe for the Tea Squares says: "They're simply divine, especially when faintly warm."

Bar cookies are so versatile because you can custom-cut them. The size depends mainly on whom you are cutting them for. So consider the sizes indicated in our recipes as suggestions.

Naturally, you want smaller, daintier cookies to serve at a women's party than to pack in a lunchbox or tote to the field to refresh men at work.

Some of our bar cookies can be served for dessert —Frosted Carrot Bars, for instance (cut them somewhat larger than usual). They taste so good that no one will dream the humble vegetable is an ingredient.

Bar cookies make good snacks for people of all ages. Plantation Peanut Cookies or Chocolate Chip Bars will generate special enthusiasm among teen-agers.

Bars are the easiest cookies to bake. You skip rolling, cutting, dropping or shaping the dough and there's only one batch to put in and take from the oven.

Do cut the bars when the cookie is slightly warm or completely cooled unless the recipe designates otherwise. If cut when hot, some bars crumble. Here are other pointers:

Avoid overmixing the dough—makes cookie tops hard. Overmixing the dough will result in a tough textured cookie.

Spread the dough evenly in the pan so all the bars will have the same thickness and texture (some areas in the pan may overbake if spread thinly).

Use the pan size the recipe indicates. If larger, the dough will be thin and unless you reduce the baking time, the cookie will be dry and tough; if smaller, the dough will be thick and may require a longer baking time.

Bake cookies only until they are done. Overbaked cookies are hard and dry; if underdone, doughy. Use the time given in the recipe as a guide for doneness, but also apply the standard tests. Cookies are done if when pressed lightly with a finger, they retain a slight imprint; a toothpick inserted in the center of cake-like bars comes out clean.

BROWNIES FOR A CROWD

Save time—bake cookies in one big pan; they're moist and keep well

½ c. regular margarine	¼ tsp. salt
1 c. sugar	½ c. chopped walnuts
4 eggs	6 tblsp. regular margarine
1 tsp. vanilla	6 tblsp. milk
1 (1 lb.) can chocolate syrup (1½ c.)	1 c. sugar
1 c. plus 1 tblsp. sifted flour	½ c. semisweet chocolate pieces
½ tsp. baking powder	1 tsp. vanilla

Beat ½ c. margarine with 1 c. sugar until light and fluffy. Beat in eggs, two at a time, and 1 tsp. vanilla. Mix well. Stir in chocolate syrup.

Sift together flour, baking powder and salt. Stir into chocolate mixture. Add nuts. Pour into well-greased 15½ × 10½ × 1″ jelly roll pan and spread evenly.

Bake in moderate oven (350°) 22 to 25 minutes, or until slight imprint remains when touched lightly with finger. Remove pan to rack, and let cookies cool.

Meanwhile, combine 6 tblsp. margarine, milk and 1 c. sugar in saucepan; stir to mix. Bring to a boil and boil 30 seconds. Add chocolate pieces; stir until mixture thickens slightly and cools. Stir in 1 tsp. vanilla. Spread over cooled cookies, then cut in 2½ × 1″ bars. Makes 5 dozen.

CANDY-TOP BROWNIES

These candy-like cookies win compliments; they're good travelers

2 c. sugar	2 tsp. vanilla
2 eggs	½ c. chopped walnuts
4 squares unsweetened chocolate	1 egg, beaten
½ c. butter or regular margarine	2 tblsp. light cream
½ c. flour	2 tblsp. butter or regular margarine

Combine 1 c. sugar and 2 eggs; beat.

Melt 2 squares chocolate with ½ c. butter; add to egg mixture. Blend in flour, 1 tsp. vanilla and nuts. Spread in greased 8″ square pan.

Bake in moderate oven (350°) 25 to 35 minutes; cool on rack.

Combine remaining 1 c. sugar, beaten egg, cream, 2 squares chocolate, 2 tblsp. butter and 1 tsp. vanilla. Bring to a boil, stirring constantly. Remove from heat and stir until of spreading consistency. Spread over cooled brownies. Cut in 2″ squares. Makes 16.

CALIFORNIA CHOCOLATE BROWNIES

These are less sweet than most brownies so you may want to frost them or sprinkle on confectioners sugar ... they're good keepers

½ c. shortening	¾ c. sifted cake flour
1 c. light corn syrup	¼ tsp. baking powder
2 squares unsweetened chocolate, melted	¼ tsp. salt
	¾ c. chopped nuts
2 eggs, well beaten	Vanilla Cream Icing
½ tsp. vanilla	(see Index)

Cream shortening until fluffy. Gradually beat in corn syrup until thoroughly mixed and light and fluffy. Stir in melted chocolate. Add eggs and vanilla.

Sift together cake flour, baking powder and salt. Add ¼ c. at a time to creamed mixture. Fold in nuts. Pour into well-greased 8″ square pan.

Bake in moderate oven (350°) 30 to 35 minutes, or until slight imprint remains when touched lightly with finger. Set pan on rack to cool completely. Then frost with Vanilla Cream Icing, if desired. Cut in 2″ squares. Makes 16.

VARIATIONS

Brownies Made with Cocoa: Omit unsweetened chocolate. Sift 6 tblsp. cocoa with flour. Add 2 tblsp. additional shortening.

Snow Peaked Brownies: When brownies in pan are cool, cut in squares. Do not frost. Remove brownies, one at a time, to baking sheet covered with waxed paper. Beat ½ c. heavy cream until it peaks when beater is removed. Beat in 2 tblsp. sugar and ½ tsp. vanilla. Top each brownie with a teaspoonful of whipped cream, forming a peak. Freeze. When frozen, place in plastic bag and return to freezer. Will keep in good condition up to 3 months.

COTTAGE CHEESE BROWNIES

Two chocolate layers with luscious cheese filling between

3 squares unsweetened chocolate	3 eggs
½ c. butter	½ tsp. lemon juice
1¼ c. sugar	½ c. unsifted flour
1½ tsp. vanilla	½ tsp. baking powder
1 tblsp. cornstarch	¼ tsp. salt
¾ c. creamed cottage cheese	½ c. chopped walnuts
	½ tsp. almond extract

Melt chocolate and 6 tblsp. butter over hot water.

Cream remaining 2 tblsp. butter, ¼ c. sugar and ½ tsp. vanilla. Add cornstarch, cottage cheese, 1 egg and lemon juice; beat until smooth. Set aside.

Beat remaining 2 eggs until thick. With a spoon, gradually stir in remaining 1 c. sugar. Beat with spoon until thoroughly mixed. Stir in chocolate mixture.

Mix and sift together flour, baking powder and salt. Stir into chocolate mixture. Mix in nuts, remaining 1 tsp. vanilla and almond extract. Spoon half of batter into bottom of greased 9" square pan. Spread evenly.

Cover with cottage cheese mixture. Carefully spoon remaining batter over top. With a spoon, zigzag through batter. Bake in moderate oven (350°) 35 minutes. Cool in pan set on rack 10 minutes, or cool completely. Cut in 2¼" squares. Makes 16.

HALLOWEEN THREE-DECKER BROWNIES

These orange-and-black treats are brownies in gala, holiday dress

First Deck:

2 squares unsweetened chocolate	2 eggs, beaten
½ c. butter	½ tsp. vanilla
1 c. sugar	½ c. sifted flour
	½ c. chopped pecans

Second Deck:

1 c. confectioners sugar	3 or 4 drops orange food
2 tblsp. soft butter	color (or use mixture of
2 tsp. milk	yellow and red to make
½ tsp. vanilla	orange)

Third Deck:

| ¼ square unsweetened chocolate | 1½ tsp. butter |

To make first deck, combine chocolate and butter;

melt over hot water. Beat in sugar, eggs and vanilla. Stir in flour and nuts. Bake in greased 8″ square pan in slow oven (325°) 30 to 35 minutes. Cool in pan on rack.

To make second layer, combine confectioners sugar, butter, milk and vanilla to make a smooth mixture. Tint orange with food color. Spread over brownies in pan. Chill 10 minutes.

To make third deck, combine chocolate and butter; melt over hot water. Drizzle from small spoon over top of brownies. Cool in pan on rack, and cut in 2″ squares. Makes 16.

MOCHA BROWNIES

The chocolate/coffee team is tops—do try the frosted brownies

2 squares unsweetened chocolate
⅓ c. butter or regular margarine
2 eggs
1 c. sugar
1 tsp. vanilla

¾ c. sifted flour
½ tsp. baking powder
¼ tsp. salt
2 tblsp. instant coffee powder
½ to ¾ c. chopped walnuts (optional)

Melt chocolate and butter together over very low heat, stirring constantly. Set aside to cool.

Beat eggs until light; gradually add sugar and beat until light and fluffy. Add vanilla. Combine with chocolate mixture and mix well.

Sift together flour, baking powder, salt and coffee powder; stir into chocolate mixture and mix well. Fold in nuts. Pour into greased 8″ square pan.

Bake in moderate oven (350°) 30 minutes, or until a slight imprint remains when fingertips touch center top. Cool in pan set on rack, then cut in 2″ squares. Makes 16.

VARIATION

Frosted Mocha Brownies: Bake brownies as directed. After brownies in pan are cool, but before cutting them, spread with this frosting: Melt 1 square unsweetened chocolate with 1 tblsp. butter or margarine over hot water (or over very low heat, stirring constantly). Blend in 1½ tblsp. very hot and strong liquid coffee and about 1 c. sifted confectioners sugar, enough to make a frosting that spreads smoothly and easily.

ORANGE BROWNIES

The new twist in these brownies is the delicate fresh orange taste

2 squares unsweetened chocolate	1 tsp. vanilla
½ c. butter	½ tsp. grated orange peel
2 eggs	½ c. sifted flour
1 c. sugar	⅛ tsp. salt
	1 c. chopped walnuts

Melt chocolate and butter. Beat eggs; beat in sugar gradually. Beat in butter and chocolate, vanilla and orange peel.

Stir in flour, salt and nuts. Pour into greased 8″ square pan.

Bake in moderate oven (350°) 20 to 25 minutes. Do not overbake. Cut in 2″ squares. Cool on racks. Makes 16.

VARIATION

Double Chocolate Brownies: Stir in ½ c. semisweet chocolate pieces along with the nuts.

PINEAPPLE/CHOCOLATE BARS

Pineapple and chocolate unite tastily in these two-tone specials

¾ c. shortening	1 c. sifted flour
½ c. sugar	¼ c. chopped nuts
3 eggs	2 squares semisweet chocolate, melted
1 tsp. vanilla	1 (8½ oz.) can crushed pineapple, well drained (⅔ c.)
½ tsp. ground cinnamon	
½ tsp. salt	
1 tsp. baking powder	

Combine shortening, sugar, eggs and vanilla; beat until mixture is creamy.

Sift together cinnamon, salt, baking powder and flour. Add to shortening mixture. Stir in nuts.

Divide batter in half. To one half add melted chocolate; spread in greased 9″ square pan. To second half add pineapple; spread over chocolate mixture in pan.

Bake in moderate oven (350°) 35 minutes. Cool in pan on rack. When cool, cut in 3 × 1″ bars. Makes 27.

TWO-TONE BROWNIES

Color contrast of the dark and light layer
provides a happy change

⅓ c. shortening
1 c. sugar
2 eggs
½ c. sifted flour
½ tsp. baking powder

½ tsp. salt
1 tsp. vanilla
1 c. chopped nuts
1½ squares unsweetened
   chocolate, melted

Cream shortening and sugar until light and fluffy; beat in eggs.

Sift dry ingredients together and add to creamed mixture. Mix thoroughly. Stir in vanilla and nuts.

Divide dough in half. To one half, add chocolate and spread in greased 8″ square pan. Spread remaining half of dough on top.

Bake in moderate oven (375°) about 20 minutes, or until a toothpick inserted in center comes out clean. Cool in pan set on rack 10 minutes, or cool completely, then cut in 2″ squares. Makes 16.

BUTTERSCOTCH BROWNIES

Quick-and-easy cookie squares have glossy,
caramel-colored tops

1 (6 oz.) pkg. butterscotch
   pieces
¼ c. shortening
1 c. brown sugar, firmly
   packed
2 eggs

½ tsp. vanilla
1 c. sifted flour
1 tsp. baking powder
½ tsp. salt
½ c. coarsely chopped
   walnuts

Melt butterscotch pieces and shortening in double boiler over hot water. Remove from heat and stir in brown sugar; cool 5 minutes.

Stir eggs and vanilla into butterscotch mixture to blend thoroughly.

Sift together flour, baking powder and salt. Blend into batter. Stir in nuts. Spread in greased 13 × 9 ×

2″ pan and bake in moderate oven (350°) about 25 minutes. Set pan on rack. While still warm, cut in 2″ (about) squares (cookies are especially good warm from the oven). Makes about 2 dozen.

PEANUT BUTTER BROWNIES

Delightful treat for those in your family
who like a chewy cookie

6 eggs
3 c. sugar
1½ c. brown sugar, firmly packed
1 c. peanut butter
½ c. shortening

1 tblsp. vanilla
4 c. unsifted flour
1½ tblsp. baking powder
1½ tsp. salt
½ c. chopped peanuts

Combine eggs, sugars, peanut butter, shortening and vanilla; blend thoroughly.

Add dry ingredients; mix only until dough is smooth. Spread evenly in two lightly greased 15½ × 10½ ×1″ jelly roll pans (or three 13 × 9 × 2″ pans). Sprinkle with peanuts.

Bake in moderate oven (350°) 25 minutes. Cut in 3 × 1″ bars and cool in pans on racks. Makes about 8 dozen.

ALMOND BRITTLE BARS

These cookies remind you of almond brittle—
they're really that good

1 c. butter or regular margarine
2 tsp. instant coffee powder
1 tsp. salt
¾ tsp. almond extract

1 c. sugar
2 c. sifted flour
1 (6 oz.) pkg. semisweet chocolate pieces
½ c. finely chopped almonds

Beat together butter, coffee powder, salt and almond extract. Gradually beat in sugar; beat until light and fluffy.

Stir in flour and chocolate pieces. Press batter into ungreased 15½ × 10½ × 1″ jelly roll pan. Sprinkle almonds over top.

Bake in moderate oven (375°) 23 to 25 minutes,

or until golden brown. Set pan on rack; cut in 2½ × 1½″ bars while warm. When cool, remove from pan. Makes 40.

NOTE: If you want to break the cookies in irregular pieces, cool baked cookie dough in pan on rack, then break it in pieces with your fingers. Cookies are crisp.

CHOCOLATE CHIP BARS

*Keep your cookie jar filled with these
for a good hostess reputation*

1 c. butter or regular margarine	2 c. sifted flour
1 c. light brown sugar, firmly packed	1 (6 oz.) pkg. semisweet chocolate pieces
1 tsp. vanilla	1 c. chopped pecans or walnuts
⅛ tsp. salt	

Beat butter with sugar until mixture is light and fluffy. Beat in vanilla.

Blend salt with flour and stir into beaten mixture, mixing well. Fold in chocolate pieces and nuts. Press into ungreased 15½ × 10½ × 1″ jelly roll pan.

Bake in moderate oven (350°) 20 minutes. While warm, cut in 2½ × 1½″ bars. Cool in pan on rack. Makes 3 dozen.

CHOCOLATE FUDGE COOKIES

*There's a citrus tang in these rich bars fast-made
with a cake mix*

2 eggs	½ c. sifted flour
½ tsp. baking soda	1 (6 oz.) pkg. semisweet chocolate pieces
½ c. melted butter	⅔ c. chopped walnuts
1 tblsp. grated orange peel	Confectioners sugar
1 (about 19 oz.) pkg. devil's food cake mix	

In a mixing bowl, beat eggs with baking soda. Beat in butter. Add orange peel, cake mix and flour. Stir until all ingredients are moistened (mixture will be stiff). Stir in chocolate pieces and nuts.

Turn batter into greased 15½ × 10½ × 1″ jelly roll pan; spread dough evenly over bottom of pan using fork tines. Bake in moderate oven (350°) 12 to 13 minutes, or until toothpick inserted in center comes out clean. (Cookies will not appear to be done.) Place pan on rack to cool. While still warm, cut in 1½" squares; sift confectioners sugar generously over top. Makes about 5½ dozen.

CHOCOLATE MERINGUE BARS

This cookie has everything—eye and appetite appeal and fine flavor

¾ c. shortening
½ c. sugar
½ c. brown sugar, firmly packed
3 eggs, separated
1 tsp. vanilla
1 tsp. baking powder
¼ tsp. baking soda
¼ tsp. salt
2 c. sifted flour
1 (6 oz.) pkg. semisweet chocolate pieces
½ c. flaked coconut
½ c. chopped nuts
1 c. brown sugar, firmly packed

Beat together shortening, white sugar and ½ c. brown sugar until light and fluffy. Beat in egg yolks and vanilla to mix well.

Sift together baking powder, baking soda, salt and flour. Add to creamed mixture. Pat into greased 13 × 9 × 2" pan. Sprinkle top with chocolate pieces, coconut and nuts.

Beat egg whites until frothy; gradually add 1 c. brown sugar, beating constantly. Beat until stiff. Spread over cookie dough in pan.

Bake in moderate oven (375°) 25 to 30 minutes. Set pan on rack to cool, then cut in 3 × 1" bars. Makes about 3 dozen.

CHOCOLATE MOLASSES COOKIES

You mix these in a saucepan. Molasses gives the new flavor

½ c. butter or regular margarine
¼ c. molasses
¾ c. brown sugar, firmly packed
1 egg
1 c. sifted flour
½ tsp. salt
½ tsp. baking soda
1 (6 oz.) pkg. semisweet chocolate pieces

Heat butter and molasses. Add brown sugar; stir over low heat until sugar is melted. Cool.

Beat egg until light. Add to cooled molasses mixture.

Sift together flour, salt and baking soda. Add with chocolate pieces to molasses mixture. Mix well. Spread in greased 13 × 9 × 2" pan.

Bake in moderate oven (350°) 20 minutes. Set pan on rack to cool. When cool, cut in 3 × 1" bars. Makes 39.

CHOCOLATE/ORANGE BARS

Delicately spiced, orange-flavored bars
with chocolate-nut topping

1 c. butter or regular margarine
1 c. light brown sugar, firmly packed
1 egg yolk
1 tblsp. grated orange peel

2½ c. sifted flour
⅛ tsp. salt
½ tsp. ground allspice
2 (6 oz.) pkgs. milk chocolate pieces
⅓ c. chopped walnuts

Beat butter, brown sugar and egg yolk until well blended. Beat in orange peel.

Sift together flour, salt and allspice. Stir into beaten mixture. Mix well. Spread batter in greased 13 × 9 × 2" pan.

Bake in moderate oven (375°) 15 to 20 minutes, until browned. Remove from oven and top at once with milk chocolate pieces, spreading with spatula as they melt. Sprinkle with nuts. Cool in pan set on rack, then cut in 3 × 1" bars. Makes 39.

CHOCOLATE WALNUT COOKIES

Black walnuts lend flavor to these country-kitchen
chocolate cookies

1 c. sugar
2 eggs, well beaten
2 squares unsweetened chocolate
½ c. butter or regular margarine
1 c. sifted flour

1 tsp. baking powder
¼ tsp. salt
1 c. finely chopped black walnuts
1 tsp. vanilla
Sifted confectioners sugar

Gradually add sugar to eggs. Melt chocolate with butter; stir into eggs.

Sift together flour, baking powder and salt. Add to first mixture with nuts and vanilla.

Bake in greased 15½ × 10½ × 1″ jelly roll pan in moderate oven (350°) 12 to 15 minutes. Cool slightly in pan; dust with confectioners sugar. Cool completely in pan on rack; cut in diamonds, triangles or 1¾″ bars. Makes about 7 dozen.

COCOA BARS

A cake-like bar with economical nut and cereal topping—good

2½ c. shortening	1 tblsp. vanilla
2½ c. sugar	2 tsp. salt
1 c. light corn syrup	2½ c. unsifted flour
8 eggs	1 c. chopped walnuts
1⅓ c. cocoa	1 c. oven-toasted rice cereal

Cream shortening and sugar until fluffy. Beat in corn syrup; beat in eggs, one at a time. Blend in cocoa. Add vanilla, salt and flour and blend.

Spread dough into two lightly greased 15½ × 10½ × 1″ jelly roll pans (or three 13 × 9 × 2″ pans). Combine nuts and cereal; sprinkle over dough.

Bake in moderate oven (350°) about 30 minutes. Cool in pans on racks, then cut in 3 × 1″ bars. Makes about 8 dozen.

NOTE: Cereal topping may absorb moisture during storage. To restore crispness, open container of cookies 2 hours before serving.

FUDGE NUT BARS

Luscious fudge nut filling bakes between two layers of cookie mixture

1 c. butter or regular margarine	1 (12 oz.) pkg. semisweet chocolate pieces
2 c. light brown sugar, firmly packed	1 c. sweetened condensed milk (not evaporated)
2 eggs	2 tblsp. butter or regular margarine
2 tsp. vanilla	½ tsp. salt
2½ c. sifted flour	1 c. chopped nuts
1 tsp. baking soda	2 tsp. vanilla
1 tsp. salt	
3 c. quick-cooking rolled oats	

Cream together 1 c. butter and sugar. Mix in eggs and 2 tsp. vanilla.

Sift together flour, soda and 1 tsp. salt; stir in rolled oats. Add dry ingredients to creamed mixture. Set aside while you make filling.

In a saucepan over boiling water, mix together chocolate pieces, sweetened condensed milk, 2 tblsp. butter and ½ tsp. salt. Stir until chocolate pieces are melted and mixture is smooth. Remove from heat, and stir in nuts and 2 tsp. vanilla.

Spread about two-thirds of cookie dough in bottom of a greased 15½ × 10½ × 1″ jelly roll pan. Cover with fudge filling. Dot with remainder of cookie dough and swirl it over fudge filling.

Bake in moderate oven (350°) 25 to 30 minutes, or until lightly browned. Cut in small (2 × 1″) bars. Cool in pan on racks. Makes about 6 dozen.

HOSTESS BAR COOKIES

Tempting layered cookies with chocolate tops resemble candy bars

¾ c. butter
¾ c. sifted confectioners sugar
1 tsp. vanilla
1 tblsp. light or heavy cream
2 c. sifted flour
1 (6 oz.) pkg. butterscotch pieces
2 tblsp. light or heavy cream
¼ c. confectioners sugar
1 c. chopped pecans
½ c. semisweet chocolate pieces
2 tblsp. light or heavy cream
¼ c. confectioners sugar
1 tsp. vanilla

Combine butter, ¾ c. confectioners sugar, 1 tsp. vanilla, 1 tblsp. cream and flour in bowl; mix well to form dough. Pat into ungreased 13 × 9 × 2″ pan. Bake in slow oven (325°) 25 minutes. Set pan on rack to cool.

Meanwhile, melt butterscotch pieces in small saucepan over low heat, stirring constantly until smooth. Remove from heat; add 2 tblsp. cream and ¼ c. confectioners sugar and beat until smooth. Fold in pecans. Spread over baked cookie in pan.

Melt chocolate pieces over low heat, stirring constantly. Remove from heat; stir in 2 tblsp. cream, ¼ c. confectioners sugar and 1 tsp. vanilla. Spread on top of filling on cookies. Cut in 3 × 1½″ bars. Makes about 2 dozen.

INDIAN BARS

They're extra-moist chocolate brownies,
and that means wonderful

1 c. butter or regular margarine	4 eggs, slightly beaten
2 squares unsweetened chocolate	1½ c. sifted flour
	1 tsp. baking powder
	2 tsp. vanilla
2 c. sugar	1 c. chopped pecans

Melt butter and chocolate over low heat. Add sugar and eggs; mix thoroughly.

Sift flour with baking powder; stir into creamed mixture. Mix in vanilla and nuts.

Bake in a greased 13 × 9 × 2″ pan in moderate oven (350°) 35 to 40 minutes. Cool completely in pan set on rack. Cut in 3 × 1½″ bars. Makes about 2 dozen.

NOTE: You can cut the recipe in half to make 12 cookie bars. Use an 8″ square pan for baking the cookie mixture.

MARBLEIZED SQUARES

Light brown and dark chocolate variegate attractive,
crinkled tops

½ c. butter or regular margarine	1 c. sifted flour
	½ tsp. salt
6 tblsp. sugar	½ tsp. baking soda
6 tblsp. brown sugar, firmly packed	½ c. broken walnuts
	1 (6 oz.) pkg. semisweet chocolate pieces
1 egg	
½ tsp. vanilla	

Beat butter until light; add white and brown sugars and beat until light and fluffy. Beat in egg and vanilla to mix thoroughly.

Sift together flour, salt and baking soda, and add to first mixture. Stir in nuts. Spread in greased 13 × 9 × 2″ pan. Sprinkle chocolate pieces evenly over top.

Place in moderate oven (350°) 1 minute. Remove

from oven and run a knife through dough to marbleize it. Return to oven and bake 12 to 14 minutes. Set pan on rack. When cool, cut in 2" (about) squares. Makes 2 dozen.

OATMEAL/CHOCOLATE BARS

Thick chewy bars that carry well
to picnics and other gatherings

1½ c. brown sugar, firmly packed	1 tsp. baking soda
¾ c. sugar	1 tsp. salt
1 c. shortening	1½ tsp. ground cinnamon
3 eggs	¾ c. milk
1 tsp. vanilla	4 c. quick-cooking rolled oats
2¼ c. sifted flour	1 (12 oz.) pkg. semisweet chocolate pieces

Cream sugars with shortening until light and fluffy. Beat in eggs and vanilla.

Sift together flour, soda, salt and cinnamon. Add to creamed mixture along with milk. Stir in oats and chocolate pieces.

Spread batter in greased 15½ × 10½ × 1" jelly roll pan. Bake in moderate oven (350°) about 30 minutes. While warm, cut in 2 × 1" bars, but cool completely in pan on rack. Makes about 6 dozen.

SEA FOAM COOKIES

They get their name from meringue top;
excellent flavor combination

½ c. shortening	1 tsp. baking soda
½ c. sugar	½ tsp. salt
½ c. brown sugar, firmly packed	3 tblsp. milk
2 eggs, separated	1 (6 oz.) pkg. semisweet chocolate pieces
1 tsp. vanilla	1 c. brown sugar, firmly packed
2 c. sifted flour	¾ c. chopped salted peanuts
2 tsp. baking powder	

Cream shortening with sugar and ½ c. brown sugar until light and fluffy. Beat in egg yolks and vanilla.

Sift together flour, baking powder, soda and salt;

stir into creamed mixture alternately with milk. (The dough will be stiff.) Press dough into greased 13 × 9 × 2" pan. Sprinkle evenly with chocolate pieces.

Beat egg whites until soft peaks form; gradually add remaining 1 c. brown sugar and beat, until very stiff and glossy. Spread over dough in pan. Scatter peanuts evenly over top.

Bake in slow oven (325°) 30 to 35 minutes. Cool in pan set on rack, then cut in 3 × 1" bars. Makes 39.

SPICY CHOCOLATE BARS

Chocolate, always good, is even better
in this richly spiced cookie

1½ c. shortening	2 tsp. baking soda
1½ c. sugar	2 tsp. salt
1½ c. brown sugar, firmly packed	4 tsp. ground cinnamon
	1 tsp. ground cloves
4 eggs	1 tsp. ground nutmeg
2 tsp. vanilla	2 c. semisweet chocolate
4 c. unsifted flour	pieces (12 oz. pkg.)

Cream shortening and sugars until fluffy. Beat in eggs, one at a time. Add vanilla.

Blend in dry ingredients; add chocolate pieces. Spread evenly in two ungreased 15½ × 10½ × 1" jelly roll pans. Bake in moderate oven (375°) 20 minutes. Cut in 3 × 1" bars; cool in pans on racks. Makes about 8 dozen.

NOTE: Instead of adding chocolate pieces to the batter, you can sprinkle them over top of dough before baking. Cookies may also be baked in three 13 × 9 × 2" pans instead of the two jelly roll pans.

TOFFEE COOKIE SQUARES

Rich cookies that taste like toffee.
Bake them for Christmas presents

½ c. butter or regular margarine	1 tsp. vanilla
	½ tsp. salt
½ c. shortening	2 c. sifted flour
1 c. brown sugar, firmly packed	1 (6 oz.) pkg. semisweet chocolate pieces
1 egg yolk, unbeaten	½ c. chopped nuts

Cream together butter, shortening, brown sugar and egg yolk. Stir in vanilla, salt and flour.

Pat mixture into lightly greased 15½ × 10½ × 1″ jelly roll pan.

Bake in slow oven (325°) 15 to 20 minutes.

Melt chocolate pieces; spread over warm baked mixture. Sprinkle with chopped nuts; cut in 2″ squares while warm. Cool in pan on rack. Makes 3 dozen.

COCONUT/MOLASSES WUNDERBARS

A molasses/coconut candy, chocolate-coated,
inspired this duplicate of the flavor combination
in cookies—they're mighty good eating

½ c. butter or regular margarine	1 tsp. vanilla
¾ c. brown sugar, firmly packed	1 c. sifted flour
	¼ tsp. salt
¼ c. dark molasses	1 c. flaked coconut
2 eggs	4 (¾ oz.) milk chocolate candy bars

Cream butter and brown sugar until light and fluffy. Beat in molasses, eggs and vanilla to mix well.

Mix flour and salt thoroughly; gradually stir into creamed mixture. Stir in coconut.

Spread in greased 9″ square pan. Bake in moderate oven (350°) about 25 minutes, or until lightly browned. Remove from oven and set pan on rack. Immediately place chocolate candy, broken in pieces, over the top. When chocolate melts, spread it evenly over top.

Cool completely in pan, then cut in 1½″ squares. Makes 3 dozen.

FILLED OATMEAL BARS

It's the taste of chocolate-coated raisins
that makes these so good

1 (15 oz.) can sweetened condensed milk (not evaporated)	1⅓ c. brown sugar, firmly packed
	1½ tsp. vanilla
2 squares unsweetened chocolate	2 c. sifted flour
	¾ tsp. salt
2 c. seedless raisins	½ tsp. baking soda
1 c. butter or regular margarine	2½ c. quick-cooking rolled oats

Combine sweetened condensed milk and chocolate; heat over boiling water until chocolate melts, stirring occasionally. Remove from heat; stir in raisins. Set aside to cool slightly.

Beat butter until light; beat in brown sugar and vanilla until fluffy.

Sift together flour, salt and baking soda; add rolled oats. Mix with creamed mixture until crumbly.

Press half of dough evenly into ungreased 13 × 9 × 2″ pan. Cover with chocolate mixture. Sprinkle with remaining half of dough; press down slightly.

Bake in moderate oven (375°) about 25 minutes, or until golden brown. Set pan on rack to cool. Cut, while slightly warm, in 2 × 1″ bars. Makes about 4 dozen.

SPICY APPLE BARS

Cut cookies larger and serve warm with vanilla
ice cream on top for a compliment-winning dessert

½ c. shortening	1 tsp. ground cinnamon
1 c. sugar	½ tsp. ground nutmeg
2 eggs	¼ tsp. ground cloves
1 c. sifted flour	1 c. quick-cooking rolled oats
1 tsp. baking powder	1½ c. diced peeled apples
½ tsp. baking soda	½ c. coarsely chopped
½ tsp. salt	walnuts
1 tblsp. cocoa	Sifted confectioners sugar

Cream together shortening and sugar until light and fluffy; beat in eggs, one at a time.

Sift together flour, baking powder, baking soda, salt, cocoa and spices; add to creamed mixture. Stir in rolled oats, apples and nuts. Spread in greased 13 × 9 × 2″ pan.

Bake in moderate oven (375°) about 25 minutes. Cool slightly in pan on rack; cut in 2 × 1½″ bars. Sprinkle with confectioners sugar. Makes about 2½ dozen.

APPLESAUCE FUDGIES

The applesauce keeps the cookies moist
longer than most brownies

2 squares unsweetened
  chocolate
½ c. butter
½ c. sweetened applesauce
2 eggs, beaten
1 c. brown sugar, firmly
  packed

1 tsp. vanilla
1 c. sifted flour
½ tsp. baking powder
¼ tsp. baking soda
¼ tsp. salt
½ c. chopped walnuts

Melt chocolate and butter together.

Mix applesauce, eggs, sugar and vanilla. Sift dry ingredients into applesauce mixture. Stir until blended; add chocolate and stir well.

Pour into greased 9″ square pan. Sprinkle with walnuts. Bake in moderate oven (350°) 30 minutes. Cut in 2¼″ squares and cool in pan on racks. Makes 16.

APRICOT BARS

Color-bright bits of apricot and fruity topping make these luscious

1 c. dried apricots
1 c. boiling water
½ c. butter or regular
  margarine
2 c. brown sugar, firmly
  packed
2 eggs
1 tsp. vanilla
1 tsp. grated orange peel

1¾ c. sifted flour
1 tsp. baking powder
¾ tsp. salt
2 tsp. orange juice
2 tsp. lemon juice
1 tsp. grated orange peel
2 tsp. soft butter
1 c. sifted confectioners sugar
½ c. chopped walnuts

Put apricots in small bowl; pour on boiling water. Let stand 5 minutes. Then drain and cut in small bits with kitchen scissors.

Cream together ½ c. butter and brown sugar until light and fluffy; beat in eggs, vanilla and 1 tsp. orange peel.

Sift together flour, baking powder and salt; blend into creamed mixture. Stir in apricots.

Spread in greased 15½ × 10½ × 1″ jelly roll pan and bake in moderate oven (350°) about 20 minutes. Let cool in pan set on rack 10 minutes.

Meanwhile, blend orange and lemon juices, 1 tsp. orange peel, 2 tsp. butter and confectioners sugar, beating until smooth. Spread on cookies that have cooled

10 minutes in pan. Sprinkle with walnuts, pressing them in lightly so they will adhere to cookies. Complete cooling, then cut in 2¼ × 1¼″ bars. Makes about 56.

LUSCIOUS APRICOT BARS

Tang of apricots makes these special

⅔ c. dried apricots
½ c. butter
¼ c. sugar
1⅓ c. sifted flour
1 c. brown sugar, firmly
   packed
2 eggs, well beaten

½ tsp. baking powder
¼ tsp. salt
½ tsp. vanilla
½ c. chopped almonds
Confectioners sugar (optional)

Rinse apricots; cover with water and simmer 10 minutes. Drain, cool and chop.

Combine butter, white sugar and 1 c. flour; mix until crumbly. Pack into greased 9″ square pan. Bake in moderate oven (375°) 20 minutes.

Gradually beat brown sugar into eggs. Sift together remaining flour, baking powder and salt. Add to egg mixture; mix well. Add vanilla, ¼ c. almonds and apricots. Spread on baked layer. Sprinkle with remaining nuts.

Bake in moderate oven (350°) about 20 minutes. Cool in pan on rack. Cut in 1½″ squares. If you wish, sprinkle lightly with confectioners sugar. Makes 2½ dozen.

CRAN/APRICOT SCOTCHIES

Red filling has luscious tang, contrasts beautifully with snowy coating

1 c. apricot pulp (cooked
   dried apricots put through
   food mill), or drained and
   strained canned apricots
½ c. cooked or canned whole
   cranberry sauce
½ c. sugar
1 tblsp. flour
1 tblsp. lemon juice
2 tblsp. orange juice
2 tsp. butter

1½ c. brown sugar, firmly
   packed
¾ c. butter or regular
   margarine
2 eggs
1 c. flaked coconut
3¾ c. sifted flour
2 tsp. cream of tartar
1 tsp. baking soda
1 tsp. salt
Confectioners sugar (for
   coating)

Combine apricot pulp, cranberry sauce, sugar mixed with 1 tblsp. flour, lemon and orange juices and 2 tsp. butter in saucepan. Bring to a boil, stirring constantly. Reduce heat and simmer, stirring constantly, 5 minutes. Set filling aside to cool before using.

Cream together brown sugar and ¾ c. butter until light and fluffy. Beat in eggs. Add coconut; stir to mix.

Sift together flour, cream of tartar, baking soda and salt; stir into creamed mixture. Pat half of mixture into greased 13 × 9 × 2″ pan.

Spoon cooled filling evenly over dough in pan. Sprinkle remaining half of dough over top (it will be crumbly, but will spread and cover during baking).

Bake in moderate oven (350°) 30 minutes. Cool in pan on rack. Cut in 3 × 1″ bars and roll in confectioners sugar. Makes about 3 dozen.

NOTE: The filling is rather soft when cookies come from oven, but it firms when cooled completely. If you want to serve cookies before thorough cooling, use 1½ tblsp. flour instead of 1 tblsp. to thicken filling.

CHERRY/WALNUT BARS

Pink-frosted cookies with shortbread base,
rich candy-like topping

2¼ c. sifted flour	½ tsp. vanilla
½ c. sugar	1 (2 oz.) jar maraschino
1 c. butter	cherries
2 eggs	½ c. chopped walnuts
1 c. brown sugar, firmly	1 tblsp. softened butter
packed	1 c. confectioners sugar
½ tsp. salt	½ c. flaked coconut
½ tsp. baking powder	(optional)

Mix flour, sugar and 1 c. butter until crumbly. Press into ungreased 13 × 9 × 2″ pan. Bake in moderate oven (350°) 20 minutes, or until crust is lightly browned.

Blend together eggs, brown sugar, salt, baking powder and vanilla.

Drain and chop cherries, reserving liquid. Stir chopped cherries and walnuts into blended mixture. Spread on top of baked crust. Return to oven and bake 25 minutes. Remove from oven; cool in pan on rack.

Combine softened butter and confectioners sugar with enough reserved cherry liquid to spread. Spread on cookies; sprinkle with coconut, if you wish. When icing has set, cut in 2 × 1" bars. Makes 48.

MARSHMALLOW/CHERRY BARS

*Tall, dainty-pink marshmallow topping
with dots of red cherries*

¾ c. butter or regular
   margarine
⅓ c. brown sugar, firmly
   packed
1½ c. sifted flour
2 envelopes unflavored gelatin
½ c. cold water
2 c. sugar

½ c. cherry juice and water
1 (8 oz.) jar maraschino
   cherries, drained and
   chopped
½ c. chopped almonds
3 drops red food color
½ tsp. almond extract

Combine butter, brown sugar and flour; mix well and press into ungreased 13 × 9 × 2" pan. Bake in slow oven (325°) 30 minutes. Set aside to cool.

Soften gelatin in ½ c. water.

Combine white sugar and juice drained from cherries (with enough water added to make ½ c.). Bring to a boil over medium heat and boil 2 minutes. Remove from heat and stir in softened gelatin. Beat with electric mixer at medium speed until very stiff, about 20 minutes (mixture climbs beaters as it thickens).

Fold in cherries and almonds. Add food color and almond extract. Spread on top of baked crust in pan. Let stand at room temperature until topping sets. Cut in 2 × 1" bars. Cover pan with lid or foil and leave in a cool place until time to serve. Makes about 48.

Hermits—Sea-Voyage Cookies

You don't have to tax your imagination to appreciate how marvelous New England Hermits tasted to men at sea. Canisters, lovingly filled and tucked into chests, went on clipper ships from Massachusetts to many far-away places. Eyes brightened when the cookies appeared, for they brought remembrances of home. Good travelers and keepers.

These hearty American cookies, spiced and fruited, never went out of style. Good today served with hot coffee. Our recipe comes from Cape Cod.

NEW ENGLAND HERMITS

Roll cookies in confectioners sugar for a homey, quick dress-up

½ c. butter	1 tsp. ground cinnamon
½ c. sugar	½ tsp. ground cloves
2 eggs	¼ tsp. ground nutmeg
½ c. molasses	⅛ tsp. ground allspice
2 c. sifted flour	3 tblsp. chopped citron
½ tsp. salt	½ c. chopped raisins
¾ tsp. baking soda	½ c. currants
¾ tsp. cream of tartar	¼ c. chopped walnuts

Cream butter with sugar until light and fluffy. Beat in eggs and molasses.

Sift together flour, salt, baking soda, cream of tartar and spices; stir into creamed mixture. Stir in citron, raisins, currants and nuts.

Spread batter evenly in greased 13 × 9 × 2″ pan. Bake in moderate oven (350°) about 20 minutes, or until done. (Touch lightly with fingertip. If no imprint remains, cookies are done.)

Set pan on rack to cool, cutting in 3 × 1″ bars while slightly warm. Cool completely before removing from pan. Makes 39.

TEATIME CURRANT COOKIES

Remember how Grandma's currant teacakes tasted? Moist, tender!

1 c. dried currants	1¾ c. sifted flour
1 c. water	¼ tsp. salt
½ c. salad oil	1 tsp. baking soda
1 egg	½ c. chopped pecans
1 c. sugar	1 c. sifted confectioners sugar

Place currants and water in 1-qt. saucepan; bring to a boil. Remove from heat, add salad oil and let cool.
Beat egg slightly; gradually add sugar, beating until

thoroughly mixed. Beat in thoroughly cooled currant mixture.

Sift flour, salt and baking soda together and add to currant mixture. Stir in nuts.

Spread in greased 13 × 9 × 2″ pan; bake in moderate oven (375°) 20 minutes (test for doneness with a wooden toothpick). Remove from oven and set pan on rack to cool 10 minutes. Cut in 2¼ × 1″ bars (about) and roll in confectioners sugar. Cool completely on racks. Makes 4 dozen.

CHINESE CHEWS

Distinctive, marvelous in taste and good keepers if you hide them

1 c. sugar	1 c. chopped pitted dates
¾ c. sifted flour	1 c. chopped nuts
1 tsp. baking powder	2 eggs, beaten
¼ tsp. salt	Confectioners sugar

Sift sugar, flour, baking powder and salt into bowl. Stir in dates and nuts.

Add eggs; mix thoroughly. Spread in greased 15½ × 10½ × 1″ jelly roll pan. Bake in moderate oven (375°) about 20 minutes.

Cut in 2 × 1″ bars while warm; sprinkle lightly with confectioners sugar. Cool in pan set on rack. Makes about 6 dozen.

DATE-FILLED OAT COOKIES

Lemon peel and spices give tantalizing fragrance, distinctive taste

1 c. chopped dates	½ c. light brown sugar, firmly
½ c. sugar	packed
¼ c. orange juice	1 tsp. grated lemon peel
½ c. water	½ c. butter or regular
1 c. sifted flour	margarine
¼ tsp. salt	¼ c. milk
¼ tsp. baking soda	1½ c. quick-cooking rolled
¼ tsp. ground nutmeg	oats
¾ tsp. ground cinnamon	

Combine dates, sugar, orange juice and water in

small saucepan. Cook, stirring, until thick; set aside to cool. You'll have about 1¾ c. filling.

Sift together flour, salt, baking soda, nutmeg and cinnamon. Add brown sugar and lemon peel, blending well. Blend in butter with pastry blender, as for pie crust. Add milk; stir in rolled oats.

Spread half of dough in greased 8″ square pan. Spread date filling evenly over top.

Roll remaining half of dough between sheets of waxed paper into an 8″ square to fit pan. Fit dough over filling.

Bake in moderate oven (350°) 25 to 30 minutes. Cool in pan set on rack. Cut in bars about 2½ × 1″. Makes 2 dozen.

DATE/NUT BARS

These cake-like cookies and coffee make great evening refreshments

1 c. sifted confectioners sugar	½ tsp. baking powder
1 tblsp. oil	¾ c. chopped nuts
2 eggs, beaten	1 c. chopped dates
¼ c. sifted cake flour	1 tsp. vanilla
¼ tsp. salt	Confectioners sugar (for tops)

Add 1 c. confectioners sugar and oil to eggs; blend well.

Add sifted dry ingredients. Stir in nuts, dates and vanilla.

Pour into greased 9″ square pan. Bake in slow oven (325°) 25 minutes. Cool slightly in pan on rack. Cut in 3 × 1″ bars; sprinkle with confectioners sugar. Makes 27.

DATE SANDWICH BARS

Easy to tote when you're asked to bring cookies. They'll win praise

¼ c. sugar	1¾ c. sifted flour
3 c. cut-up dates	½ tsp. baking soda
1½ c. water	1 tsp. salt
¾ c. soft butter or regular margarine	1½ c. quick-cooking rolled oats
1 c. brown sugar, firmly packed	

Mix sugar, dates and water, and cook over low heat until mixture thickens. Stir to prevent scorching. Set aside to cool.

Thoroughly mix butter and brown sugar. Beat until fluffy.

Stir flour, baking soda and salt together. Stir into the brown sugar-butter mixture. Add rolled oats and mix well. Divide in half and spread one part into greased 13 × 9 × 2″ pan. Flatten and press it down with hands so the mixture will cover the bottom of the pan.

Spread the cooled date mixture on top. Sprinkle evenly with the second half of the rolled oat mixture. Pat it down lightly with hands.

Bake in hot oven (400°) 25 to 30 minutes, or until a delicate brown. Remove from oven; while warm, cut in 2 × 1½″ bars. Remove bars at once from pan to racks to finish cooling. Makes about 30.

FRENCH BARS

Delicate as spice cake. Dress up cookies with Orange Butter Frosting

2¼ c. brown sugar, firmly packed	1 tsp. ground cinnamon
4 eggs, well beaten	½ tsp. salt
1½ c. soured evaporated milk (see Note)	1½ c. chopped walnuts
	1½ c. cut-up dates
1½ tsp. baking soda	1 c. toasted flaked coconut
2¼ c. unsifted flour	Orange Butter Frosting (recipe follows)

Add sugar to eggs and beat until thick. Stir in soured evaporated milk.

Blend in dry ingredients. Stir in nuts, dates and coconut. Do not overmix batter.

Spread dough evenly in two lightly greased 15½ × 10½ × 1″ jelly roll pans (or three 13 × 9 × 2″ pans). Bake in moderate oven (350°) about 20 minutes. Cool in pans on racks. Frost if desired, and cut in 2½ × 1″ bars. Makes 80.

NOTE: To sour evaporated milk, pour 1½ tblsp. vinegar into a 2-cup measure. Add evaporated milk until measurement is 1½ c. Stir well and set aside a few minutes before using.

Orange Butter Frosting: Combine 1 lb. confectioners sugar, sifted, with ¼ c. butter, ¼ c. orange juice, ½ tsp. salt and 1 tsp. grated orange peel. Beat until creamy. Spread on cooled bars. (Let frosting set before cutting cookies).

NUT AND FRUIT BARS

It's wonderful how fast these date cookies sell at Christmas bazaars

3 eggs	1 c. chopped walnuts
1 tsp. vanilla	1 (8 oz.) pkg. pitted dates
1 c. sugar	1 (6 oz.) jar maraschino
1 c. sifted flour	cherries, drained
½ tsp. salt	Confectioners sugar
1 tsp. baking powder	

Combine eggs and vanilla. Beat well. Add sugar and flour sifted with salt and baking powder; blend well. Stir in nuts and fruits.

Bake in greased 15½ × 10½ × 1″ jelly roll pan in moderate oven (350°) 30 minutes. Cool in pan on rack. Cut in 2″ squares. Sprinkle with confectioners sugar. Store in airtight box. Makes 3 dozen.

ORANGE/DATE BARS

These are "candy cookies"; roll moist bars in confectioners sugar

½ lb. pitted dates	2 eggs
2 tblsp. flour	1 tsp. baking soda
1 c. water	1¾ c. sifted flour
¾ c. shortening	½ tsp. salt
1 c. brown sugar, firmly	½ c. chopped nuts (optional)
packed	1 (16 oz.) pkg. candy orange
1 tsp. vanilla	slices (gumdrops)

Put dates, 2 tblsp. flour and water in small saucepan. Bring to a boil and cook until mixture is thick. Set aside to cool.

Cream shortening, brown sugar and vanilla until light and fluffy. Beat in eggs.

Sift together baking soda, 1¾ c. flour and salt; add

to creamed mixture. Stir in nuts. Spread half of dough in bottom of greased 13 × 9 × 2″ pan.

Cut candy orange slices in lengthwise thirds; cover dough in pan with candy arranged in straight rows crosswise in pan. Spread cooled date mixture on top of orange slices. Carefully top with remaining half of dough.

Bake in moderate oven (350°) 40 minutes. Cool in pan on rack, then cut between orange slices to make bars about 2 × 1″. Makes about 4 dozen.

ORANGE/DATE DAINTIES

Orange/date flavors blend and lift these out of the commonplace

1 c. finely cut dates	1 c. sifted cake flour
1 c. orange juice	¼ tsp. baking soda
2 tsp. grated orange peel	½ tsp. baking powder
¼ c. regular margarine	⅛ tsp. salt
½ c. sugar	¼ c. orange juice
1 egg	¾ c. crushed corn flakes

Combine dates and 1 c. orange juice in heavy pan. Cook over low heat, stirring, until mixture is thick and smooth. Cool slightly; stir in orange peel and set aside.

Beat together margarine and sugar until light and fluffy. Beat in egg to blend well.

Sift together cake flour, baking soda, baking powder and salt. Add alternately with ¼ c. orange juice to beaten mixture, beating after each addition.

Spread batter in lightly greased 15½ × 10½ × 1″ jelly roll pan. Top batter with reserved orange-date mixture, spreading evenly. Sprinkle corn flakes over the top.

Bake in moderate oven (375°) about 25 minutes. Set pan on rack; while still hot, cut in 2″ squares. Makes about 40.

TREASURE BARS

Nuts, coconut, dates or chocolate are the hidden treasure in these

1 c. sifted flour	1 tblsp. flour
1/2 c. brown sugar, firmly packed	1/2 tsp. baking powder
1/2 c. butter	1/4 tsp. salt
2 eggs	1 c. chopped walnuts
1 c. brown sugar, firmly packed	1 c. shredded coconut
1 tsp. vanilla	1/2 c. chopped dates or semisweet chocolate pieces

Combine 1 c. flour and 1/2 c. brown sugar; cut in butter. Press into greased 13 × 9 × 2" pan. Bake in moderate oven (350°) 12 minutes. Cool on rack 5 minutes.

Meanwhile, beat eggs slightly. Add 1 c. brown sugar gradually, beating until light and fluffy. Blend in vanilla.

Sift together 1 tblsp. flour, baking powder and salt. Stir into egg mixture. Stir in nuts, coconut and dates. Spread over baked crust. Return to oven and bake 25 minutes. Cool in pan on rack, then cut in 2 1/2 × 1 1/2" bars. Makes about 2 1/2 dozen.

CALIFORNIA LEMON BARS

Hostess favorite—rich cookies, great with beverages and ice cream

1 c. sifted flour	2 tblsp. lemon juice
1/2 c. butter or regular margarine	2 tblsp. flour
1/4 c. confectioners sugar	1 1/2 c. confectioners sugar
2 eggs, beaten	1 tsp. vanilla
1 c. sugar	2 tblsp. melted butter or margarine
1/2 tsp. baking powder	1 tblsp. milk (about)

Blend 1 c. flour, 1/2 c. butter and 1/4 c. confectioners sugar as for pastry. Press into ungreased 8" square pan. Bake in moderate oven (350°) 20 minutes.

Combine eggs, sugar, baking powder, lemon juice and 2 tblsp. flour. Pour onto baked bottom layer and bake in moderate oven (350°) 25 minutes. Cool slightly in pan.

Combine 1 1/2 c. confectioners sugar, vanilla, 2 tblsp. butter and enough milk to make mixture of spreading consistency. Spread on top of baked cookies in pan. Cool in pan on rack, then cut in 2 1/2 × 1 1/4" bars. Makes 1 1/2 dozen.

LEMON MERINGUE BARS

These cookies taste like lemon meringue pie—and that's good!

½ c. butter or regular
  margarine
½ c. sifted confectioners
  sugar
2 eggs, separated
1 c. sifted flour

¼ tsp. salt
2 tsp. finely grated lemon
  peel
½ c. sugar
½ c. chopped walnuts
16 walnut halves

Cream butter until light and fluffy. Gradually beat in confectioners sugar. Beat in egg yolks to blend.

Combine flour and salt; sift into egg yolk mixture. Stir in lemon peel. Spread evenly in greased 8″ square pan.

Bake in moderate oven (350°) about 10 minutes, until lightly browned. Remove from oven. Set oven regulator to hot (400°).

Beat egg whites until they form stiff moist peaks; gradually beat in ½ c. sugar, blending well. Stir in chopped nuts. Spread meringue evenly over baked layer. Return to hot oven (400°) and bake about 5 to 7 minutes, until lightly browned. Remove from oven and partially cool in pan set on wire rack. Cut in 2″ squares and top each square with a walnut half. Makes 16.

LEMON/COCONUT SQUARES

Delicate texture, fresh lemon flavor make these cookies special

Cookie Dough:

1½ c. sifted flour
½ c. brown sugar, firmly
  packed

½ c. butter or regular
  margarine

Filling:

2 eggs, beaten
1 c. brown sugar, firmly
  packed
1½ c. flaked or shredded
  coconut

1 c. chopped nuts
2 tblsp. flour
½ tsp. baking powder
¼ tsp. salt
½ tsp. vanilla

Frosting:

1 c. confectioners sugar
1 tblsp. melted butter or
   regular margarine

Juice of 1 lemon

Mix together ingredients for cookie dough; pat down well in buttered 13 × 9 × 2″ pan. Bake in very slow oven (275°) 10 minutes.

To make filling, combine eggs, sugar, coconut, nuts, flour, baking powder, salt and vanilla. Spread on top of baked mixture. Bake in moderate oven (350°) 20 minutes.

While still warm, spread with frosting made by combining confectioners sugar, melted butter and lemon juice. Cool slightly; cut in 2″ squares. Complete cooling in pan on racks. Makes about 24.

LEMON LOVE NOTES

Snowy confectioners sugar coating contributes to the cookies' charms

½ c. butter
1 c. sifted flour
¼ c. confectioners sugar
1 c. sugar
2 tblsp. flour

½ tsp. baking powder
2 eggs, beaten
2 tblsp. lemon juice
2 tsp. grated lemon peel

Mix butter, 1 c. flour and confectioners sugar. Press into an ungreased 8″ square pan. Bake in moderate oven (350°) 8 minutes or until golden. Cool in pan on rack.

Combine sugar, 2 tblsp. flour and baking powder. Add eggs, lemon juice and peel. Mix well. Pour evenly over baked, cooled mixture in pan.

Bake in moderate oven (350°) 25 minutes. (Top puffs up in baking, but falls in cooling.) Cool in pan on rack and cut in 2″ squares. Sprinkle with confectioners sugar, if desired. Makes 16.

COFFEE COOKIE BARS

A hearty cookie, moist and tasty—a fine coffee accompaniment

1 c. brown sugar, firmly packed	½ tsp. baking powder
¼ c. shortening	½ tsp. baking soda
1 egg	½ tsp. salt
1 tsp. vanilla	½ c. hot, strong coffee
1½ c. sifted flour	½ c. raisins
½ tsp. ground cinnamon	½ c. chopped nuts
	Caramel Icing (recipe follows)

Cream sugar and shortening until light and fluffy. Beat in egg and vanilla.

Sift together flour, cinnamon, baking powder, baking soda and salt, and add alternately with hot coffee to creamed mixture. Stir in raisins and nuts.

Spread dough in greased 13 × 9 × 2″ pan. Bake in moderate oven (350°) 25 minutes. While hot, spread with Caramel Icing. Set pan on rack to cool, then cut in 2 × 1″ bars. Makes about 4 dozen.

Caramel Icing: Combine 3 tblsp. brown sugar, firmly packed, 3 tblsp. butter and 1 tblsp. dairy half-and-half, light cream or milk in 1-qt. saucepan. Bring to a boil. Remove from heat and gradually add 1 c. sifted confectioners sugar, beating constantly. If icing is not smooth, place over low heat, stirring constantly, until lumps of sugar disappear. Makes enough to ice cookies baked in a 13 × 9 × 2″ pan.

FRUIT BARS

Excellent cookies to mail for gifts—they're good keepers

2 c. seedless raisins	1 c. sugar
1½ c. chopped mixed candied fruit	1 c. brown sugar, firmly packed
1 c. chopped walnuts	2 eggs, beaten
½ c. orange or pineapple juice	4½ c. sifted flour
2 tsp. vanilla	2 tsp. ground cinnamon
1 c. butter or regular margarine	2 tsp. baking powder
	1 tsp. baking soda

Rinse raisins in hot water, drain; dry on towel.

Combine raisins, candied fruit, nuts, juice and vanilla; let stand.

Cream together butter, sugars and eggs. Sift together dry ingredients and add in thirds to creamed mixture;

mix until smooth. Add fruit mixture; blend well. Let stand 1½ hours in refrigerator, or overnight.

When ready to bake, spread dough in greased 15½ × 10½ × 1″ jelly roll pan. Bake in hot oven (400°) 15 to 20 minutes, until lightly browned. Cool in pan set on rack. When cool, cut in bars about 3 × 1″. Makes about 4 dozen.

RAISIN-FILLED BARS

Cooked raisin filling produces cookies that are good— like raisin pie

2 c. raisins
1⅓ c. water
3 tblsp. cornstarch
2 tblsp. cold water
1 c. sugar
1 tsp. vanilla
1 c. brown sugar, firmly packed

1½ c. quick-cooking or regular rolled oats
1 c. melted butter or regular margarine
1½ c. sifted flour
1 tsp. baking soda
½ tsp. salt
1 c. chopped nuts

To make filling, cook raisins in 1⅓ c. water until tender. Dissolve cornstarch in 2 tblsp. cold water. Add sugar and cornstarch to raisins; stir until mixture thickens. Remove from heat, add vanilla and set aside to cool.

Add brown sugar and oats to melted butter; mix well.

Sift together flour, soda and salt; add to sugar-butter mixture. Stir in nuts. Pack half of mixture into bottom of greased 9″ square pan. Spread raisin filling evenly on top. Then top with remaining crumb mixture.

Bake in moderate oven (350°) 30 minutes. Set pan on rack to cool 10 minutes, or cool completely, then cut in 3 × 1″ bars. Makes about 27.

FAVORITE HONEY BARS

These chewy cookies are good. Play smart and double the recipe

½ c. shortening
½ c. sugar
½ c. honey
1 egg, well beaten
⅔ c. sifted flour
½ tsp. baking soda
½ tsp. baking powder
¼ tsp. salt
1 c. quick-cooking rolled oats
1 c. flaked coconut
1 tsp. vanilla
½ c. chopped nuts

Cream shortening, sugar and honey until light and fluffy. Add egg and blend.

Sift flour with soda, baking powder and salt; add to creamed mixture. Add oats, coconut, vanilla and nuts.

Spread in greased 15½ × 10½ × 1″ jelly roll pan; bake in moderate oven (350°) 20 to 25 minutes. Cool in pan on rack. When cool, cut in 2½ × 1½″ bars. Makes about 3 dozen.

NOTE: To trim, sprinkle confectioners sugar over tops of bars before serving.

HONEY/ALMOND TRIANGLES

A honey-almond topping bakes right on these rich, tasty cookies

½ c. butter
¼ c. sugar
2 tblsp. honey
2 tblsp. milk
1 c. chopped, slivered or
    sliced almonds
1 tsp. almond extract
1¾ c. sifted flour
½ c. sugar
2 tsp. baking powder
¼ tsp. salt
½ c. butter
1 egg

In saucepan combine ½ c. butter, ¼ c. sugar, honey, milk, almonds and almond extract. Bring to a full rolling boil, stirring constantly. Set aside to cool slightly.

Sift together flour, ½ c. sugar, baking powder and salt. With pastry blender, cut in ½ c. butter until particles are very fine.

Beat egg with a fork until blended; add to crumb mixture, tossing with a fork to mix. Gather dough and work with hands until mixture holds together. With lightly floured fingertips, press evenly over bottom of lightly greased 15½ × 10½ × 1″ jelly roll pan.

Pour honey-almond topping over dough and spread evenly. Bake in moderate oven (350°) 20 to 25 minutes, or until a deep golden color. Place pan on rack at least 10 minutes, or until cool. Cut in 2½″ squares, then cut each square diagonally to make triangles. Makes 4 dozen.

HONEYED LEMON SLICES

Honey and lemon blend their flavors in these superlative cookie bars

1 c. brown sugar, firmly
   packed
2 c. sifted flour
½ c. butter or regular
   margarine

1 c. cookie coconut
1 c. honey
2 tblsp. butter
¼ c. lemon juice
3 eggs, beaten

Blend together brown sugar, flour, ½ c. butter and coconut. Pat two-thirds of mixture into ungreased 9″ square pan.

In small saucepan, cook together honey, 2 tblsp. butter, lemon juice and eggs, stirring constantly, until mixture thickens. Cool and spread over mixture in pan. Sprinkle remainder of brown sugar mixture over top.

Bake in moderate oven (350°) 40 minutes. Cut in 1½″ squares and cool in pan on rack. Makes about 3 dozen.

LEBKUCHEN

Spicy German Christmas cookies with glazed tops— good keepers

¾ c. honey
¾ c. sugar
1 large egg
1 tsp. grated lemon peel
1 tblsp. milk
2¾ c. sifted flour
½ tsp. salt
1 tsp. ground cinnamon

1 tsp. ground allspice
¼ tsp. ground cloves
⅓ c. chopped citron
½ c. chopped blanched
   almonds
1 c. sifted confectioners sugar
4 tsp. water (about)

In large saucepan heat honey slightly, but do not boil. Remove from heat and stir in sugar. Beat in egg, then add lemon peel and milk.

Sift together flour, salt, cinnamon, allspice and cloves. Stir, a little at a time, into honey mixture. Stir in citron and almonds. Form dough into a ball; wrap in waxed paper and chill several hours or overnight.

Divide dough in half and let stand 15 to 20 minutes to warm slightly to make spreading in pans easier. Spread each half in a greased 13 × 9 × 2″ pan (use a metal spoon moistened in water to spread dough).

Bake pans of dough separately in hot oven (400°) about 15 minutes, or until lightly browned. (Or test for doneness by touching lightly with fingertip. If no imprint remains, cookies are done.)

Place pans on cooling racks and brush cookie tops at once with confectioners sugar mixed with enough water to make a smooth icing. While still warm, cut in 3 × 1″ bars or diamond shapes; remove from pans to cool on racks. When cool, store cookies in airtight containers. They will keep several weeks. Four or five days before serving, a cut apple or orange placed in canisters mellows and improves flavor of cookies. Makes about 6 dozen.

ENGLISH TEA SQUARES

Jam-filled bars are all-purpose cookies—serve with tea or coffee

¾ c. butter or regular margarine	¼ tsp. ground allspice
1 c. sugar	1 c. chopped almonds or walnuts
1 egg	½ c. strawberry jam
1 tsp. vanilla	3 tblsp. confectioners sugar
2 c. sifted flour	

Beat butter until light; add sugar and beat until light and fluffy. Beat in egg and vanilla to blend well. Stir in flour, allspice and almonds.

Spoon about half of mixture into lightly greased 9″ square pan. Carefully spread strawberry jam over top. Top with remaining dough.

Bake in moderate oven (350°) 40 to 45 minutes, or until delicately browned. Remove to cooling rack and sift confectioners sugar over top. When cool, cut in 1½″ squares. Makes 3 dozen.

JINGLE JAM BARS

You bake cake-like batter on berry jam and cut it in luscious ribbons

¼ c. butter
1 c. red raspberry jam
4 eggs
¾ c. sugar
1 tsp. vanilla

¾ c. sifted cake flour
1 tsp. baking powder
1 tsp. salt
Confectioners sugar

Melt butter in 15½ × 10½ × 1″ jelly roll pan. Mix jam with butter and spread evenly over bottom of pan.

Beat eggs until thick and lemon colored. Add sugar, 1 tblsp. at a time, beating after each addition. Add vanilla.

Sift together remaining dry ingredients and fold into egg mixture in 2 parts. Spread batter evenly over jam mixture in pan. Bake in hot oven (400°) 15 to 18 minutes. Remove from oven and let stand in pan for 5 minutes.

Then invert pan on sheet of wrapping paper or towel lightly dusted with confectioners sugar. Let stand 2 or 3 minutes. Then lift pan gradually, allowing cake to fall out slowly. Assist carefully with spatula, if necessary.

Cut cake crosswise in two equal pieces. Invert one piece over the other so that jam edges are together. Use paper to assist in turning one piece over the other. Cut in 2½ × 1½″ bars. Cool on racks. Makes 20.

NOTE: You can use strawberry, apricot or other jam instead of raspberry.

MARMALADE BARS

If you're looking for a superb go-with for tea or coffee, here it is

1 c. orange marmalade
½ c. chopped pecans
½ c. flaked coconut
½ c. regular margarine
1 c. brown sugar, firmly
   packed
1 egg
2 tblsp. orange juice

1½ c. sifted flour
1 tsp. baking powder
¼ tsp. baking soda
¼ tsp. salt
1 c. quick-cooking rolled oats
Orange Confectioners
   Frosting (recipe follows)

Combine marmalade, pecans and coconut. Set aside.

Beat margarine and brown sugar until light and fluffy. Beat in egg and orange juice to mix well.

Sift together flour, baking powder, soda and salt.

54

Add to beaten mixture. Fold in rolled oats. Spread half of dough into well-greased 13 × 9 × 2″ pan. Drop teaspoonfuls of marmalade mixture over dough and spread evenly to cover. Drop remaining half of dough over top. Carefully spread over filling.

Bake in moderate oven (350°) 35 to 38 minutes. While warm, frost with Orange Confectioners Frosting. Cool in pan set on rack, then cut in 3 × 1″ bars. Makes 39.

Orange Confectioners Frosting: Combine 2 tblsp. soft margarine, 1½ c. sifted confectioners sugar and 2 to 3 tblsp. orange juice (or enough to make a frosting of spreading consistency). Beat until smooth.

SWEDISH ALMOND SHORTBREAD

A crisp bar, subtly flavored with toasted almonds; sugar-sprinkled

2 c. butter
1 c. sugar
6 c. unsifted flour
1 tblsp. vanilla

½ tsp. salt
1 c. toasted slivered almonds
Sugar (for top)

Cream butter and sugar until fluffy. Work in flour, vanilla and salt. Roll out dough to fit two ungreased 15½ × 10½ × 1″ jelly roll pans (or three 13 × 9 × 2″ pans).

Sprinkle with almonds and sugar. Cut unbaked dough in 2½ × 1½″ bars. Bake in moderate oven (350°) about 15 minutes. Immediately recut bars along same lines. Cool in pans on racks. Makes 80.

BRAZIL NUT BARS

Distinctive holiday cookies with a rich, nutty flavor— try them

2 c. sifted flour
2 tsp. baking powder
¾ tsp. salt
½ tsp. ground cinnamon
½ c. shortening
⅓ c. butter or regular margarine

1 c. light brown sugar, firmly packed
2 eggs, beaten
1 tsp. vanilla
1 c. thinly sliced or chopped Brazil nuts
1 egg white

Sift together flour, baking powder, salt and cinnamon.

Cream together shortening, butter and brown sugar until light and fluffy. Add eggs and vanilla; beat until light. Add sifted dry ingredients and half of nuts. Spread in greased 15½ × 10½ × 1″ jelly roll pan, or two 8″ square pans.

Beat egg white slightly. Brush over dough; sprinkle with remaining nuts. Bake in moderate oven (350°) 20 to 30 minutes. Cut in 2 × 1″ bars. Cool in pans on racks. Makes about 6 dozen.

BROWN SUGAR CHEWS

No-fat cookies have crisp crust, and chewy, sweet walnut centers

1 egg	½ c. sifted flour
1 c. brown sugar, firmly packed	¼ tsp. salt
	¼ tsp. baking soda
1 tsp. vanilla	1 c. chopped walnuts

Combine egg, brown sugar and vanilla. Mix thoroughly.

Sift together flour, salt and baking soda; stir into brown sugar mixture, then stir in nuts.

Spread in greased 8″ square pan. Bake in moderate oven (350°) 15 to 18 minutes. Cool in pan on rack, then cut in 1½″ bars. (Chews are soft when warm.) Makes 25.

BROWN SUGAR/NUT BARS

Cut these chewy cookies in small squares—they're rich, satisfying

1 lb. brown sugar	1 tsp. baking powder
1 c. butter	½ tsp. salt
2 eggs	1 c. coarsely chopped walnuts
2 c. sifted flour	

Cook sugar and butter in top of double boiler over hot water until sugar dissolves. Cool.

Add eggs, one at a time, beating thoroughly after each addition. Stir in remaining ingredients. Spread in ungreased 15½ × 10½ × 1″ jelly roll pan. Bake in moderate oven (350°) 25 minutes. While hot, cut in 2″ squares or desired size. Cool in pan on rack. Makes about 35.

BUTTERSCOTCH STRIPS

Cookies three ways—strips, man-size squares and a four-layer stack

½ c. butter	2 tsp. baking powder
2 c. brown sugar, firmly packed	½ c. chopped nuts
	½ tsp. salt
2 eggs	2 tsp. vanilla
2 c. sifted flour	Confectioners sugar

Melt butter, add to sugar and cool. Blend in eggs. Stir in remaining ingredients.

Spread in lightly greased 13 × 9 × 2″ pan. Bake in slow oven (325°) about 30 minutes. While still warm, cut into 24 strips about 3 × 1½″. Roll in confectioners sugar. Cool on racks. Makes 2 dozen.

NOTE: These may be cut in 12 (3 × 3″) squares for man-size cookies.

VARIATION

Butterscotch Stack: Mix dough as directed and divide into four equal portions. Roll or pat out each portion into an 8″ circle between two pieces of waxed paper (draw an 8″ circle on counter top for guide).

Chill circles in refrigerator until top piece of paper can be peeled off easily; transfer circles on waxed paper to lightly greased baking sheets.

Bake in slow oven (325°) about 20 minutes. You may bake two at a time by using both oven shelves; be sure to exchange top and bottom baking sheets after 10 minutes in the oven for even browning.

Remove from baking sheet and cool on rack. When cool, peel off paper. Stack circles, spreading each with filling of whipped cream or scoops of softened ice cream. Freeze. To serve, let stand at room temperature about 15 minutes. Cut into wedges. Makes 10 to 12 servings.

CHEESECAKE BARS

They taste like cheesecake and that means rich and luscious

⅓ c. butter or regular margarine
⅓ c. brown sugar, firmly packed
1 c. sifted flour
½ c. chopped walnuts
¼ c. sugar
1 (8 oz.) pkg. cream cheese
1 egg, beaten
2 tblsp. milk
1 tblsp. lemon juice
½ tsp. vanilla

Cream butter and brown sugar until light; add flour and chopped walnuts. Cream with spoon until mixture forms crumbs. Set aside 1 c. mixture for topping. Press remaining crumb mixture into ungreased 8″ square pan.

Bake in moderate oven (350°) 12 to 15 minutes. Set pan on rack to cool.

Combine white sugar and cream cheese; beat until smooth. Add egg, milk, lemon juice and vanilla. Beat thoroughly to mix. Spread evenly in pan over baked crumbs. Sprinkle reserved 1 c. crumbs over top.

Bake in moderate oven (350°) 25 to 30 minutes. Set pan on rack to cool. Cut in 2 × 1″ bars and store in refrigerator. (Cookies are perishable and must be kept in refrigerator until eaten.) Makes 32.

FROSTED CARROT BARS

Carrots are the mystery ingredient in these wonderfully moist cookies

4 eggs
2 c. sugar
1½ c. salad oil
2 c. sifted flour
2 tsp. baking soda
2 tsp. ground cinnamon
1 tsp. salt
3 c. finely grated carrots (9 medium)
1½ c. flaked coconut
1½ c. chopped walnuts
Cream Cheese Frosting (recipe follows)

Beat eggs until light; gradually beat in sugar. Alternately add salad oil and flour sifted with soda, cinnamon and salt. Mix well.

Fold in carrots, coconut and walnuts. Spread evenly in two greased 13 × 9 × 2″ pans.

Bake in moderate oven (350°) 25 to 30 minutes. Set pans on racks and cool. Spread with Cream Cheese Frosting, then cut in 3 × 1" bars. Remove from pans and place in covered container. Store in refrigerator or freezer. Makes 6½ dozen.

Cream Cheese Frosting: Blend 1 (3 oz.) pkg. cream cheese with 1 tblsp. dairy half-and-half or whole milk. Add 2½ c. sifted confectioners sugar, 3 tblsp. dairy half-and-half or whole milk (or enough to make a frosting of spreading consistency), 1 tsp. vanilla and ⅛ tsp. salt. Beat to mix.

PENUCHE DREAM BARS

And we give you a chocolate variation—try both and take your pick

Bottom Layer:

½ c. shortening	1 c. sifted flour
½ c. brown sugar, firmly packed	½ tsp. salt
	2 tblsp. milk

Top Layer:

2 eggs	2 tblsp. flour
1 c. brown sugar, firmly packed	⅓ tsp. baking powder
1 tsp. vanilla	1 (3½ oz.) can flaked coconut (1⅓ c.)
½ tsp. salt	1 c. chopped pecans

For bottom layer, cream shortening and brown sugar until light and fluffy. Mix together flour and salt; add to creamed mixture. Stir in milk. Pat evenly in greased 9" square pan.

Bake in slow oven (325°) about 20 minutes, until light brown. Remove from oven.

To make top layer, combine eggs, brown sugar and vanilla; beat until mixture thickens.

Sift together salt, flour and baking powder; add to egg mixture. Mix well; stir in coconut and pecans. Spread evenly over baked bottom layer.

Bake in slow oven (325°) about 20 minutes, until golden brown. Set pan on rack and let cool, then cut in 2¼ × 1" bars. Makes 3 dozen.

Chocolate Dream Bars: Make and bake bottom layer as for Penuche Dream Bars, but use ⅓ c. butter or regular margarine instead of ½ c. shortening. Make top layer, substituting 1 (6 oz.) pkg. semisweet chocolate pieces for the coconut. Spread on baked layer and bake 15 to 20 minutes. Cool in pan on rack. Spread Easy Chocolate Icing on top and cut in 2¼ × 1″ bars.

Easy Chocolate Icing: Melt 1 tsp. butter with 1 square unsweetened chocolate over warm, not boiling, water. Remove from heat and stir in 1½ to 2 tblsp. hot water. Add enough sifted confectioners sugar (about 1 c.) to make icing that spreads easily. Beat until smooth. Makes enough to ice from 3 to 4 dozen cookies, depending on size, or a 9″ square pan of cookies.

PLANTATION PEANUT COOKIES

Cookies look and taste much like peanut brittle—a teen-age favorite

½ c. butter or shortening	1 c. sifted flour
½ c. brown sugar, firmly packed	¼ tsp. baking soda
1 egg, slightly beaten	½ tsp. ground cinnamon
1 tsp. vanilla	½ c. coarsely chopped salted peanuts
½ c. finely chopped salted peanuts	

Cream butter until light; beat in brown sugar until fluffy. Beat in 2 tblsp. beaten egg and vanilla to mix well. Add the ½ c. finely chopped peanuts.

Blend together flour, baking soda and cinnamon; add to creamed mixture. With floured fingers, pat dough on greased baking sheet to make a rectangle 14 × 10″. Brush top with remaining egg and sprinkle with coarsely chopped peanuts.

Bake in slow oven (325°) 20 to 22 minutes. Press lightly with finger. If a slight imprint remains, cookies are done. Use care not to overbake. While warm, cut in 3½ × 1½″ bars (or break in irregular pieces). Cool in pan on rack. Makes 2 dozen.

PECAN CHEWS

Easy-to-make cookies with a caramel, toasted-nut flavor

¾ c. butter
1½ c. brown sugar, firmly
   packed
1 egg

1 tsp. vanilla
½ tsp. salt
2 c. sifted flour
1 c. chopped toasted pecans

Cream butter and brown sugar until light and fluffy. Beat in egg, vanilla and salt. Blend in flour and nuts.

Spread dough in lightly greased 15½ × 10½ × 1" jelly roll pan. Bake in moderate oven (375°) about 15 minutes, or until lightly browned. Cool in pan on rack, then cut in 3 × 1" bars. Makes about 4 dozen.

NUT-CRESTED COOKIE SQUARES

Serve these candy-like cookies during the holidays with fruit punch

1 c. butter
1 c. brown sugar, firmly
   packed
1 tsp. vanilla
1 egg

2 c. sifted flour
⅛ tsp. salt
1 (6 oz.) pkg. semisweet
   chocolate pieces
½ c. finely chopped nuts

Cream butter until fluffy; add brown sugar and beat until light. Add vanilla and egg; then add the flour and salt. Blend well.

Spread evenly about ¼" thick on greased baking sheet. Bake in moderate oven (350°) 15 minutes.

Meanwhile melt chocolate pieces.

Remove baking sheet from oven and at once spread melted chocolate over top to frost evenly. Sprinkle with nuts. Cut in 2" squares while still hot. Cool in pan on racks. Makes about 4 dozen.

SOUTHERN PRALINE BARS

Rich butterscotch flavor makes these chewy, frosted bars favorites

½ c. lard
1½ c. brown sugar, firmly
  packed
2 eggs
1½ c. sifted flour
1 tsp. baking powder

1 tsp. salt
2 tsp. vanilla
¾ c. chopped pecans
Praline Frosting (recipe
  follows)

Melt lard in 2-qt. saucepan. Add remaining ingredients, except frosting, and mix well. Spread in greased 13 × 9 × 2″ pan.

Bake in moderate oven (350°) 25 to 30 minutes. Cool slightly in pan on rack, then spread with Praline Frosting. When cool, cut in 2 × 1½″ bars. Makes about 2½ dozen.

Praline Frosting: Melt together in saucepan 2 tblsp. butter, ¼ c. brown sugar, firmly packed, and 2 tblsp. light cream or milk. Stir in about 1 c. sifted confectioners sugar (enough to make a frosting of spreading consistency) and beat until smooth.

VARIATION

Coconut Praline Bars: Substitute ¾ c. flaked coconut for the pecans and bake as directed.

SWEDISH HEIRLOOM BARS

*Dainty tea-party cookies accented with cinnamon—
a women's special*

1 c. sugar
1 c. shortening
½ tsp. vanilla
1 egg, separated

2 c. sifted flour
½ tsp. salt
1 tblsp. ground cinnamon
1 c. finely chopped nuts

Cream sugar, shortening and vanilla until mixture is light and fluffy. Beat in egg yolk.

Sift together flour, salt and cinnamon; stir into creamed mixture and mix well. Spread dough in greased 15½ × 10½ × 1″ jelly roll pan (dough will be spread thin).

Beat egg white until frothy and spread over top of dough. Sprinkle nuts evenly over egg white topping.

Bake in moderate oven (350°) about 20 minutes. Cool in pan on rack 10 minutes, then cut in 2 × 1½″ bars. Makes about 50.

SPEEDY COOKIES SUPREME

Quick and easy—youngsters like the pronounced brown sugar flavor

2 c. brown sugar, firmly
   packed
2 eggs

½ c. butter or shortening
2 c. sifted flour
1 c. broken nuts

Combine 1 c. brown sugar, 1 egg, beaten, butter and flour. Blend thoroughly. Press dough onto greased large baking sheet (about 17 × 14″).

Beat the remaining egg and spread over top of dough on baking sheet; sprinkle with ½ c. brown sugar, then with nuts. Scatter remaining ½ c. brown sugar over top.

Bake in moderate oven (350°) about 15 minutes, until light brown. Cool on baking sheet set on rack 10 minutes, then cut in 2″ squares, or desired shapes. Makes about 4½ dozen.

TOFFEE STICKS

These take more time to make than many bars, but they are worth it

¾ c. butter or regular
   margarine
½ c. brown sugar, firmly
   packed
1 egg yolk
1 tsp. vanilla
¼ tsp. salt
1½ c. sifted flour

2 tblsp. shortening
1 (6 oz.) pkg. butterscotch
   pieces
¼ c. light corn syrup
1 tblsp. water
¼ tsp. salt
Toasted slivered almonds
   (for top)

Blend together butter, brown sugar, egg yolk, vanilla and salt. Stir in flour. Spread mixture in greased 13 × 9 × 2″ pan.

Bake in moderate oven (350°) 20 minutes, or until nicely browned. Cool slightly in pan on rack.

Combine shortening, butterscotch morsels, corn syrup, water and salt in saucepan. Heat and stir until smooth; spread over top of baked dough. Sprinkle on almonds. Allow topping to set, then cut in 2 × 1″ sticks. Makes about 4 dozen.

WALNUT BARS

Chewy nut cookies have crackly tops—
they disappear fast

¾ c. sifted flour
¼ tsp. salt
¼ tsp. baking soda

2 c. brown sugar, lightly
  packed
2 eggs
1 c. coarsely chopped walnuts

Sift together flour, salt and soda. Add sugar and eggs, mix well; then beat quickly until fluffy. Add nuts.

Bake in greased 9″ square pan in moderate oven (350°) 30 minutes. Cool in pan on rack, then cut in 2 × 1″ bars. Makes about 32.

WALNUT/CINNAMON SQUARES

This recipe and variations make eight different
kinds of cookies

1 c. butter
1 c. sugar
1 egg, separated

2 c. sifted flour
1 tsp. ground cinnamon
1 c. finely chopped walnuts

In a mixing bowl, cream together butter and sugar. Beat in egg yolk to mix thoroughly.

Sift together flour and cinnamon; stir into creamed mixture and mix thoroughly. Spread dough evenly over bottom of lightly greased 15½ × 10½ × 1″ jelly roll pan.

Beat egg white slightly; brush over top of dough. With fingertips, smooth surface. Sprinkle nuts over dough and press in.

Bake in very slow oven (275°) 1 hour. While still hot, cut in 1½″ squares; cool in pans on racks. Makes about 5½ dozen.

VARIATIONS

Austrian Almond Squares: Make dough for Walnut/ Cinnamon Squares, but substitute 1 tsp. ground nutmeg for the cinnamon and 1 c. chopped or sliced almonds for the walnuts. Bake as directed.

Orange/Pecan Flats: Make cookies as directed for

Walnut/Cinnamon Squares, but add 1 tblsp. grated orange peel along with egg yolk. Omit cinnamon and use chopped pecans instead of walnuts.

Turkish Cardamoms: Make cookies as directed for Walnut/Cinnamon Squares, but substitute 1 tsp. ground cardamom for the cinnamon and 1 c. chopped filberts or hazelnuts for the walnuts.

Macadamia Nut Gingers: Make cookies as directed for Walnut/Cinnamon Squares, but substitute 1 tsp. ground ginger for the cinnamon and use finely chopped roasted salted macadamia nuts instead of walnuts.

Peanut Salts: Make cookies as directed for Walnut/ Cinnamon Squares, except use 1 c. brown sugar, firmly packed, instead of white sugar. Omit cinnamon, and use salted roasted peanuts instead of walnuts.

Brown Sugar Spice Crisps: Make cookies as directed for Walnut/Cinnamon Squares, substituting 1 c. light brown sugar, firmly packed, for the white sugar. Use 1½ tsp. ground cinnamon instead of 1, and add ¾ tsp. ground nutmeg, ¾ tsp. ground ginger and ¼ tsp. ground cloves along with cinnamon. Omit walnuts, topping only with egg whites.

Lemon or Lime Sugar Crisps: Make cookies as directed for Walnut/Cinnamon Squares, but add 2 tblsp. grated lemon or lime peel along with egg yolk. Omit cinnamon and walnuts.

GOLDEN COCONUT DIAMONDS

You brush icing on these Danish cookies
luscious with coconut

1 c. butter	1 c. sifted confectioners sugar
1 c. sugar	(about)
Few drops yellow food color	2 tblsp. light rum, or about
1 c. flaked coconut	1 tsp. rum flavoring plus
2 c. sifted flour	2 tsp. water

Cream together butter and sugar until light and fluffy. Beat in food color; stir in coconut. Gradually stir in flour to make a smooth dough.

With lightly floured fingertips, press dough evenly over bottom of greased 15½ × 10½ × 1″ jelly roll pan. Bake in slow oven (325°) 25 to 30 minutes, or until lightly browned.

Mix confectioners sugar and rum to make a thin icing. While cookies are hot, drizzle on icing and quickly brush it over cookies to form a glaze. While still warm, cut cookies in 8 lengthwise strips, then diagonally in 1″ wide strips to make diamonds. Cool in pan on rack. Makes about 80.

CRUMBLE COOKIES

This three-generation family recipe came from England with the homemaker's grandmother. Easy to make, great with tea or milk

1 c. dark brown sugar, firmly packed	1 c. butter 2¼ c. sifted flour

Combine all ingredients in large bowl of electric mixer; beat at medium speed to mix thoroughly. Press over bottom of ungreased 13 × 9 × 2″ pan.

Bake in moderate oven (350°) 15 to 17 minutes, or until golden brown. Set pan on rack. Cut in 2″ squares while warm; let cool a few minutes before removing from pan. Makes about 28.

FROSTED MOLASSES CREAMS

Coffee flavors these molasses cookies and the frosting they wear

½ c. shortening	¾ tsp. salt
½ c. sugar	¼ tsp. baking soda
1 egg, beaten	1 tsp. ground cinnamon
½ c. molasses	½ tsp. ground cloves
⅓ c. strong, hot coffee	Creamy Coffee Icing (recipe
1½ c. sifted flour	follows)
1½ tsp. baking powder	

Cream together shortening and sugar; blend in egg, molasses and coffee.

Sift together dry ingredients; add to creamed mixture and blend well. Pour into greased and waxed-paper lined 13 × 9 × 2″ pan.

Bake in moderate oven (350°) 25 minutes. While warm, frost with Creamy Coffee Icing. Cool in pan on rack, then cut in 3 × 1″ bars. Makes about 39.

Creamy Coffee Icing: Cream ¼ c. butter or margarine

with 2 c. confectioners sugar. Add about 2 tblsp. cold coffee, enough to make an icing of spreading consistency; mix until smooth.

OATMEAL SHORTBREADS

Try these nutty, not-too-sweet cookies as an accompaniment to cheese

1½ c. sifted flour
⅔ c. brown sugar, firmly
   packed

⅔ c. quick-cooking rolled
   oats
1 c. butter

Combine all ingredients in large mixing bowl. With pastry blender or fingers, cut or rub ingredients together until well blended and crumbly. Press firmly and evenly into greased 15½ × 10½ × 1″ jelly roll pan. (Lightly flour fingertips if necessary to prevent sticking.)

Bake in slow oven (300°) 40 to 45 minutes, or until deep golden. While still hot, cut in 2 × 1½″ bars. Cool in pan on rack. Makes about 4 dozen.

Drop Cookies

BITE INTO plump, golden drop cookies and you'll often discover happy surprises in our recipes—dates, raisins, currants, cherries, nuts, chocolate pieces, citron, coconut and other treats. These are the substantial family cookies that usually travel successfully and keep well (if you hide them). They fill more cookie jars than any other kind and contribute much to the fame of country kitchens.

Next to bars, drop cookies are the easiest type to make. True, you do have several bakings, but if pressed for time, you can divide the dough and freeze part of it to bake when you have a little leisure or want to serve freshly baked cookies with coffee to business callers or neighbors who stop by.

Many cookies that once were rolled and cut now are represented in the drop cookie family. Try Grandma's Soft Sugar Cookies in this section and see if they don't remind you of the rolled cookies you used to eat at your grandmother's house. They're big and fat, with a glistening sprinkle of sugar and a raisin decoration in the center.

It's a real sacrifice not to give honorable mention to many of our drop cookie recipes. For instance, Hampshire Hermits, in which the flavors of citron and Lemon Glaze blend so harmoniously. And if you like fig cookies, you'll want to try California Fig Cookies. They're *really* good.

The dough for drop cookies is soft enough to drop from a spoon. Use a kitchen spoon rather than a measuring spoon, and take slightly rounded rather than level spoonfuls (unless recipe specifies otherwise.) Push dough off the spoon with a rubber spatula or another spoon. Make the drops the same size and peak them up so they will bake evenly and look attractive. Bake them *just until done,* or until a slight imprint remains when you touch a cookie lightly with your finger. Remove from baking sheet unless the recipe directs otherwise. If left on a hot sheet, they continue to bake and may overbake.

You also will find several crisp cookies in this section that start as drops of dough. Sesame Wafers are an excellent example. So are see-through, party lace cookies, flat or rolled (after baking) the Swedish way.

The generous collection of oatmeal cookie recipes includes the favorites of the countryside, be they crisp, chewy or soft. Among them are Rookie Cookies, which, as some women know from experience, greatly please men.

ALMOND JEWELS

Cookies bright as a Mexican fiesta with that Chinese-almond taste

2 c. sifted flour	1 egg
½ tsp. baking powder	¾ tsp. vanilla
¼ tsp. salt	¾ c. chopped almonds
½ c. butter or regular margarine	Gumdrops
	Almonds (for tops)
¾ c. sifted brown sugar, firmly packed	

Sift together flour, baking powder and salt.

Cream butter; add sugar gradually; cream until light and fluffy. Beat in egg and vanilla; stir in chopped nuts. Add dry ingredients and mix.

Drop teaspoonfuls of dough 1½ to 2" apart onto lightly greased baking sheet. Decorate tops with pieces of bright gumdrops (not licorice) and insert lengthwise slices of almonds in cookie centers.

Bake in moderate oven (350°) 12 to 15 minutes. Cool cookies on racks. Makes 3½ dozen.

ANISE DROPS

Cookies make their own creamy white topping while they bake

3 eggs
1 c. plus 2 tblsp. sugar
1¾ c. sifted flour
½ tsp. baking powder

½ tsp. salt
1 tsp. anise extract or 3 tblsp.
  anise seeds

Beat eggs with electric mixer at medium speed until fluffy. Gradually add sugar, beating constantly. Continue to beat for 20 minutes.

Reduce speed of mixer to low and add flour sifted with baking powder and salt. Beat in anise extract. Drop dough by teaspoonfuls about ½" apart onto well-greased baking sheet, swirling dough to make a round cookie. Let stand at least 8 hours to dry, preferably overnight.

Bake in slow oven (325°) about 10 minutes, or until cookies are a creamy golden color, not brown, on bottom. Remove cookies to rack to cool. Makes about 50.

BLACK WALNUT COOKIES

Tastes like sour cream cookies Grandma served with applesauce

½ c. shortening
¾ c. sugar
1 egg
½ tsp. vanilla
2 c. sifted flour
1 tsp. baking powder

1 tsp. ground cinnamon
½ tsp. salt
¼ tsp. baking soda
½ c. dairy sour cream
½ c. chopped black walnuts

Cream shortening and sugar until light and fluffy. Beat in egg and vanilla.

Sift together dry ingredients. Add to creamed mixture, alternately with sour cream. Stir in walnuts.

Drop by teaspoonfuls about 2" apart onto greased baking sheet. Press flat with bottom of drinking glass, dipping glass into sugar before pressing each cookie.

Bake in moderate oven (375°) 9 to 12 minutes. Remove cookies and cool on racks. Makes 4½ dozen.

BEST-EVER BUTTERSCOTCH COOKIES

*One of the best-tasting cookies ever baked
in Countryside Kitchens*

1 tblsp. vinegar
1 c. evaporated milk (about)
½ c. butter or regular
  margarine
1½ c. brown sugar, firmly
  packed
2 eggs
1 tsp. vanilla
2½ c. sifted flour

1 tsp. baking soda
½ tsp. baking powder
½ tsp. salt
⅔ c. chopped walnuts or
  pecans
Brown Butter Frosting (recipe
  follows)
Walnut or pecan halves

Put vinegar in a 1-cup measure; add evaporated milk and set aside.

Beat butter until light; add brown sugar and beat until mixture is light and fluffy. Beat in eggs and vanilla to blend thoroughly.

Sift together flour, baking soda, baking powder and salt.

Stir evaporated milk and add alternately with dry ingredients to creamed mixture. Stir in chopped nuts. Drop rounded tablespoonfuls of dough about 2½" apart onto lightly greased baking sheet.

Bake in moderate oven (350°) 10 to 12 minutes, or until lightly browned and barely firm to touch. Remove cookies and cool on racks. When cool, spread with Brown Butter Frosting and press a walnut or pecan half in each cookie. Makes about 5 dozen.

Brown Butter Frosting: Melt ½ c. butter in small saucepan and cook over medium heat, stirring constantly, until butter stops bubbling and is nut-brown in color (do not scorch). Combine with 2 c. sifted confectioners sugar and 2 to 4 tblsp. boiling water; beat until smooth and of spreading consistency. Makes enough to frost about 5 dozen cookies.

BUTTERSCOTCH DROPS

*These soft, chewy, delicious, easy, economical
cookies always please*

1 c. shortening
2 c. brown sugar, firmly
  packed
2 eggs

½ c. buttermilk or water
3½ c. sifted flour
1 tsp. baking soda
1 tsp. salt

Mix shortening, brown sugar and eggs. Stir in buttermilk.

Sift together flour, soda and salt, and add to first mixture. Chill.

Drop by teaspoonfuls about 2″ apart onto lightly greased baking sheet. Bake in hot oven (400°) 8 to 10 minutes until set (almost no imprint when touched with finger). Makes 6 dozen.

CASHEW DROPS

Pleasant surprise: biting into a whole-cashew center

½ c. butter or regular
  margarine
1 c. brown sugar, firmly
  packed
1 egg
½ tsp. vanilla
2 c. sifted flour

¾ tsp. baking powder
¾ tsp. baking soda
¼ tsp. salt
⅓ c. dairy sour cream
1¾ c. whole cashew nuts
Golden Butter Glaze (recipe
  follows)

Cream butter and sugar until light and fluffy. Beat in egg and vanilla to mix thoroughly. Add sifted dry ingredients alternately with sour cream, blending well. Carefully fold in nuts.

Drop by well-rounded teaspoonfuls 2″ apart onto greased baking sheet.

Bake in hot oven (400°) 8 to 10 minutes. Remove cookies and cool on racks. Top with Golden Butter Glaze, if desired. Makes about 4 dozen.

Golden Butter Glaze: Melt ½ c. butter in saucepan over medium heat until it turns *light* golden brown (use care not to overbrown). Remove from heat and add 3 c. sifted confectioners sugar, 1 tsp. vanilla and enough hot water (3 to 4 tblsp.) to make a glaze that will spread smoothly. Beat well. Makes enough to frost or glaze 4 dozen cookies, depending on size.

CORN FLAKE COOKIES

*Coconut takes the spotlight in these
extra-good, crisp cookies*

2 c. sifted flour
1 tsp. baking soda
½ tsp. salt
½ tsp. baking powder
1¼ c. shortening
1 c. sugar

1 c. brown sugar, firmly
  packed
2 eggs, well beaten
1 tsp. vanilla
2 c. flaked or shredded
  coconut
2 c. corn flakes

Sift together flour, soda, salt and baking powder.

Cream shortening; gradually add sugars; beat until light. Add eggs and vanilla.

Combine dry ingredients and creamed mixture; add coconut and corn flakes.

Drop small teaspoonfuls 1½" apart onto greased baking sheet.

Bake in moderate oven (350°) 8 to 10 minutes, or until delicately browned. Spread on racks to cool. Makes 8 dozen.

CREAM CHEESE DROP COOKIES

*Lemon and cheese flavors blend tastily
in these drop cookies*

¾ c. butter
1 (3 oz.) pkg. cream cheese
1 c. sifted confectioners sugar
1 tblsp. lemon juice
1 tsp. vanilla

2 tsp. grated lemon peel
2 c. sifted cake flour
1 c. chopped pecans
Sifted confectioners sugar (for
  rolling)

Cream butter and cream cheese until light and fluffy. Gradually add 1 c. confectioners sugar, beating thoroughly. Stir in lemon juice, vanilla and lemon peel. Add flour and mix well. Stir in nuts.

Drop by scant teaspoonfuls about 2" apart onto ungreased baking sheet. Bake in a slow oven (300°) about 25 minutes, until set but not brown. While hot roll in sifted confectioners sugar. Cool on racks. Makes 4 dozen.

GUESS-AGAIN COOKIES

*The slightly salty, crisp bits in these rich cookies
are potato chips!*

1 c. butter or regular
  margarine
½ c. sugar
1 tsp. vanilla

2 c. sifted flour
½ c. crushed potato chips
½ c. chopped pecans

Beat butter, sugar and vanilla until light and fluffy.
Add flour, potato chips and nuts; mix well.

Drop by scant teaspoonfuls 2″ apart onto ungreased
baking sheet. Flatten by pressing with bottom of drinking glass, greased and dipped in sugar (grease and
sugar glass as needed).

Bake in moderate oven (350°) 10 to 11 minutes.
Remove to racks to cool. Makes about 5 dozen.

MAPLE WAFERS

*You can bake these maple cookies even if you live
far from sugar bush country. Try frosting
on your favorite sugar cookies, too*

3 tblsp. butter or regular
  margarine
½ c. maple-blended syrup
1 egg, beaten
2 tblsp. milk
1 c. sifted flour

1 tsp. cream of tartar
½ tsp. baking soda
¼ tsp. salt
¾ c. chopped nuts
Maple Frosting (recipe
  follows)

Melt butter. Remove from heat and stir in maple
syrup. Add egg and milk and mix well.

Sift together flour, cream of tartar, baking soda and
salt. Add to maple syrup mixture; blend well. Fold in
nuts. Chill thoroughly (batter thickens).

Drop dough by teaspoonfuls 2″ apart onto lightly
greased baking sheet. Bake in hot oven (400°) 8 to 10
minutes. Remove cookies and cool on racks. When cool,
spread with Maple Frosting. Makes about 2 dozen.

Maple Frosting: Heat ¼ c. butter until light golden
brown. Stir in 1 c. sifted confectioners sugar, ⅛ tsp.
salt, ¾ to 1 tsp. maple flavoring and 1 tblsp. hot water,
or enough to make frosting that will spread smoothly
on wafers.

POTATO CHIP COOKIES

*Something different! These chewy cookies
will be the talk of your next coffee party
when you reveal what's in them*

1 c. shortening	2 eggs
1 c. sugar	1 tsp. vanilla
1 c. brown sugar, firmly packed	2 c. sifted flour
	1 c. crushed potato chips

Beat shortening until light; gradually add white and brown sugars, beating constantly. When light and fluffy, add eggs, one at a time, beating after each addition. Add vanilla and beat to blend thoroughly.

Stir in flour, then fold in potato chips. Drop by rounded teaspoonfuls 2″ apart onto lightly greased baking sheet. Flatten with floured fork tines.

Bake in moderate oven (350°) 12 to 15 minutes, or until light golden brown. Spread on racks to cool. Makes about 5 dozen.

SALTED PEANUT COOKIES

*Red-skinned and creamy white peanuts
dot these brown cookies*

1 c. shortening	1 tsp. baking powder
2 c. brown sugar, firmly packed	½ tsp. baking soda
2 eggs	2 c. quick-cooking rolled oats
1 tsp. vanilla	1 c. corn flakes
2 c. sifted flour	1 c. salted peanuts (skins on)

Cream shortening and brown sugar until light and fluffy. Beat in eggs to mix thoroughly. Beat in vanilla.

Sift together flour, baking powder and soda; stir into creamed mixture. Then fold in rolled oats, corn flakes and peanuts. Drop by rounded teaspoonfuls 2″ apart onto greased baking sheet.

Bake in moderate oven (350°) 10 to 12 minutes. Spread on racks to cool. Makes about 7 dozen.

SESAME WAFERS

Dainty, crisp and rich-flavored—
taste-testers were enthusiastic

¾ c. melted butter or regular
   margarine
1½ c. light brown sugar,
   firmly packed
1 tsp. vanilla
1 egg

1 c. Toasted Sesame Seeds
   (recipe follows)
1¼ c. sifted flour
¼ tsp. baking powder
¼ tsp. salt

Cream butter and sugar until light and fluffy. Add vanilla and egg; beat to mix thoroughly. Stir in sesame seeds.

Sift together flour, baking powder and salt; stir into creamed mixture. Drop half teaspoonfuls of dough about 2″ apart onto lightly greased baking sheet.

Bake in moderate oven (375°) about 5 to 6 minutes, or until edges brown (bottoms of cookies brown and burn quickly). Remove from oven and transfer cookies at once to racks to cool. Makes about 7 dozen.

Toasted Sesame Seeds: Spread seeds in a shallow pan and heat in a moderate oven (350°) about 20 minutes, until they turn a pale brown; stir occasionally. Remove from oven and cool. (Watch while they are in the oven to prevent scorching.)

SOUR CREAM DROP COOKIES

New version of old-time sour cream cookies
uses dairy sour cream

1 c. shortening
2 c. sugar
1 tsp. vanilla
3 eggs
1 c. dairy sour cream
5 c. sifted flour

½ tsp. baking soda
3 tsp. baking powder
1 tsp. salt
1½ c. chopped walnuts
2 tblsp. sugar
1 tsp. ground cinnamon

Beat shortening until light; add 2 c. sugar and beat until fluffy. Beat in vanilla and eggs to mix thoroughly. Beat in sour cream.

Sift together flour, baking soda, baking powder and salt. Add to creamed mixture. Fold in chopped nuts. Chill 1 hour, or until dough is easy to handle.

Drop dough by teaspoonfuls about 2″ apart onto lightly greased baking sheet.

Combine 2 tblsp. sugar with cinnamon. Lightly grease bottom of drinking glass (2¼″ in diameter) and dip in cinnamon/sugar mixture. Press cookies flat.

Bake in moderate oven (350°) about 12 minutes. Remove to racks to cool. Makes about 6 dozen.

CHOCOLATE BANANA COOKIES

Delicious way to salvage very ripe bananas— tasty, moist cookies

1 c. sugar
⅔ c. shortening
2 eggs
1 tsp. vanilla
1 c. mashed bananas (2½ medium)
1 (6 oz.) pkg. semisweet chocolate pieces, melted

2½ c. sifted flour
2 tsp. baking powder
¼ tsp. salt
¼ tsp. baking soda
Chocolate Frosting (recipe follows)

Beat together sugar and shortening until mixture is light and fluffy. Beat in eggs and vanilla, mixing well. Add bananas and melted chocolate.

Sift together flour, baking powder, salt and baking soda. Add to beaten mixture. Drop by teaspoonfuls about 2″ apart onto lightly greased baking sheet.

Bake in moderate oven (350°) 10 minutes. Remove cookies and cool on racks; then frost with Chocolate Frosting, if desired. Makes about 5 dozen.

Chocolate Frosting: Combine 2 tblsp. soft butter, 2 squares unsweetened chocolate, melted, 3 tblsp. warm water and 2 c. sifted confectioners sugar. Beat until smooth.

CHOCOLATE CHEESE COOKIES

Crisp cookies with a delicate flavor of chocolate and cream cheese

½ c. butter
½ c. shortening
1 (3 oz.) pkg. cream cheese
1½ c. sugar
1 egg
½ tsp. vanilla

2 squares semisweet chocolate, melted and cooled slightly
2¼ c. sifted flour
1½ tsp. baking powder
½ tsp. salt
2 tblsp. milk
½ c. chopped nuts (optional)

Beat butter, shortening and cream cheese until light. Gradually add sugar, beating until mixture is light and fluffy. Beat in egg, vanilla and melted chocolate.

Sift together flour, baking powder and salt. Add alternately with milk to chocolate mixture. Stir in nuts.

Drop by teaspoonfuls 2" apart onto lightly greased baking sheet. Bake in moderate oven (350°) about 15 minutes. Remove cookies and cool on racks. Makes about 4½ dozen.

NOTE: Use unsweetened instead of semisweet chocolate for a more pronounced chocolate flavor.

CHOCOLATE HERMITS

Make dainty, tea-size or man-size cookies according to your needs. Top with a chocolate confectioners sugar frosting (see Index)—a decorative curl for dainty cookies, a generous covering for others

1⅓ c. sifted flour	3 squares unsweetened
2 tsp. baking powder	chocolate, melted
½ tsp. salt	1 tsp. vanilla
1 tsp. ground cinnamon	⅓ c. milk
½ c. shortening	1 c. chopped raisins
1 c. sugar	1 c. chopped nuts
1 egg, well beaten	

Sift together flour, baking powder, salt and cinnamon.

Cream shortening; add sugar gradually; cream until fluffy.

Add egg to creamed mixture with chocolate; blend well. Add vanilla and milk. Stir in dry ingredients, raisins and nuts. Mix well; chill 30 minutes.

Drop by teaspoonfuls about 2" apart onto greased baking sheet. Bake in moderate oven (350°) 15 minutes. Remove cookies and cool on racks. Makes 2 dozen.

CHOCOLATE MARSHMALLOW CAKELETS

Cookies resemble little cakes, ideal for cold weather because chocolate topping sometimes gets sticky when it's hot and humid

½ c. shortening
1 c. brown sugar, firmly
   packed
1 egg
1¾ c. sifted flour
½ tsp. baking soda
½ tsp. salt
½ c. cocoa

½ c. milk
½ c. chopped walnuts
18 regular marshmallows
   (about), cut in halves
1 (6 oz.) pkg. semisweet
   chocolate pieces
2 tblsp. butter
½ tsp. ground cinnamon

Beat shortening until light; add brown sugar and beat until fluffy. Beat in egg to blend.

Sift together flour, baking soda, salt and cocoa. Beat flour mixture alternately with milk into creamed mixture. Stir in walnuts.

Drop rounded teaspoonfuls of dough 2″ apart onto lightly greased baking sheet. Bake in moderate oven (350°) 12 to 15 minutes. Remove from oven and top with marshmallow halves. Set pan on rack until cookies are cool enough to handle.

Melt chocolate pieces with butter; stir in cinnamon. Holding cookies in hand, use a small spatula and swirl their tops with chocolate mixture to cover marshmallows. Cool cookies on racks. Makes about 3 dozen.

CHOCO-MARSHMALLOW COOKIES

*Fat marshmallows atop chocolate cookies
go fancy with frosting*

1¾ c. sifted cake flour
½ tsp. salt
½ tsp. baking soda
½ c. cocoa
½ c. shortening
1 c. sugar
1 egg

1 tsp. vanilla
¼ c. milk
18 regular marshmallows, cut
   in halves
Cocoa Frosting (recipe
   follows)
36 pecan halves (½ c.)

Sift together flour, salt, soda and cocoa.

Cream shortening and sugar; add egg, vanilla and milk, beating well. Add dry ingredients and mix. Drop by teaspoonfuls about 2″ apart onto greased baking sheet.

Bake in moderate oven (350°) 8 minutes (don't overbake). Remove from oven and press a marshmallow half, cut side down, on top of each cookie. Bake

2 minutes longer. Remove cookies and cool on racks. Top with Cocoa Frosting, then with a pecan half. Makes 3 dozen.

Cocoa Frosting: Combine 2 c. sifted confectioners sugar, 5 tblsp. cocoa and ⅛ tsp. salt. Add 3 tblsp. soft butter or margarine and 4 to 5 tblsp. light cream. Blend until smooth.

CHOCOLATE POTATO COOKIES

A homey pioneer favorite made with buttermilk— moist, good keepers

½ c. shortening	1½ c. sifted flour
1 c. brown sugar, firmly packed	½ tsp. salt
	½ tsp. baking soda
1 egg	¾ c. buttermilk
1 tsp. vanilla	½ c. chopped walnuts or pecans
2 squares unsweetened chocolate, melted	½ recipe for Chocolate Frosting (see Index)
½ c. unseasoned mashed potatoes (room temperature)	

Cream together shortening and brown sugar until light and fluffy. Beat in egg and vanilla to mix well. Add chocolate and mashed potatoes and beat until smooth.

Sift together flour, salt and baking soda; add alternately with buttermilk to creamed mixture. Stir until smooth, then add nuts. Drop by rounded teaspoonfuls 2″ apart onto greased baking sheet.

Bake in hot oven (400°) about 10 minutes, or until cookies, when touched with finger, spring back (do not overbake). Let remain on baking sheet a minute or two before removing to racks for cooling. While *still warm,* spread on Chocolate Frosting. Makes 4½ dozen.

CHOCOLATE SANDWICH TREASURES

Favorite of a Pennsylvania woman— keeps well, sells fast at bazaars

1 c. milk	4 c. sifted flour
5 tblsp. flour	2 tsp. baking soda
1 c. confectioners sugar	½ tsp. baking powder
1 c. shortening	½ tsp. salt
¼ tsp. salt	1 c. buttermilk
½ c. shortening	¾ c. boiling water
2 c. sugar	½ c. cocoa
2 eggs	2 drops red or green food
1 tsp. vanilla	color (optional)

To make filling, combine ½ c. milk with 5 tblsp. flour and mix to a smooth paste. Add remaining ½ c. milk. Cook over medium heat, stirring, until mixture thickens. Set aside to cool.

In large mixer bowl, beat at medium speed confectioners sugar, 1 c. shortening and ¼ tsp. salt until light and fluffy. Add cooked mixture and continue beating until fluffy. Set aside while you bake cookies. (You'll have 2½ cups.)

To make cookie dough, beat ½ c. shortening until light; gradually add white sugar and beat until mixture is light and fluffy. Beat in eggs and vanilla to mix well.

Sift together 4 c. flour, baking soda, baking powder and ½ tsp. salt. Alternately add with buttermilk to creamed mixture.

Pour boiling water over cocoa and stir to mix. Cool and add to dough, mixing well.

Drop by teaspoonfuls (not heaping) 1″ apart onto lightly greased baking sheet. Bake in moderate oven (350°) 8 minutes. Remove from pan and cool on racks.

When cookies are cool, put together in pairs with filling spread between. You'll use 2 c. to fill cookies. Tint remaining ½ c. filling a delicate pink or green with 2 drops red or green food color, or leave filling untinted. Drop a little on top of each cookie sandwich. A nut or flaked coconut may be placed on top for decoration. Makes 5 dozen filled cookies.

NOTE: When the Pennsylvania homemaker who contributed this recipe wants to give the cookies a special appeal for guests, she divides the filling in quarters and places each part in a small bowl. She leaves one part creamy white, tints the other three delicately with food color—pink, green and yellow-orange. Then she decorates the tops of the sandwiches with a bit of the filling, adding nuts or flaked coconut for a trim.

Florentines Direct from Italy

Many American tourists in Europe resolve, once they get home, to duplicate the Florentines they ate in Italy. These cookies are almost a confection—half candy, half cookie. They are rich, sweet and excellent with coffee for evening refreshments. It's the combination of flavors—candied orange peel, chocolate and cream—plus the crisp texture that makes the cookies so rewarding.

Their name comes from the city of Florence, according to most food historians, back in the 15th or 16th century.

Our taste tests revealed that many people on this side of the Atlantic Ocean prefer a little less candied orange peel than Europeans like. Our recipe calls for ¾ cup finely chopped peel, but there's no law against using 1 to 1½ cups of it.

FLORENTINES

Lacy cookies for special occasions, painted
with melted chocolate

¾ c. heavy cream	¾ c. very finely chopped
¼ c. sugar	candied orange peel (4 oz.
¼ c. sifted flour	pkg.)
½ c. very finely chopped	2 (4 oz.) bars sweet cooking
slivered blanched almonds	chocolate

Stir cream and sugar together to blend well. Stir in flour, almonds and orange peel. Drop by scant teaspoonfuls about 1¼" apart onto heavily greased and floured baking sheet. *Flatten cookies with spatula;* they will be about ½ to ¾" apart after flattening.

Bake in moderate oven (350°) about 10 to 12 minutes, until cookies brown lightly around edges. (Centers of cookies will be bubbling when you remove them from oven.) Let stand 2 or 3 minutes or until they become firmer. Place on wire rack or waxed paper to cool.

Meanwhile, melt chocolate over hot, not boiling, water. When cookies are cool, turn upside down and brush with melted chocolate. Let dry several hours or overnight at room temperature to give chocolate time to set. (In hot, humid weather, use chocolate confection coating, melted, instead of sweet cooking chocolate.) Store in covered container in refrigerator or freezer. Makes about 4 dozen.

FROSTED DROP BROWNIES

Frost some cookies white, some with chocolate to provide interest

½ c. butter or regular margarine	½ tsp. salt
¾ c. sugar	½ c. milk
1 egg	1 tsp. vanilla
2 squares unsweetened chocolate, melted	½ c. chopped nuts
1¾ c. sifted flour	Shiny White Icing or Chocolate Icing
½ tsp. baking soda	36 walnut or pecan halves

Cream butter and sugar until fluffy. Add egg and beat well. Stir in melted chocolate.

Sift together flour, baking soda and salt. Add alternately with the milk to the chocolate mixture. Stir in vanilla and nuts.

Drop by teaspoonfuls 2″ apart onto ungreased baking sheet; bake in hot oven (400°) 8 to 10 minutes. Remove cookies and cool on racks. Drop 1 tsp. Shiny White or Chocolate Icing onto center of each cookie and swirl with a fork. Top with walnut or pecan halves. Makes 3 dozen cookies.

Shiny White Icing: Add enough cream or milk to 2 c. sifted confectioners sugar to make icing of spreading consistency. Add ½ tsp. vanilla. (Tint part of the icing a delicate pink with a few drops red food color. Flavor with peppermint extract, if you like.)

Chocolate Icing: Add 1 square unsweetened chocolate, melted, to 1 c. sifted confectioners sugar; beat in enough cream or milk to make icing of spreading consistency. Add ½ tsp. vanilla.

MALTED CHOCOLATE DROPS

Just the cookie chocolate lovers adore—try the frosted variation

⅔ c. butter or regular margarine
¾ c. sugar
2 eggs
1 tsp. vanilla
2 c. sifted flour
2 tsp. baking powder
¼ tsp. salt
¼ c. cocoa
1 c. chocolate-flavored instant malted milk powder
¼ c. water
1 c. chopped wanluts

Beat butter and sugar together until light and fluffy. Beat in eggs and vanilla to mix well.

Sift together flour, baking powder, salt, cocoa and malted milk powder. Add alternately with water to creamed mixture. Fold in nuts. Chill several hours.

Drop teaspoonfuls of dough 2″ apart onto greased baking sheet. Bake in moderate oven (350°) about 12 minutes. Remove cookies and cool on racks. Makes about 4 dozen.

VARIATION

Frosted Malted Chocolate Drops: When cookies are cool frost with Chocolate Malt Frosting.

Chocolate Malt Frosting: Melt 1 square unsweetened chocolate and 1 tblsp. butter over very low heat (or over hot water), stirring constantly. Mix in 1 tblsp. warm water, 2 tblsp. chocolate-flavored instant malted milk powder, 2 tblsp. light cream or dairy half-and-half and 1 c. sifted confectioners sugar, or enough to make a frosting of spreading consistency.

PENNSYLVANIA DUTCH COOKIE-PIES

A teen-age enthusiasm. Filling is good with other cookies, too

1½ c. sugar
¼ c. shortening
½ c. cocoa
1 egg
1 tsp. vanilla
2 c. sifted flour
½ tsp. cream of tartar
½ tsp. baking soda
1 tsp. salt
¾ c. buttermilk
Fluffy Refrigerator Filling (recipe follows)

Cream together sugar and shortening until light and fluffy. Beat in cocoa and egg. Add vanilla.

Sift together flour, cream of tartar, baking soda and salt; add alternately with buttermilk to creamed mixture. Mix well.

Drop by teaspoonfuls about 2" apart onto greased baking sheet. Bake in moderate oven (375°) 10 to 12 minutes. Remove cookies to racks and cool.

Spread flat sides (bottoms) of cooled cookies with Fluffy Refrigerator Filling and put together in pairs. (If you like, you can sprinkle filling with flaked coconut before putting together.) Makes 26 cookie-pies.

Fluffy Refrigerator Filling: Place 2½ tblsp. flour in 1-qt. saucepan. Measure ½ c. milk. Add a little milk to flour and stir to make a smooth paste. Add remaining milk; cook and stir until mixture thickens. Cool.

In a small mixing bowl, cream together ½ c. butter or shortening, ½ c. sugar, ⅛ tsp. salt and 1 tsp. vanilla until light and fluffy. Slowly add thickened flour-milk mixture, beating constantly, until filling is light and fluffy. Makes about 1¾ cups.

NOTE: You will have ⅓ to ⅔ c. filling left over after using for Pennsylvania Dutch Cookie-Pies. The woman who shares this recipe says it's a planned leftover. She stores the filling in a covered jar in the refrigerator and uses it to spread on other cookies or cupcakes she bakes. The filling in the refrigerator remains soft and fluffy. She often doubles the recipe to make more filling to refrigerate.

PINEAPPLE/CHOCOLATE CHIP COOKIES

Big recipe for family—good keepers, have mild pineapple flavor

½ c. butter
½ c. shortening
1 c. brown sugar, firmly packed
1 c. white sugar
2 eggs
1 tsp. vanilla

1 c. crushed pineapple with juice
4 c. sifted flour
½ tsp. baking soda
½ tsp. salt
1 c. chopped walnuts
1 (6 oz.) pkg. semisweet chocolate pieces

Cream together butter, shortening and sugars until light and fluffy. Beat in eggs, one at a time, and vanilla. Stir in pineapple.

Sift together flour, baking soda and salt; divide in half. Add first half to creamed mixture. When well blended, add second half. Stir in nuts and chocolate pieces.

Drop batter by teaspoonfuls 2″ apart onto greased baking sheet. Bake in hot oven (400°) 15 minutes. Remove cookies to racks and cool. Makes about 7 dozen.

SOFT CHOCOLATE CHIPPERS

Children like to come home to these chocolate-dotted goodies

½ c. shortening
1 c. brown sugar, firmly
   packed
1 egg
1 tsp. vanilla
1¾ c. sifted flour

½ tsp. baking soda
½ tsp. salt
¼ c. buttermilk
1 (6 oz.) pkg. semisweet
   chocolate pieces

Beat shortening until light; add brown sugar and beat until light and fluffy. Beat in egg and vanilla to blend well.

Sift together flour, baking soda and salt. Add alternately with buttermilk to creamed mixture. Beat until smooth. Add chocolate pieces and mix well.

Drop about 2″ apart onto greased baking sheet. Flatten with a spoon. Bake in moderate oven (375°) 8 to 10 minutes, until lightly browned. Remove to cooling racks. Makes about 3 dozen.

SOUR CREAM CHOCOLATE COOKIES

These quick-to-make cookies have the good taste sour cream imparts

½ c. butter
1 c. brown sugar, firmly
   packed
1 egg
2 squares unsweetened
   chocolate, melted
1½ c. sifted flour
¼ tsp. baking powder

¼ tsp. salt
¼ tsp. baking soda
½ c. dairy sour cream
1 c. chopped walnuts
1 tsp. vanilla
Cocoa Frosting (recipe
   follows)

Cream together butter and brown sugar. Add egg and blend well. Beat in chocolate.

Sift together flour, baking powder, salt and soda; add to creamed mixture alternately with sour cream. Stir in nuts and vanilla.

Drop by teaspoonfuls about 2″ apart onto greased baking sheet. Bake in moderate oven (375°) 8 minutes. Remove cookies and cool on racks, then frost with Cocoa Frosting. Makes 5 dozen.

Cocoa Frosting: Heat 3 tblsp. milk. Add 1½ c. sifted confectioners sugar, 3 tblsp. butter and 3 tblsp. cocoa. Blend together until of spreading consistency.

TWO-TONE JUMBLES

Try these 2-in-1 cookies—plain and chocolate sour cream treats

¼ c. shortening	1 c. chopped walnuts or
¼ c. butter	pecans
1 c. brown sugar, firmly packed	2¾ c. sifted flour
	½ tsp. baking soda
½ c. sugar	1 tsp. salt
1 tsp. vanilla	1 c. dairy sour cream
2 eggs	1 square unsweetened chocolate, melted

Beat together shortening, butter, brown and white sugars and vanilla until light and fluffy. Beat in eggs to mix well. Stir in ½ c. walnuts.

Sift together flour, baking soda and salt. Add alternately to creamed mixture with sour cream. Divide dough in half. Add chocolate to one half.

Drop chocolate dough from teaspoon 2″ apart onto lightly greased baking sheet. Drop equal size spoonfuls of plain dough next to and touching chocolate mounds (they will bake together as one). Sprinkle with remaining ½ c. nuts, pressing them in lightly.

Bake in moderate oven (375°) about 12 minutes, until almost no imprint remains after touching center of cookie with finger and until lightly browned. Remove cookies to racks to cool. Makes about 3½ dozen.

TWO-WAY COOKIES

As easy to bake chocolate/orange and coconut cookies as one kind

4 c. sifted flour
1 tsp. salt
1 tsp. baking soda
1 c. regular margarine
1 c. sugar
1¼ c. light brown sugar, firmly packed

3 eggs
1 tsp. vanilla
½ tsp. orange extract
1 (6 oz.) pkg. semisweet chocolate pieces
1 (3½ oz.) can flaked coconut

Sift together flour, salt and baking soda.

Cream margarine until fluffy; gradually add sugars. Add eggs, one at a time, beating thoroughly after each addition. Add vanilla; blend.

Add sifted dry ingredients. Mix well. Divide batter in half.

Add orange extract and chocolate pieces to one half dough and coconut to other half. Drop by rounded teaspoonfuls about 2″ apart onto greased baking sheet.

Bake in moderate oven (350°) 12 to 15 minutes. Remove cookies and cool on racks. Makes about 6 dozen.

CARAMEL APPLE COOKIES

You can frost the cookies before freezing or just before serving

½ c. shortening
1⅓ c. brown sugar, firmly packed
1 egg
2¼ c. sifted flour
1 tsp. baking soda
½ tsp. salt
1 tsp. ground cinnamon

1 tsp. ground cloves
½ tsp. ground nutmeg
1 c. grated peeled apples
1 c. light raisins
½ c. apple juice
1 c. chopped walnuts
Caramel Icing (recipe follows)

Cream shortening, sugar and egg until light and fluffy. Sift together dry ingredients and add to creamed mixture. When well blended, stir in remaining ingredients, except icing.

Drop by level tablespoonfuls 3″ apart onto greased baking sheet. Bake in moderate oven (350°) about 12 minutes, or until lightly browned.

Remove cookies and cool on racks. When cool, spread with Caramel Icing. Makes about 4 dozen

Caramel Icing: Combine ¼ c. butter and ¼ c. brown sugar, firmly packed, in saucepan; cook until sugar dissolves, about 3 minutes. Add 1½ c. sifted confectioners sugar, ¼ tsp. salt and 2½ tblsp. dairy half-and-half or light cream; beat until smooth. (If frosting becomes too thick when spreading on cookies, thin it by adding a little more cream.)

GLAZED APPLE COOKIES

These big, spicy cookies travel and keep well, taste wonderful

½ c. shortening	1 c. finely chopped peeled
1⅓ c. brown sugar, firmly	apple (2 medium)
packed	1 c. raisins
1 egg	¼ c. milk
2 c. sifted flour	1½ c. sifted confectioners
1 tsp. baking soda	sugar
½ tsp. salt	1 tblsp. butter
1 tsp. ground cinnamon	½ tsp. vanilla
½ tsp. ground cloves	2½ tblsp. light cream or
¼ tsp. ground nutmeg	dairy half-and-half
1 c. coarsely chopped nuts	(about)

Beat together shortening and brown sugar until light and fluffy. Beat in egg to blend thoroughly.

Sift together flour, baking soda, salt, cinnamon, cloves and nutmeg. Stir half the dry ingredients into creamed mixture. Stir in nuts, apple and raisins; then stir in remaining half of dry ingredients and milk. Mix well.

Drop from tablespoon 1½″ apart onto lightly greased baking sheet. Bake in hot oven (400°) 10 to 12 minutes. Remove cookies to racks and while still warm, spread with glaze.

To make glaze, combine confectioners sugar, butter, vanilla and enough cream to make glaze of spreading consistency. Beat until smooth. Spread on warm cookies. Makes about 3 dozen.

BANANA DROP COOKIES

*Cake-like banana cookies are coated with
cinnamon-sugar and bran*

1 c. whole bran cereal	1½ tsp. vanilla
6 tblsp. sugar	1 c. mashed bananas (3
½ tsp. ground cinnamon	medium)
1 c. sugar	2½ c. sifted flour
½ c. shortening	3 tsp. baking powder
¼ c. butter	1 tsp. salt
2 eggs	

Place bran cereal on sheet of waxed paper; roll fine
with rolling pin. Add 6 tblsp. sugar and cinnamon;
mix well. Set aside.

Beat 1 c. sugar, shortening and butter until light and
fluffy. Beat in eggs and vanilla to mix thoroughly. Stir
in bananas.

Sift together flour, baking powder and salt. Stir into
banana mixture. Drop by teaspoonfuls into bran mixture and tumble until they are well coated. Place 2"
apart on greased baking sheet.

Bake in hot oven (400°) about 10 minutes. Remove
cookies and cool on racks. Makes 4½ dozen.

CITRUS/NUT DROPS

*Cookies flavored with orange and lemon, wear red
cherry hats*

½ c. shortening	1 tsp. grated lemon peel
¼ c. sugar	1¼ c. sifted flour
1 egg yolk	1 egg white, slightly beaten
½ tsp. vanilla	¾ c. finely chopped nuts
2 tblsp. evaporated milk	Candied cherry halves
1 tsp. grated orange peel	(for tops)

Cream together shortening and sugar until light and
fluffy. Beat in egg yolk, vanilla, evaporated milk and
orange and lemon peels. Mix in flour.

Dip tablespoonfuls of dough in egg white. Lift out
with fork, and dip one side in nuts. Place nut side up
2" apart on greased baking sheet; press a cherry half
into each.

Bake in slow oven (325°) 20 minutes. Remove
cookies and cool on racks. Makes about 2 dozen.

CHRISTMAS DROP COOKIES

Gay with holiday colors, but festive for parties at all seasons

1 lb. dates, chopped
½ c. chopped walnuts
½ c. chopped maraschino
   cherries
1 c. sugar

1 tsp. vanilla
3 egg whites, stiffly beaten
1 c. sifted flour
Maraschino cherry pieces
   (for tops)

Combine dates, nuts and cherries. Mix in sugar and vanilla. Add egg whites to fruit mixture alternately with flour. (If mixture is dry, add a little cherry juice.)

Drop by teaspoonfuls about 2″ apart onto greased baking sheet. Top with pieces of cherries.

Bake in moderate oven (350°) about 20 minutes, until lightly browned. Remove cookies and cool on racks. Store in tightly covered container. (They keep indefinitely, and are better with aging.) Makes 4 dozen.

CRY BABY COOKIES

They're favorites of men. That's why we give you a giant-size recipe

1 c. plus 2 tblsp. shortening
1 c. plus 2 tblsp. sugar
1 c. light molasses
2 eggs, well beaten
4¾ c. sifted cake flour
1 tblsp. baking powder

1 tsp. salt
1½ tsp. baking soda
2 c. shredded coconut
2 c. chopped walnuts
1½ c. raisins
1 c. milk

Cream shortening; beat in sugar, molasses and eggs.

Sift together flour, baking powder, salt and soda; combine with coconut, walnuts and raisins. Add alternately with milk to creamed mixture.

Drop tablespoonfuls 2″ apart onto greased baking sheet. Bake in moderate oven (375°) 10 minutes. Remove cookies and cool on racks. Makes about 9½ dozen.

DATE/NUT DROPS

Chewy cookies rich flavored with nuts, dates and brown sugar—good

2 c. chopped dates	3 eggs
½ c. sugar	1 tsp. vanilla
½ c. water	4 c. sifted flour
1 c. butter or regular margarine	1 tsp. baking soda
	1 tsp. salt
1 c. sugar	1 tsp. ground cinnamon
1 c. brown sugar, firmly packed	1½ c. chopped nuts

Combine dates, ½ c. sugar and water in saucepan. Cook, stirring occasionally, until mixture is the consistency of very thick jam. Cool.

Cream butter; add sugars gradually, beating until light and fluffy. Beat in eggs and vanilla.

Sift together dry ingredients. Add to creamed mixture, blending thoroughly. Stir in nuts and date mixture.

Drop by rounded teaspoonfuls about 2″ apart onto greased baking sheet. Bake in a moderate oven (375°) 12 to 15 minutes. Remove cookies and cool on racks. Makes 12 dozen.

OREGON DATE SURPRISES

Walnut-stuffed dates are the unusual ingredient in these cookies

36 pitted dates (8 oz.)	1¼ c. sifted flour
½ c. large walnut pieces (36)	½ tsp. baking soda
¼ c. butter or regular margarine	1 tsp. baking powder
	¼ tsp. salt
¾ c. brown sugar, firmly packed	½ c. dairy sour cream
	Vanilla Cream Icing
1 egg	(see Index)
1 tsp. vanilla	

Stuff each date with a walnut piece. Set aside.

Beat together butter and brown sugar until light and fluffy. Beat in egg and vanilla to blend well.

Sift together flour, baking soda, baking powder and salt. Add to creamed mixture alternately with sour cream. Add stuffed dates and stir until they are well coated with batter.

Drop from teaspoon about 2″ apart onto lightly greased baking sheet, allowing 1 date to each cookie. Bake in moderate oven (375°) about 10 minutes. Remove cookies and cool on racks. If you like, frost with Vanilla Cream Icing. Makes 3 dozen.

NOTE: If you shell walnuts, first soak them overnight in salt water. Then the nut meats will come out whole.

RAGGED ROBINS

These dainty cookies are ideal for serving with ice cream, puddings

2 eggs	1 c. chopped dates
½ c. sugar	2 c. corn flakes
1 tsp. vanilla	¼ c. confectioners sugar
1 c. chopped walnuts	

Beat eggs until lemon-colored; gradually beat in sugar and vanilla to blend thoroughly. Stir in walnuts and dates. Fold in corn flakes.

Drop by teaspoonfuls 2″ apart onto lightly greased baking sheet. Bake in moderate oven (350°) 12 to 15 minutes. Cool 1 or 2 minutes on baking sheet, then remove to cooling rack. While still warm, roll in confectioners sugar. When cool, store cookies in loosely covered container. Makes about 3½ dozen.

CALIFORNIA FIG COOKIES

A recipe from the state that grows figs—and knows how to use them

1 c. chopped golden or black figs (½ lb.)	1 egg
⅓ c. water	1 tsp. vanilla
1 c. butter or regular margarine	2 c. sifted flour
½ c. sugar	2 tsp. baking powder
½ c. brown sugar, firmly packed	½ tsp. salt
	Walnut or pecan halves (optional)

Cook figs with water, stirring frequently, until thickened, about 5 minutes. Set aside to cool.

Beat butter with both sugars until light and fluffy; beat in egg and vanilla to blend well.

Sift together flour, baking powder and salt. Mix into creamed mixture. Then stir in cooled figs.

Drop by teaspoonfuls about 2″ apart onto lightly

greased baking sheet. Press a walnut half on top of each cookie. Bake in moderate oven (375°) 10 to 12 minutes, until lightly browned. Remove cookies and cool on racks. Makes 4 dozen.

FAMILY COOKIES

These soft cookies contain healthful vegetable and fruit ingredients

1 c. regular margarine	4½ c. sifted flour
2 c. sugar	½ tsp. salt
3 eggs	1 tsp. baking soda
1 c. cut-up carrots, ground	¼ tsp. ground allspice
1 large apple, ground	¼ tsp. ground cloves
1 large orange, ground	½ tsp. ground nutmeg
1 c. dates, ground	1 tsp. ground cinnamon
1 c. raisins, ground	1 c. chopped walnuts

Beat margarine until light; gradually add sugar and beat until light and fluffy. Beat in eggs until well blended. Fold in carrots and fruits.

Sift together flour, salt, baking soda and spices. Add to first mixture. Fold in nuts.

Drop by teaspoonfuls 2″ apart onto lightly greased baking sheet and bake in moderate oven (350°) 10 to 12 minutes. Remove cookies and cool on racks. Store in airtight container. Makes about 7½ dozen.

HOLIDAY FRUITCAKE COOKIES

Glamor cookies with gay green and red topknots—a yuletide treat

4 c. sifted flour	1 c. chopped pecans
1 tsp. baking soda	1 c. candied cherries, cut in quarters
1 tsp. salt	
1 c. shortening	2 c. cut-up dates
2 c. brown sugar, firmly packed	1 c. candied fruits and peels
2 eggs, beaten	Red or green candied cherries (for tops)
⅔ c. buttermilk	

Sift together flour, soda and salt.

Cream shortening; add brown sugar and eggs; beat until light and fluffy. Add buttermilk and sifted dry ingredients, then fold in nuts, cherries, dates and candied fruits. Chill dough.

Drop dough by teaspoonfuls about 2″ apart onto lightly greased baking sheet. Top each cookie with green or red cherry half.

Bake in moderate oven (375°) 8 to 10 minutes. Remove cookies and cool on racks. Makes 8 dozen.

Fruited Drop Cookies

There are many ways to introduce healthful fruit, wheat germ and rolled oats in meals, but when it comes to pleasant eating, none surpasses Fruited Drop Cookies. The recipe comes from a Tennessee woman who invented it; she says the cookies are husband-inspired. Because her husband is a great cookie fan, she decided to make them contribute to his nutrition. Result: Fruited Drop Cookies. Once you make them, you'll know why the hearty, good-for-you cookies are so popular in her family.

FRUITED DROP COOKIES

Serve these with glasses of milk or with hot coffee for a treat

½ c. finely cut dried apricots	1 tblsp. lemon juice
½ c. chopped dried prunes	1½ c. quick-cooking rolled oats
½ c. seedless raisins	
¾ c. water	2 tblsp. wheat germ
½ c. regular margarine	2 c. sifted flour
½ c. sugar	1 tsp. baking soda
½ c. brown sugar, firmly packed	½ tsp. baking powder
	½ tsp. salt
1 egg	½ c. chopped nuts

Combine apricots, prunes and raisins with water in saucepan. Heat and simmer about 5 minutes, stirring frequently. (Mixture is thick; watch carefully.) Set aside to cool.

Beat margarine until light; gradually add white and brown sugars, beating until light and fluffy. Beat in egg and lemon juice to blend well. Add fruit, rolled oats and wheat germ and mix well.

Sift together flour, baking soda, baking powder and salt. Fold into fruit mixture along with nuts. Chill.

Drop dough by teaspoonfuls 1″ apart onto lightly greased baking sheet. Bake in moderate oven (375°) 12 to 15 minutes. Remove cookies and cool on racks. Store in tightly covered container. Makes about 4½ dozen.

FRUITY GUMDROP COOKIES

Apples, gumdrops and raisins—no wonder the cookies are so tasty

2 c. sifted flour	1 egg, beaten
½ tsp. salt	¾ c. thick applesauce
2 tsp. baking powder	1 c. gumdrops, cut in small
½ tsp. ground cinnamon	pieces (no black candies)
½ c. shortening	1 c. raisins
½ c. sugar	

Sift together flour, salt, baking powder and cinnamon.

Cream shortening and sugar; add egg and applesauce; mix well.

Add flour mixture; stir until well blended; stir in gumdrops (no black candies) and raisins.

Drop by teaspoonfuls about 2″ apart onto lightly greased baking sheet. Bake in hot oven (400°) 10 to 15 minutes, until lightly browned. Transfer to cooling rack. Makes 4 dozen.

NOTE: You can use drained, crushed pineapple or canned peaches, drained and mashed, instead of applesauce. Rolled oats may be substituted for the gumdrops.

HAMPSHIRE HERMITS

Tangy Lemon Glaze is perfect on these citron-flavored cookies

⅔ c. butter or regular margarine
1 c. light brown sugar, firmly packed
2 eggs
2 tblsp. dairy sour cream or buttermilk
1¾ c. sifted flour
1¾ tsp. ground cinnamon
¼ tsp. ground ginger
¼ tsp. cloves
¼ tsp. baking soda
⅛ tsp. salt
1 c. chopped nuts
½ c. chopped raisins or currants
½ c. finely chopped citron
Lemon Glaze (recipe follows)

Beat butter until light. Gradually add brown sugar and beat after each addition until light and fluffy. Beat in eggs, one at a time, beating to mix thoroughly. Stir in sour cream.

Sift together flour, spices, baking soda and salt. Add to creamed mixture and beat until batter is smooth. Gradually add nuts, raisins and citron.

Drop batter from tablespoon 2″ apart onto greased baking sheet. Bake in moderate oven (350°) about 12 to 15 minutes, until cookies are golden brown. Remove cookies to racks and while warm, brush with Lemon Glaze. Makes about 3 dozen.

Lemon Glaze: Add 2 tblsp. lemon juice to 1 c. sifted confectioners sugar. Stir until smooth; brush over warm cookies (glaze is thin and tart).

LEMON DROP COOKIES

Crushed candy sweetens, adds lemony flavor to dotted cookies

½ c. boiling water (about)
¼ c. dried currants
2 c. sifted flour
3 tsp. baking powder
1 tsp. salt
1 c. finely crushed candy lemon drops
¼ c. shortening
½ c. chopped candied cherries
1 egg, beaten
½ tsp. vanilla
⅓ c. milk

Pour boiling water over currants to cover; let stand 5 minutes. Drain and spread currants on paper toweling.

Sift together flour, baking powder and salt. Crush about ¼ c. lemon drops at a time between two sheets

97

of aluminum foil; measure and stir each fourth at once into mixture before they stick together. Mix flour mixture and crushed lemon candy well. Blend in shortening with pastry blender until crumbly. Add cherries and currants.

Combine egg, vanilla and milk, and stir into flour mixture with fork. Stir until dough clings together in a ball.

Drop by teaspoonfuls about 1″ apart onto greased baking sheet. Bake in moderate oven (350°) about 15 minutes. Transfer cookies to rack to cool. Makes about 3½ dozen.

MULTI-FRUITED DROPS

Crisp cookies—grated citrus peel enhances other fruit flavors

1 c. butter or regular margarine	½ tsp. baking soda
1 c. sugar	1½ c. quick-cooking rolled oats
1 c. brown sugar, firmly packed	1 tblsp. grated orange peel
2 eggs	1 tblsp. grated lemon peel
1 tsp. vanilla	1 c. chopped dates
2 c. sifted flour	1 c. seedless raisins
½ tsp. salt	1 c. chopped nuts
1 tsp. baking powder	1 c. flaked coconut

Cream together butter and sugars until light and fluffy. Beat in eggs and vanilla to mix thoroughly.

Sift together flour, salt, baking powder and soda. Mix into creamed mixture. Add remaining ingredients and mix well.

Drop from teaspoon about 2″ apart onto greased baking sheet. Bake in moderate oven (375°) 12 minutes. Remove to racks to cool. Makes about 8 dozen cookies.

OLD-FASHIONED HERMITS

Seeded raisins make country-kitchen treats tasty— good travelers

1 c. shortening	1 tsp. salt
2 c. brown sugar, firmly packed	1 tsp. ground nutmeg
	1 tsp. ground cinnamon
2 eggs	1½ c. chopped nuts
½ c. cold coffee	2½ c. seeded raisins or currants
3½ c. sifted flour	
1 tsp. baking soda	

Thoroughly mix together shortening, sugar and eggs. Stir in cold coffee.

Sift together dry ingredients and stir into shortening mixture. Stir in nuts and raisins. Chill at least 1 hour.

Drop rounded teaspoonfuls of dough 2" apart onto lightly greased baking sheet. Bake in moderate oven (375°) 8 to 10 minutes. Test for doneness by touching lightly with fingertip. If almost no imprint remains, cookies are done. Use care not to overbake. Remove to racks to cool. Makes about 7½ dozen.

ORANGE COOKIES

For parties spread Orange Icing over tops of cake-like treats

⅔ c. shortening	½ tsp. salt
1 c. sugar	½ tsp. baking soda
2 eggs, slightly beaten	½ c. orange juice
1 tblsp. grated orange peel	½ c. chopped nuts
2¼ c. sifted flour	

Cream together shortening and sugar.

Combine eggs, creamed mixture and orange peel.

Sift together flour, salt and baking soda.

Add to creamed mixture alternately with orange juice; mix until well blended. Add nuts.

Drop by tablespoonfuls about 2" apart onto greased baking sheet. Bake in moderate oven (375°) 10 minutes, or until golden brown. Remove cookies and cool on rack. Makes 3 dozen.

Orange Icing: Blend together 2½ tblsp. butter or regular margarine and 1½ c. sifted confectioners sugar. Stir in 1½ tblsp. orange juice and 2 tsp. grated orange peel. Blend until smooth.

ORANGE/CARROT COOKIES

Cheerful as Kansas sunflowers and kind to the budget—attractive, too

1 c. shortening	2 c. sifted flour
¾ c. sugar	2 tsp. baking powder
1 c. mashed cooked carrots	½ tsp. salt
1 egg	Golden Glow Topping
1 tsp. vanilla	(recipe follows)

Cream shortening and sugar until fluffy. Add carrots, egg and vanilla; mix well.

Sift together flour, baking powder and salt; add to carrot mixture; mix well. Drop batter by teaspoonfuls about 2" apart onto greased baking sheet.

Bake in moderate oven (350°) about 20 minutes. Place cookies on racks to cool. While warm, spread with Golden Glow Topping. Makes 5 dozen.

Golden Glow Topping: Combine juice of ½ orange, grated peel of 1 orange, 1 tblsp. butter or regular margarine and 1 c. sifted confectioners sugar. Blend until smooth.

ORANGE/COCONUT CRISPS

Friends will make a point to stop by for these crisp 3" cookies

2 eggs	2½ c. sifted flour
⅔ c. salad oil	2 tsp. baking powder
1 c. sugar	½ tsp. salt
¼ c. thawed frozen orange juice concentrate	1 c. cookie coconut

Beat eggs with fork until well blended. Stir in oil. Blend in sugar until mixture thickens. Stir in orange juice concentrate.

Sift together flour, baking powder and salt; add with coconut to egg mixture. Stir until well blended.

Drop by teaspoonfuls about 2" apart on ungreased baking sheet. Stamp each cookie flat with bottom of drinking glass dipped in sugar. (Lightly oil glass, then dip in sugar. Continue dipping in sugar for each cookie.)

Bake in hot oven (400°) 8 to 10 minutes. Remove immediately from baking sheet to cooling rack. Makes 3 dozen.

NOTE: Balls of cookie dough, rolled in sugar, may be packaged and frozen for future use. To bake: remove as many balls as desired from package, place on baking sheet and let stand about 30 minutes at room temperature. Bake as directed.

ORANGE-GLAZED PRUNE COOKIES

Brown cookies with yellow topknots hold prune and orange flavors

2 c. brown sugar, firmly packed	1 tsp. baking soda
1 c. butter or shortening	1 tsp. ground cinnamon
2 eggs, beaten	½ tsp. salt
½ c. milk	2 c. chopped cooked prunes
3½ c. sifted flour	1 c. chopped walnuts
1 tsp. baking powder	1 tsp. vanilla
	Orange Glaze (recipe follows)

Cream together sugar and butter; stir in eggs and milk.

Sift together flour, baking powder, soda, cinnamon and salt; stir into creamed mixture. Add prunes, nuts and vanilla.

Drop by teaspoonfuls onto greased baking sheet. Bake in moderate oven (350°) 15 to 20 minutes, until lightly browned. Remove cookies and cool on racks.

Spread tops of cooled cookies with a thin layer of Orange Glaze. Makes 8½ dozen.

Orange Glaze: Combine 3 c. confectioners sugar, grated peel of 1 orange and ¼ c. orange juice. Blend thoroughly until smooth.

PRUNE COOKIES

Spiced drop cookies topped with prune hats—try these soon

2 c. sugar	½ tsp. ground allspice
1 c. shortening	1 tsp. ground cinnamon
3 eggs	¼ tsp. ground nutmeg
1 c. finely cut cooked prunes	¼ tsp. ground cloves
3 c. sifted flour	¾ c. chopped walnuts
1 tsp. baking soda	Cooked prunes, pitted
½ tsp. salt	(for tops)

Combine sugar, shortening, eggs and prunes; beat until well blended.

Sift together dry ingredients; add in thirds to beaten mixture. Stir in walnuts.

Drop dough from teaspoon about 2″ apart onto ungreased baking sheet. Top each with a quarter of a cooked prune, skin side up.

Bake in moderate oven (375°) 12 to 14 minutes. Remove cookies and cool on racks. Makes about 5 dozen.

NOTE: If batter seems too stiff, add a small amount of prune juice.

GOLDEN PINEAPPLE COOKIES

You paint cookie tops with pineapple juice-confectioners sugar icing

½ c. shortening	2 c. sifted flour
1 c. brown sugar, firmly packed	1½ tsp. baking powder
1 egg	¼ tsp. baking soda
1 tsp. vanilla	⅛ tsp. salt
1 (8½ oz.) can crushed pineapple	1 c. sifted confectioners sugar

Cream shortening with brown sugar until light and fluffy. Add egg and vanilla and beat well to mix thoroughly.

Drain pineapple, reserving juice. Add pineapple to creamed mixture. Sift together flour, baking powder, baking soda and salt; stir into creamed mixture.

Drop by teaspoonfuls 1½ to 2″ apart onto greased baking sheet. Bake in slow oven (325°) about 15 minutes, until golden. Remove from baking sheet and cool on racks.

Stir 4 tsp. reserved pineapple juice into confectioners

sugar. Beat until smooth. Brush on cookies. Makes about 4 dozen.

PUMPKIN COOKIES

Children eat these soft cookies without making crumbs

½ c. shortening
1¼ c. brown sugar, firmly
    packed
2 eggs
1 tsp. vanilla
1½ c. mashed cooked or
    canned pumpkin

2½ c. sifted flour
4 tsp. baking powder
½ tsp. salt
½ tsp. ground cinnamon
½ tsp. ground nutmeg
1 c. raisins
1 c. chopped nuts

Cream together shortening and brown sugar. Add eggs; beat thoroughly. Mix in vanilla and pumpkin.

Sift together dry ingredients. Blend into creamed mixture. Stir in raisins and nuts.

Drop dough by heaping teaspoonfuls about 2″ apart onto greased baking sheet. Bake in a moderate oven (375°) about 15 minutes, until lightly browned. Remove cookies and cool on racks. Makes 5 dozen.

PUMPKIN/PINEAPPLE COOKIES

Taste like your best pumpkin pie with faint pineapple undertone

½ c. butter or regular
    margarine
1 c. brown sugar, firmly
    packed
½ c. sugar
1 egg
1 c. canned pumpkin
½ c. drained crushed
    pineapple

1 c. coarsely cut-up pecans
1 c. quick-cooking rolled oats
2 c. sifted flour
½ tsp. baking powder
½ tsp. baking soda
½ tsp. salt
2 tsp. ground cinnamon
¼ c. milk

Cream butter and sugars until light and fluffy. Beat in egg, then beat in pumpkin and pineapple. Stir in nuts and oats.

Sift together dry ingredients and add alternately with milk to creamed mixture.

Drop by teaspoonfuls about 2″ apart onto greased baking sheet. Bake in moderate oven (350°) 8 to 10 minutes. Place cookies on racks to cool. Makes 6 dozen.

GRANDMA'S RAISIN COOKIES

To keep cookies until mealtime, hide them from your family

1½ c. seedless raisins
1½ c. water
1½ c. shortening
2 c. sugar
2 eggs
1 tsp. vanilla
4 c. sifted flour (about)

2 tsp. baking powder
1 tsp. baking soda
½ tsp. salt
1 c. chopped walnuts
Caramel Frosting (recipe
    follows)

Cover raisins with water and cook gently about 20 minutes. Drain, saving 1 c. liquid. Cool.

Beat shortening and sugar until light and fluffy. Beat in eggs and vanilla to mix thoroughly.

Sift together flour, baking powder, baking soda and salt. Stir into creamed mixture alternately with reserved 1 c. raisin liquid. Stir in raisins and nuts.

Drop dough from tablespoon 2" apart onto greased baking sheet. Spread out with bowl of spoon. Bake in moderate oven (375°) 10 to 12 minutes. Place cookies on racks and while still warm, spread tops with Caramel Frosting. Makes 5½ dozen.

Caramel Frosting: Combine in saucepan 1½ c. brown sugar, firmly packed, ¾ c. evaporated milk and ¼ c. regular margarine. Cook until sugar dissolves and margarine is melted. Remove from heat and cool slightly. Add 1 tsp. vanilla and enough sifted confectioners sugar (about 3 c.) to make a frosting of spreading consistency. If frosting gets too thick, add a few drops of milk.

RANCH HOUSE RAISIN COOKIES

You cook the raisins before you stir them into the cookie mixture

½ c. raisins
1 c. water
1 c. brown sugar, firmly
  packed
½ c. shortening
1 egg

½ tsp. vanilla
1¾ c. sifted flour
½ tsp. salt
½ tsp. baking powder
½ tsp. baking soda
½ c. chopped nuts

Bring raisins to a boil with water. Cool thoroughly.

Cream sugar and shortening until fluffy. Add egg and vanilla. Beat to mix.

Sift together flour, salt, baking powder and soda. Alternately add to creamed mixture with cooled raisins (there should be ½ c. liquid with raisins; if not, add water to make ½ c.). Stir in nuts.

Drop dough by teaspoonfuls at least 2″ apart onto greased baking sheets.

Bake in moderate oven (350°) 10 to 12 minutes. Remove cookies and cool on racks. Makes 4 dozen.

RAISIN/CARROT COOKIES

Good family-style cookies that keep well if given a chance

1 c. sifted flour	½ c. molasses
¼ c. nonfat dry milk powder	1 egg, beaten
¼ tsp. baking soda	1 c. shredded carrots
1 tsp. baking powder	(or sweet potato)
¼ tsp. ground nutmeg	1 tsp. grated lemon peel
¼ tsp. ground cinnamon	½ c. ground or finely
½ tsp. salt	chopped raisins
⅓ c. shortening	1¾ c. quick-cooking rolled
⅓ c. brown sugar, firmly packed	oats

Sift together flour, dry milk powder, soda, baking powder, nutmeg, cinnamon and salt.

Cream together shortening, sugar and molasses; add egg, then dry ingredients; stir until well blended.

Add carrots, lemon peel, raisins and oats; mix well. (If dough is too stiff, add a few drops of milk.) Chill.

Drop by teaspoonfuls about 2″ apart onto lightly greased baking sheet. Bake in hot oven (375°) 10 to 12 minutes, until lightly browned. Remove cookies and cool on racks. Makes 5 dozen.

RAISIN/KETCHUP COOKIES

Ketchup gives cookies a rose-beige color and faint spicy taste—fresh Lemon Glaze contributes pleasing piquant flavor contrast

1 c. regular margarine	½ tsp. baking soda
½ c. sugar	⅛ tsp. salt
½ c. light brown sugar, firmly packed	¼ c. tomato ketchup
	¾ c. raisins
2 eggs	½ c. chopped nuts
1 tsp. vanilla	Lemon Glaze (recipe follows)
2¾ c. sifted flour	

Beat margarine until light. Gradually add white and brown sugars, beating constantly. Beat until light and fluffy. Beat in eggs and vanilla to blend well.

Sift together flour, baking soda and salt. Stir into creamed mixture alternately with ketchup. Fold in raisins and nuts. Drop heaping teaspoonfuls of dough 2" apart onto lightly greased baking sheet.

Bake in moderate oven (375°) 10 to 12 minutes, or until edges are browned and almost no imprint remains when touched lightly with fingertips. Remove cookies to cooling racks. Brush on Lemon Glaze while cookies are hot. Makes about 4 dozen.

Lemon Glaze: Combine 1½ c. sifted confectioners sugar with 2 tblsp. strained lemon juice; stir until smooth. If mixture is not thin enough to make a transparent glaze on cookies, add more lemon juice, 2 or 3 drops at a time until of right consistency. Makes ½ cup.

PECAN LACE ROLL-UPS

For women's luncheons tie bright ribbons around the crisp roll-ups

2 eggs	¼ c. melted butter or regular margarine
⅔ c. brown sugar, firmly packed	
	¼ c. sifted flour
1 tsp. vanilla	⅔ c. finely chopped pecans

Beat eggs until they thicken. Add brown sugar, 1 tblsp. at a time, beating constantly. Beat in vanilla to blend well. Slowly add slightly cooled butter. Fold in flour and pecans.

Place a tablespoonful of batter on well-greased baking sheet, spreading it to make a circle 4" in diameter. Repeat process, having no more than 4 cookie circles 2" apart on baking sheet at a time.

Bake in moderate oven (375°) 5 to 6 minutes, or until browned. Remove from oven and let cool about 30 seconds, then slip wide spatula under cookie to loosen it. Place the handle of a wooden spoon on one end of cookie and quickly roll up loosely to make a fat cylinder. Place on rack to cool. Repeat with other baked cookies. Then bake and roll the remainder of the batter in the same way (no more than 4 cookies at a time). Makes 15.

SWEDISH LACE COOKIES

The thin, crisp, brown lace-like cookie
saddles or roll-ups always get attention.
They're much easier to make than you may think

½ c. butter or regular margarine	⅔ c. sugar
1½ c. regular rolled oats	1 tsp. baking powder
1 egg	1 tblsp. flour
	Dash of salt

Melt butter and pour over rolled oats.

Beat egg until light; then beat in sugar. Stir together baking powder, flour and salt to blend. Add to egg mixture, then add rolled oats.

Drop tablespoonfuls of batter 3″ apart onto greased and lightly floured baking sheet. Bake in moderate oven (375°) about 8 to 10 minutes, until golden brown.

Place on cooling rack; let stand about 1 minute (cookies should still be hot and pliable). Lift cookies off quickly with wide spatula and place over broomstick, wrapped with aluminum foil, propped across two coffee or shortening cans or pans. Gently press cookies to make them the shape of a saddle. Work fast. If cookies get too cold, they break in shaping. You can return the baking sheet to the oven for a minute if they cool too fast. Makes about 20 cookies.

VARIATION

Lace Roll-Ups: While cookies are warm, roll up around handle of a wooden spoon to make fat cylinders. These cookies are easier to store than the saddle shapes.

WALNUT LACE COOKIES

These see-through cookies are thin, fragile,
crisp and delicious

⅓ c. sifted flour
½ tsp. baking powder
⅛ tsp. salt
¼ c. butter or regular
   margarine

1 c. brown sugar, firmly
   packed
1 egg, slightly beaten
1 c. chopped walnuts

Sift together flour, baking powder and salt.

Blend butter, brown sugar and sifted dry ingredients with pastry blender as for pie crust. Add egg and mix thoroughly. Stir in walnuts.

Drop thin batter by half teaspoonfuls about 2″ apart onto heavily greased baking sheet. (Cookies spread during baking). Bake in moderate oven (375°) 5 to 6 minutes. Remove from baking sheet at once and cool on racks. Makes about 5½ dozen.

GINGER NUGGETS

Team these cookies with glasses of milk
for after-school snacks

3 c. sifted flour
1 c. nonfat dry milk powder
1½ tsp. salt
2 tsp. baking soda
1 tsp. ground cinnamon
½ tsp. ground ginger

¼ tsp. ground cloves
1 c. shortening
1½ c. molasses
¼ c. sugar
1 egg

Sift together flour, dry milk powder, salt, soda and spices.

Cream together shortening, molasses and sugar.

Add egg, mix well. Add dry ingredients, and mix well. Chill.

Drop from teaspoon about 2″ apart onto greased baking sheet.

Bake in moderate oven (375°) 10 to 15 minutes, until done. Remove cookies and cool on racks. Makes about 8 dozen.

MOLASSES/WHOLE WHEAT COOKIES

Raisins and whole wheat flour
make these molasses cookies special

½ c. nonfat dry milk powder
½ tsp. baking soda
2 tsp. baking powder
½ tsp. salt
⅓ c. shortening
¾ c. molasses

1 tsp. vanilla
2 eggs, beaten
1 c. plus 2 tblsp. whole wheat
flour
½ c. raisins

Sift together dry milk powder, soda, baking powder and salt.

Cream together shortening, molasses, and vanilla; add eggs, blend well.

Add sifted ingredients and whole wheat flour; stir until thoroughly mixed. Add raisins (whole, chopped or ground).

Drop by teaspoonfuls about 2" apart onto lightly greased baking sheet. Bake in moderate oven (350°) 10 to 12 minutes, until lightly browned. Remove cookies and cool on racks. Makes 4 dozen.

PEANUT/MOLASSES COOKIES

Cookies fruited with prunes are a pleasing texture
and flavor surprise

1 c. sifted flour
½ tsp. salt
1 tsp. baking powder
¼ tsp. baking soda
¼ c. shortening
¼ c. brown sugar, firmly
packed

½ c. molasses
½ c. crunchy peanut butter
½ tsp. vanilla
1 egg
2 tblsp. milk
1 c. chopped, uncooked
prunes

Sift together flour, salt, baking powder and soda.

Cream together shortening, sugar, molasses, peanut butter and vanilla. Add egg and milk; mix well. Add dry ingredients; stir until well blended. Add chopped prunes.

Drop by teaspoonfuls onto lightly greased baking

sheet. Bake in moderate oven (375°) 10 to 15 minutes, or until done.

Transfer cookies to cooling rack. Store in tightly covered container. Makes 5 dozen.

SOFT MOLASSES COOKIES

Family-style, generous cookies like
Grandma used to make—updated

1 c. butter or regular margarine	½ tsp. salt
1 c. sugar	1 tsp. instant coffee powder
1 large egg	2 tsp. ground cinnamon
1 c. light molasses	1 tsp. ground ginger
4¾ c. sifted flour	½ tsp. ground cloves
3 tsp. baking soda	¾ c. milk
	Raisins or walnut halves

Beat butter until light; gradually add sugar and beat until fluffy. Beat in egg to blend thoroughly; then beat in molasses.

Sift together flour, baking soda, salt, coffee powder and spices. Add to first mixture alternately with milk. Beat about 30 seconds.

Drop dough by heaping teaspoonfuls about 2″ apart onto lightly greased baking sheet, using care to keep cookies round. Press a raisin in center of each cookie.

Bake in moderate oven (375°) about 12 to 15 minutes, or until done. Place cookies on racks to cool. Makes about 5½ dozen.

SOFT MOLASSES DROPS

Ideal for mailing overseas and wonderful
eating at home and abroad

¾ c. butter	2 tblsp. molasses
1½ c. brown sugar, firmly packed	1 tsp. baking soda
3 eggs	3 c. sifted flour
1 tsp. vanilla	1 c. raisins

Cream together butter and sugar until light and fluffy. Beat in eggs and vanilla to mix well.

Combine molasses and baking soda. Add to creamed mixture. Gradually stir in flour. Add raisins.

Drop by teaspoonfuls 2″ apart onto greased baking sheet. Bake in moderate oven (350°) 8 minutes, or until brown. Cool cookies on racks. Makes about 6 dozen.

SLAPJACKS

*The Pennsylvania Dutch created these molasses/
coconut cookies*

¾ c. butter or regular
  margarine
3 c. brown sugar, not firmly
  packed
1 c. light or dark molasses

1½ tsp. baking soda
3 c. sifted flour
¼ tsp. salt
½ c. cookie coconut
½ c. chopped walnuts

Cream butter and brown sugar until light and fluffy. Blend in molasses.

Sift together baking soda, flour and salt; add to creamed mixture, beating to mix thoroughly. Add coconut and nuts. Chill thoroughly for several hours, or overnight.

Drop dough by teaspoonfuls 2″ apart onto greased baking sheet. Bake in moderate oven (350°) 12 to 14 minutes. Cool 2 or 3 minutes on baking sheet before removing to cooling rack. Makes about 7 dozen.

COCONUT/NUTMEG COOKIES

*Serve these with lemon sherbet for a wonderful
flavor combination*

1 (1 lb. 3 oz.) pkg. yellow or
  white cake mix
1 c. flaked coconut
½ c. butter or regular
  margarine

1 tsp. ground nutmeg
1 egg
2 tblsp. cold water

Combine all ingredients and mix until well blended.

Drop teaspoonfuls of mixture onto lightly greased baking sheet. Bake in moderate oven (350°) 12 to 15 minutes, until lightly browned. Transfer cookies to cooling rack. Makes 3½ dozen.

HONEYED GINGERSNAPS

Sugar sparkles on top of brown cookies—
crisp outside, chewy within

⅔ c. sugar
¼ c. butter or regular
   margarine
1 tsp. ground ginger
½ tsp. ground cinnamon
½ tsp. baking soda
½ tsp. salt

½ tsp. vanilla
1 egg
½ c. honey
1½ c. sifted flour
Sugar for topping
   (about ¼ c.)

Combine ⅔ c. sugar, butter, ginger, cinnamon, baking soda, salt and vanilla in large mixing bowl. Cream until light and fluffy. Add egg and beat until very fluffy. Blend in honey. Add flour, a little at a time, and blend well.

Drop by teaspoonfuls 2½″ apart onto lightly greased baking sheet. Sprinkle with sugar.

Bake in moderate oven (350°) 10 to 15 minutes, until lightly browned. Remove at once from baking sheet to racks to cool thoroughly. Makes about 4 dozen.

SWEDISH SPICE SPECIALS

Cardamom and orange peel contribute delightful,
distinctive flavor

2 c. sifted flour
½ c. sugar
½ tsp. baking soda
½ c. light corn syrup
½ c. regular margarine or
   butter

1 tsp. ground cardamom
¼ tsp. ground ginger
¼ tsp. ground cloves
2 tsp. finely grated orange
   peel
1 egg

Sift flour with sugar and soda.

Combine corn syrup, margarine, spices and orange peel in saucepan; heat just until mixture boils and margarine melts. Remove from heat and cool.

Beat egg in large bowl. Slowly pour the cooled syrup into the egg. Stir in flour-sugar mixture all at once; blend well.

Drop by teaspoonfuls 2" apart onto greased baking sheet. Bake in moderate oven (350°) 10 to 12 minutes, until lightly browned. Transfer cookies to racks to cool. Makes about 3 dozen.

CIRCLE RANCH OAT COOKIES

Nicely spiced, big soft cookies—
store airtight to retain freshness

1 c. shortening	1 tsp. baking soda
1½ c. brown sugar, firmly packed	¾ tsp. salt
	1 tsp. ground cinnamon
2 eggs	½ tsp. ground nutmeg
½ c. buttermilk	3 c. quick-cooking rolled oats
1¾ c. sifted flour	½ c. chopped walnuts
1 tsp. baking powder	¾ c. dried currants or raisins

Beat shortening until light; add brown sugar and beat until fluffy. Beat in eggs to mix well. Stir in buttermilk.

Sift together flour, baking powder, baking soda, salt, cinnamon and nutmeg; stir into beaten mixture. Stir in rolled oats, nuts and currants.

Drop dough by tablespoonfuls 2" apart onto lightly greased baking sheet. Bake in hot oven (400°) about 8 minutes. Cool slightly on baking sheet; then remove to racks to complete cooling. Makes about 5 dozen.

NOTE: You can use sweet milk instead of buttermilk, but decrease baking soda to ¼ tsp. and increase baking powder to 2 tsp.

Fresh-from-the-Oven Cookies

The contributor of the recipe for Oatmeal/Coconut Crisps and its variations keeps the dough in a tight container in her refrigerator for several days—sometimes a few weeks. It's a great recipe; she finds it easier to bake a few cookies at a time. And, in addition, she can always serve cookies with that wonderful fresh-from-the-oven aroma and taste.

113

OATMEAL/COCONUT CRISPS

Taste-testers voted these the best oatmeal cookies they've sampled

2 c. butter or regular margarine	4 eggs
2 c. brown sugar, firmly packed	3 c. sifted flour
	2 tsp. salt
2 c. sugar	2 tsp. baking soda
2 tsp. vanilla	6 c. quick-cooking rolled oats
	1½ c. flaked coconut

Cream together butter and brown and white sugars until fluffy. Stir in vanilla; then add eggs, one at a time, beating after each addition.

Sift together flour, salt and baking soda. Add to creamed mixture. Stir in rolled oats and coconut. Drop by teaspoonfuls about 2" apart onto well-greased baking sheets.

Bake in moderate oven (350°) 10 to 15 minutes. Cool cookies on racks. Makes 14 dozen.

NOTE: You can omit the 1½ c. coconut and divide dough into thirds. Add ⅓ c. flaked coconut to one part, ⅓ c. raisins to second part and ⅓ c. chopped walnuts to the third part.

VARIATIONS

Oatmeal/Raisin Cookies: Use 1½ c. raisins instead of the coconut.
Oatmeal/Nut Cookies: Use 1½ c. chopped walnuts instead of the coconut.
Oatmeal/Butter Crisps: Omit the flaked coconut.

OATMEAL CHIPPERS

Nuggets of chocolate lift these cookies above the commonplace

½ c. butter or regular margarine	1 tsp. baking soda
	1 tsp. salt
½ c. shortening	1 tsp. ground cinnamon
1 c. sugar	1 tsp. ground nutmeg
1 c. brown sugar, firmly packed	2 c. quick-cooking rolled oats
	1 (6 oz.) pkg. semisweet chocolate pieces
2 eggs	
1 tsp. vanilla	1 c. chopped walnuts
2 c. sifted flour	

Cream together butter and shortening. Add sugars gradually, beating until light and fluffy. Beat in eggs and vanilla.

Blend in sifted dry ingredients, mixing thoroughly. Stir in oats, chocolate pieces and nuts.

Drop by rounded teaspoonfuls about 2″ apart onto greased baking sheet. Bake in moderate oven (375°) 9 to 12 minutes. Remove cookies and cool on racks. Makes 8 dozen.

OATMEAL DROP COOKIES

Coffee party treats—apricot or other fruit jam adds a color note

½ c. butter or regular margarine	1 tsp. vanilla
½ c. shortening	2½ c. sifted flour
1 c. brown sugar, firmly packed	1 tsp. baking soda
¾ c. sugar	1 tsp. salt
2 eggs	1 tsp. ground cinnamon
½ c. water	2 c. quick-cooking rolled oats
	½ c. apricot jam

Cream together butter and shortening. Gradually beat in sugars until mixture is light and fluffy. Add eggs, water and vanilla. Beat well.

Sift together flour, soda, salt and cinnamon. Blend into creamed mixture. Stir in oats.

Drop rounded teaspoonfuls about 3″ apart onto ungreased baking sheet. Make an indentation in each with tip of spoon. Fill with apricot jam (about ½ tsp.). Top with 1 tsp. dough.

Bake in hot oven (400°) 10 to 12 minutes. Remove cookies and cool on rack. Makes 4 dozen.

JEWELED OATMEAL DROPS

Gumdrops add chewy texture, color and flavor to these crisp cookies

1 c. shortening
1 c. brown sugar, firmly
packed
1 c. sugar
2 eggs
1 tsp. vanilla
2 c. sifted flour

½ tsp. baking soda
1 tsp. baking powder
¾ tsp. salt
2 c. quick-cooking rolled oats
1 c. cut-up assorted gumdrops
(no black candies)

Beat shortening until light. Add sugars and beat until fluffy. Beat in eggs and vanilla to mix thoroughly.

Sift together flour, baking soda, baking powder and salt; add to beaten mixture. Mix well.

Stir in rolled oats and gumdrops. Drop by teaspoonfuls about 2″ apart onto lightly greased baking sheet.

Bake in moderate oven (375°) about 10 to 12 minutes. Remove from baking sheet to rack and let cool. Makes 5½ dozen.

NOTE: Cut gumdrops with scissors moistened in cold water.

VARIATION

Orange Jeweled Oatmeal Drops: Substitute 18 candy orange slices, cut in small pieces, for the assorted gumdrops.

ORANGE/OATMEAL SCOTCHIES

*An orange-coconut blend flavors these crisp
brown oatmeal cookies*

¾ c. shortening
1½ c. brown sugar, firmly
packed
2 eggs
1 tblsp. grated orange peel
6 tblsp. orange juice

1½ c. quick-cooking rolled
oats
½ c. flaked coconut
2 c. sifted flour
2 tsp. baking powder
½ tsp. baking soda
½ tsp. salt

Cream shortening and sugar until light and fluffy. Beat in eggs to mix thoroughly. Then beat in orange peel and juice. Stir in rolled oats and coconut.

Sift together remaining dry ingredients; stir into first mixture.

Drop by teaspoonfuls 2″ apart onto lightly greased

baking sheet. Bake in hot oven (400°) 8 to 10 minutes. Remove cookies and cool on racks. Makes about 5½ dozen.

OVERNIGHT MACAROONS

Easy-to-make, delicious, inexpensive—
cookies look like brown lace

4 c. quick-cooking rolled oats	2 eggs, beaten
2 c. brown sugar, firmly packed	1 tsp. salt
1 c. salad oil	1 tsp. almond extract

Combine rolled oats, brown sugar and salad oil in large mixing bowl; mix well. Cover and let stand overnight.

In the morning, blend eggs, salt and almond extract into oat mixture. Let stand 5 minutes.

Drop batter from teaspoon 2″ apart onto lightly greased baking sheet. Bake in slow oven (325°) 15 minutes. Remove cookies and cool on racks. Makes 4 dozen.

SCOTCH MOLASSES COOKIES

Thin, crisp oatmeal cookies have attractive
lacy edges. Good!

¾ c. sifted flour	2½ c. quick-cooking rolled oats
½ c. sugar	
2 tsp. baking powder	1 c. raisins
½ tsp. salt	⅔ c. melted shortening
2 tsp. baking soda	1 egg, beaten
1 tsp. ground cinnamon	¾ c. molasses
½ tsp. ground nutmeg	1 tblsp. milk
⅛ tsp. ground cloves	

Sift together dry ingredients.

Combine oats and raisins; sift flour mixture over top.

Combine remaining ingredients in bowl. Pour over dry ingredients; mix well. Drop by teaspoonfuls 2 to 3″ apart onto greased baking sheet.

Bake in moderate oven (350°) 8 to 12 minutes. Spread on racks to cool. Makes 3 dozen.

PUMPKIN/OATMEAL DROPS

Not too sweet; mild, spicy and good
keepers if you hide them

¾ c. butter or regular
  margarine
1½ c. sugar
2 eggs
1 c. canned pumpkin
1 tsp. vanilla
1½ c. sifted flour
2 tsp. baking powder
½ tsp. baking soda

½ tsp. salt
1 tsp. ground cinnamon
½ tsp. ground nutmeg
⅛ tsp. ground cloves
1½ c. quick-cooking rolled
  oats
½ c. shredded coconut
½ c. chopped nuts

Cream together butter and sugar. Beat in eggs; add pumpkin and vanilla.

Sift together flour, baking powder, soda, salt and spices. Stir into creamed mixture. Add oats, coconut and nuts.

Drop by teaspoonfuls 2″ apart onto greased baking sheet. Bake in moderate oven (375°) about 12 minutes. Remove cookies and cool on racks. Makes 6 dozen.

ROOKIE COOKIES

For hearty cookies that are extra-chewy
use regular rolled oats

2 eggs
2 c. brown sugar, firmly
  packed
1 c. melted butter or regular
  margarine
2 c. sifted flour
1 tsp. baking powder

½ tsp. baking soda
½ tsp. salt
4 c. regular rolled oats
1 c. chopped nuts
1 c. shredded coconut
½ c. raisins
½ c. water (about)

Beat eggs; blend in sugar and butter.

Sift together flour, baking powder, soda and salt. Stir into egg mixture. Stir in remaining ingredients, adding enough water to moisten well. Mix thoroughly.

Drop by teaspoonfuls about 2″ apart onto greased baking sheet. Bake in moderate oven (350°) about 15 minutes. Remove cookies and cool on racks. Makes 6 dozen.

NOTE: For less chewy cookies use 3½ c. quick-cooking rolled oats instead of the regular.

WHEAT/OAT CRISPS

*It's a wonder that anything so "good for you"
can taste so good*

¾ c. shortening
1 c. brown sugar, firmly
   packed
½ c. white sugar
1 egg
¼ c. water
1 tsp. vanilla
1 c. stone ground whole
   wheat flour

1 tsp. salt
½ tsp. baking soda
3 c. quick-cooking rolled oats
2 tblsp. wheat germ
½ c. flaked coconut
½ c. chopped nuts
¼ c. semisweet chocolate
   pieces (optional)

Beat shortening with sugars until light and fluffy.
Beat in egg, water and vanilla until creamy.

Stir together flour, salt and baking soda to mix. Stir
into creamed mixture and blend well. Add rolled oats,
wheat germ, coconut and nuts. Drop by teaspoonfuls
2″ apart onto lightly greased baking sheet. Top each
cookie with a chocolate piece.

Bake in moderate oven (350°) 12 to 15 minutes.
Transfer cookies to racks to cool. Makes 5 dozen.

GRANDMA'S SOFT SUGAR COOKIES

*Grandma centered seeded raisins
in her memorable man-size cookies*

1 c. sugar
1 c. brown sugar, firmly
   packed
½ c. butter
½ c. shortening
2 eggs
1 tsp. vanilla
½ tsp. lemon extract
1 tsp. ground nutmeg

3½ c. sifted flour
2 tsp. baking powder
1 tsp. cream of tartar
¾ tsp. salt
¾ tsp. baking soda
1 c. buttermilk
⅓ c. sugar (for tops)
Seeded raisins (or seedless)

Beat together white and brown sugars, butter and
shortening until light and fluffy. Beat in eggs, vanilla
and lemon extract to mix well.

Sift together nutmeg, flour, baking powder, cream of
tartar, salt and soda. Add alternately with buttermilk
to creamed mixture.

Drop tablespoonfuls of dough 2½″ apart onto
greased baking sheet. With the back of the spoon's

bowl, spread round and round with the outer edge of the cookies a little thicker than the centers. Sprinkle generously with sugar and place a fat seeded raisin in the center of each cookie.

Bake in hot oven (400°) about 10 minutes. For softer cookies, bake in hot oven (425°) about 8 minutes, or until no indentation remains when you touch the center of the cookie with your fingertip. Remove cookies and cool on racks. Makes 4 dozen.

POWDERED SUGAR COOKIES

*Rich, dainty cookies that can be
either molded or dropped*

½ c. shortening
½ c. butter
1½ c. confectioners sugar
1 egg
1 tsp. vanilla
¼ tsp. almond extract
2½ c. sifted flour

1 tsp. baking soda
1 tsp. cream of tartar
¼ tsp. salt
1 c. chopped pecans
¾ c. confectioners sugar
(for coating)

Beat shortening and butter until light; gradually add 1½ c. confectioners sugar, beating constantly. Beat in egg, vanilla and almond extract to mix well.

Sift together flour, baking soda, cream of tartar and salt. Add to creamed mixture. Stir in nuts.

Drop by teaspoonfuls 1″ apart onto ungreased baking sheet. (Or shape in 1″ balls.) Bake in hot oven (400°) 8 to 10 minutes. Remove to cooling racks, and while still warm, roll in confectioners sugar. When cool, roll in confectioners sugar again for snowy white coating. Makes about 6 dozen.

Rolled Cookies

WHEN LIGHTS and decorations go up along main streets across the country, rolling pins and cookie cutters of many shapes soon come to light in the kitchen. Then, more than at any other season, rolled cookies have top popularity. By the time Christmas arrives, cookie stars, hearts, crescents, jaunty gingerbread boys and animals dangle from the branches of twinkling Christmas trees.

We tell you how to glamorize cookies by sprinkling them before baking with coarse white or colored decorating sugar, tiny colored candies, chocolate shot (jimmies), chopped nuts, silver and gold dragées and other simple trims. You can also spread baked cookies with frosting or a glaze, or put them together in pairs with frosting or filling. (Be sure to try our Raisin-Filled Cookies with a choice of three other fillings.)

If you want a picture-pretty tray or plate of cookies to set—as for a buffet supper—bake our beautiful Wild Rose Cookies, dainty Cheese/Jam Cookie Tarts and Frosted Diamond Cookies (a Pennsylvania Dutch specialty containing caraway seeds).

Among our rolled cookies are also some imported recipes from faraway places, all adapted to American tastes—Finnish Stars, Orange Wreaths from Mexico and Chinese Almond Cookies.

Do bake our traditionals. We recommend the Frosted Ginger Creams, an unforgettable molasses cookie. And don't miss the big recipe for Gingerbread Christmas Cookies, ideal for cutting into different shapes for yuletide. We also include Hard-Cooked Egg Cookies, a delightful yellow rolled cookie.

Some women bake rolled cookies the year around,

time being their only limitation. But beginners and women inexperienced in rolling dough are sometimes loath to try them. It's really simple to roll cookie dough if you use good recipes and follow the rules. Number one is to chill the dough if it seems soft. When it gets firm, take only the amount you can work with at a time from the refrigerator.

Roll it on a pastry cloth with a stockinet-covered rolling pin. Rub a little flour into the cloth and stockinet with your hands to discourage the dough from sticking. Repeat if necessary, but be stingy with flour —adding too much makes cookies tough.

Roll from the center of the mound of dough as you do for pie crust. When you cut dough with the cookie cutter, start at the edges and work to the center. Dip the cutter in flour and shake off the excess. Repeat as often as necessary to prevent dough from sticking. Cut with pressure and keep scraps to a minimum by cutting cookies close together. For the last baking, gather the scraps, shape into a mound, roll and cut. These cookies will be less tender than those rolled only once.

If you do not have cookie cutters in assorted shapes, why not start a collection, adding one or two a year? Many women say this is a rewarding hobby. If you (or another family member) have artistic leanings you also can draw and cut patterns from cardboard. Grease the patterns well before laying them on the rolled dough; cut around them with a pointed knife.

Lift cutouts to the baking sheet on a wide spatula to avoid stretching them out of shape. Bake cookies only until delicately browned unless recipe specifies otherwise.

ALMOND QUARTER-MOONS

Recipe for the dainty crescents
is from an almond grower's wife

2¾ c. sifted flour	1½ c. sugar
1½ tsp. baking powder	½ tsp. almond extract
¼ tsp. salt	2 eggs, beaten
¾ c. butter or regular margarine	½ c. ground unblanched almonds

Sift together flour, baking powder and salt.

Cream butter and sugar until light and fluffy. Add almond extract and eggs; beat well. Add sifted dry ingredients and almonds and mix well. Chill.

Roll dough about ⅛″ thick. Cut with crescent-shaped cutter. Place about 2″ apart on ungreased baking sheet. Bake in moderate oven (350°) 8 to 10 minutes. Remove cookies and cool on racks. Makes about 10 dozen.

Special-Occasion Jelly Cookies

Jelly in country kitchens is more than a spread for hot biscuits, toast or jelly roll. It's also a favored ingredient in many dishes, including cookies like these Almond/Jelly Cookies.

Jelly touches these crisp, rich cookies with bright color and supplies that luscious fruity flavor. They're at their best served the same day you bake them, although you can freeze them successfully to bring out on short notice when you want to give your guests a true country-kitchen treat. The combination of almond/jelly flavors makes these cookie sandwiches exceptional.

When we first made them, we used currant jelly, as suggested by the North Dakota woman who contributed this recipe. You can substitute any kind you especially like or have in your cupboard. We found both apricot and peach jams also made delightful fillings.

ALMOND/JELLY COOKIES

Grated almonds speckle cookie sandwiches filled with tart-sweet jelly

1 c. butter
1 c. plus 2 tblsp. sugar
¼ tsp. vanilla
1½ c. sifted flour
⅛ tsp. salt

1 c. grated unblanched almonds (about ¾ c. before grating)
½ c. currant jelly

Beat butter until light; add sugar and vanilla and beat until fluffy.

Add flour and salt, blended together, and then the almonds.

Cover bowl tightly and chill overnight or several hours.

Roll dough very thin with waxed paper placed over dough to make rolling easier. Cut with 2½" round cutter.

Place cookies 1" apart on lightly greased baking sheet and bake in slow oven (300°) 8 to 10 minutes, until they start to brown around edges. Remove cookies to cooling rack. While still warm, spread half of cookies with currant jelly and top with other half of cookies. Complete cooling on racks. Makes 3 dozen.

NOTE: You can crush almonds fine with a rolling pin if a hand-turned grater is not available.

APPLESAUCE ROLL-UP COOKIES

Slice and bake one roll; freeze the other
roll for baking later

1¾ c. applesauce (16½ oz. can)	2 c. brown sugar, firmly packed
¾ c. cut-up dates	1 c. shortening
½ c. sugar	3 eggs
1 tblsp. grated orange peel	4 c. sifted flour
1 c. chopped nuts	¼ tsp. salt
	½ tsp. baking soda

To make filling, combine applesauce, dates and white sugar. Cook over low heat, stirring until thick, about 12 minutes. Remove from heat; stir in orange peel and nuts. Set aside to cool (you'll have 3 c. filling).

Beat brown sugar with shortening until light and fluffy. Beat in eggs to mix well.

Sift together flour, salt and baking soda. Add to creamed mixture, and mix thoroughly. Divide in half. Roll each half about ¼" thick on waxed paper to make a 15 × 12" rectangle.

Spread 1½ c. filling over each half of dough. Roll up like jelly roll (each roll will be about 16" long). Wrap tightly in waxed paper and refrigerate overnight, or at least several hours.

With a sharp knife, cut dough in ¼″ slices; place 1½ to 2″ apart on lightly greased baking sheet. Bake in moderate oven (350°) about 12 minutes, until lightly browned. Transfer cookies to racks to cool. Store cookies in container with loose-fitting lid. Makes about 10 dozen.

NOTE: If cookies lose crispness on standing, spread on baking sheet and heat in slow oven (300°) about 5 minutes. If you like, sift confectioners sugar mixed with cinnamon over slightly warm cookies. Use the proportion of 1 tsp. ground cinnamon to ½ c. confectioners sugar. Especially good with coffee.

BROWN-EYED SUSANS

These yellow and brown cookies
bring beauty to any tea table

1 c. butter or regular margarine	3¼ c. sifted flour
1 c. sugar	1 tblsp. baking powder
1 egg	1 tsp. salt
½ tsp. almond extract	⅓ c. semisweet chocolate
¼ tsp. yellow food color	pieces (64)

Cream butter and sugar together until light and fluffy. Beat in egg, almond extract and food color.

Sift together flour, baking powder and salt. Gradually blend into creamed mixture.

Turn dough onto lightly floured surface; knead gently to form a ball. Wrap in plastic wrap or waxed paper and chill several hours, or until dough can be handled easily.

Divide dough in fourths. Roll one fourth at a time to make a 12 × 6″ rectangle. Cut each rectangle into strips ¾″ wide and 6″ long. On long side of strip cut slits ½″ apart and three-fourths of the way through to opposite side. Roll each strip like a jelly roll. (Dough has tendency to break when rolled; hold roll together with fingers and pinch slightly on bottom when placing on baking sheet. This spreads the blossoms.) Place about 1″ apart on ungreased baking sheet. Turn cut ends down a little to form flower petals. Center a chocolate piece, flat side up, in each flower.

Bake in moderate oven (375°) 8 to 10 minutes, until browned. Remove from oven; cool slightly on baking sheet set on rack. Remove from baking sheet and cool completely on racks. Makes about 64.

VARIATION

Festival Squares: Divide dough for Brown-Eyed Susans in half. Make flower cookies with one half, Festival Squares with the other half: Roll dough into two 12 × 6″ rectangles. Cut in 2″ squares with knife; then cut two ½″ slits in each side of squares. Bake and cool like Brown-Eyed Susans. Then drop Vanilla Cream Icing in irregular amounts from teaspoon onto centers of cookies. For the most charming cookies, divide icing into four parts. Leave one white and tint the other with food color in pastel shades of pink, green and yellow. Makes 3 dozen.

Vanilla Cream Icing: Stir together 2 c. sifted confectioners sugar, ¼ tsp. salt and 1 tsp. vanilla; add enough milk or water (about 2 tblsp.) to make an icing that spreads easily. Beat well. Spread on cookies with pastry brush, or drop from spoon, as directed in recipe.

BUTTER CRISPIES

Freeze some of these to bring out for company—they're good keepers

1 c. butter	⅛ tsp. salt
1 c. sugar	¾ tsp. ground nutmeg
1 egg	1 tsp. baking soda
3½ c. sifted flour	½ c. buttermilk

Cream butter until light and fluffy. Gradually beat in sugar and egg.

Combine flour, salt, nutmeg and baking soda. Sift into creamed mixture alternately with buttermilk. Chill at least an hour or until firm.

Roll out a small part of dough at a time, keeping remaining dough in refrigerator until ready to roll. Roll very thin. Cut with 2½″ round or fancy cookie cutters. Place ¼ to ½″ apart on ungreased baking sheet.

Bake in moderate oven (350°) 8 to 10 minutes, until lightly browned. Remove from baking sheet to wire racks to cool. Makes 5½ dozen.

CHEESE/JAM COOKIE TARTS

*Brown rims of cookie dough frame fruit
jams of festive colors*

1 c. butter
1 (8 oz.) pkg. cream cheese
2 c. sifted flour

½ c. jam (grape, apricot,
   peach or berry)

Beat together butter and cream cheese until light and fluffy. Blend in flour. Chill overnight.

Roll dough about ⅛" thick and cut with 2" round cutter. Spread tops with jam; arrange ½" apart on ungreased baking sheet. (Cookies shrink during baking.)

Bake in moderate oven (350°) 10 to 12 minutes. Remove cookies and cool on racks. Makes about 6 dozen.

NOTE: Store cookies in container with loose lid in a cool place, or package and freeze them. To use if frozen, thaw in wrapper at room temperature about 15 minutes. To restore crispness to stored cookies, spread them on baking sheets and heat in slow oven (300°) about 5 minutes.

Chinese Almond Cookies

An Iowa country woman, member of a gourmet club, serves these with tea for dessert after an oriental-type meal.

The inspiration to make Chinese Almond Cookies followed a trip to California and an afternoon spent browsing around San Francisco's Chinatown. Back home in her farm kitchen, she set out to duplicate the cookies she saw in an oriental bakery and tasted in a Chinese dinner. Luckily, she used lard for shortening; this gave her product that characteristic texture that all authentic Chinese almond cookies have. By baking them in a slow oven, she achieved the right color—no browning except a delicate shading around the edges. Her cookies, with almonds centered on top, capture the delightful flavor that makes this type of cookie the top oriental favorite of Americans.

127

CHINESE ALMOND COOKIES

*Go Chinese with these creamy white cookies,
a top oriental favorite*

1 c. lard, butter or regular
   margarine
1 c. sugar
1 egg
¾ tsp. almond extract
2¾ c. sifted flour

½ tsp. baking soda
½ tsp. salt
24 whole almonds (about),
   split lengthwise in halves
   (about ¼ c.)

Beat together lard and sugar until light and fluffy. Beat in egg and almond extract to blend well.

Sift together flour, baking soda and salt; add to creamed mixture. Shape dough with hands to form a ball.

Roll dough a scant ¼″ thick and cut with 2″ round cutter. Place 2″ apart on ungreased baking sheet. Put an almond half in the center of each cookie.

Bake in slow oven (325°) 15 to 20 minutes, or until cookies brown very lightly around edges. Carefully remove cookies with broad spatula to cooling rack. (They are fragile when hot.) When cool, store in covered container in a cool place, or freeze. Makes about 3½ dozen.

CLOTHESPIN COOKIES

*These fascinating cookies will be the talk
of your coffee party*

3¼ c. sifted flour
1 tsp. salt
2 tblsp. sugar
2 c. shortening

1¼ c. warm water
2 egg yolks
Chocolate/Marshmallow
   Filling (recipe follows)

Blend together flour, salt, sugar and ½ c. shortening as for pie crust. Stir in warm water. Then add egg yolks and mix well. Cover bowl and chill 1 hour.

Remove dough from refrigerator and roll in rectangle ¼″ thick. Spread with ½ c. shortening. Fold one half of dough (greased top) over on other half; refrigerate another hour. Repeat this process two more times, each time spreading ½ c. shortening on dough.

Roll a fourth of dough at a time, leaving remaining dough in refrigerator until ready to work with it. Cut in strips 1″ wide, 4″ long. Wind each strip loosely around a clean wooden clothespin. Lay in ungreased 15½ × 10½ × 1″ jelly roll pan.

Bake in hot oven (425°) 10 to 12 minutes. Place clothespins with cookies on cooling racks. In 2 or 3 minutes, gently twist pins and slip off cookies. (They are crisp and break easily so work carefully.) When cool, fill with Chocolate/Marshmallow Filling.

To fill, cut a small hole in corner of small plastic bag. Partly fill with Chocolate/Marshmallow Filling, leaving remaining filling in refrigerator until needed. Squeeze out filling, first into one end of cookie and then in other end to fill completely. Store filled cookies in refrigerator until serving time. Makes 9 dozen.

NOTE: Cookies may be refrigerated a few days and then filled. Or freeze cookies and fill them when needed.

CHOCOLATE/MARSHMALLOW FILLING

This luscious filling and the crisp cookies are great teammates

¼ c. flour
1 c. milk
½ c. butter
½ c. sugar
½ c. confectioners sugar

½ c. marshmallow creme
1 tsp. vanilla
2 to 4 squares unsweetened chocolate, melted and cooled

Mix flour with a little milk to make a smooth paste; add remaining milk and cook, stirring constantly, until mixture thickens. Set aside to cool.

Cream together butter and sugars until light and fluffy, using electric mixer on high speed. Add thickened flour-milk mixture and beat well. Then beat in the marshmallow creme and vanilla. Stir in chocolate. Cover and chill before using. Makes 2 cups.

NOTE: You can use 2 to 4 squares unsweetened or semisweet chocolate in the filling. What you use and how much is a matter of personal preference.

COCOA/MOLASSES COOKIES

*Long-time favorites in Dutch neighborhoods
in Hudson River Valley*

1 c. butter	3 c. sifted flour
½ c. sugar	1 tsp. salt
1 c. light molasses	½ c. cocoa
1 egg	Sugar Glaze (see Index)
1 tsp. vanilla	

Cream butter and sugar until light and fluffy. Beat in molasses, egg and vanilla to mix well.

Sift together flour, salt and cocoa; stir into creamed mixture. Chill dough.

Roll dough rather thick, about ¼", and cut into 4 × 2½" rectangles. (Use an empty luncheon meat can for a cutter, or a 4 × 2½" rectangular cutter or a knife. Cookies cut with the empty can or cutter have rounded corners.) Place ½" apart on lightly greased baking sheet.

Bake in moderate oven (350°) about 10 minutes. Remove cookies and cool on racks, then spread with Sugar Glaze. Makes 3 dozen.

CORNMEAL COOKIES

*The unusual ingredient in these crisp,
raisin treats is cornmeal*

1½ c. sifted flour	¾ c. sugar
½ tsp. baking powder	1 egg
½ tsp. salt	½ tsp. lemon extract
½ c. cornmeal	¼ c. milk
½ tsp. ground nutmeg	½ c. chopped raisins
½ c. shortening	5 tblsp. sugar (for topping)

Sift together flour, baking powder, salt, cornmeal and nutmeg.

Beat together shortening and ¾ c. sugar until light and fluffy. Beat in egg and lemon extract. Alternately add milk and sifted dry ingredients. Beat until smooth. Stir in raisins.

Roll dough out on lightly floured board to ¼"

thickness; cut with 2½″ round cutter. Place 1″ apart on greased baking sheet; sprinkle with sugar. Bake in moderate oven (375°) 12 to 15 minutes. Remove cookies and cool on racks. Makes 29 cookies.

DATE PINWHEELS

Two-tone pinwheels add charm to a tray
or plate of one-color cookies

1⅓ c. chopped dates	1⅓ c. brown sugar, firmly
½ c. sugar	packed
½ c. water	2 eggs
½ c. chopped nuts	2⅔ c. sifted flour
⅔ c. shortening	½ tsp. salt
	½ tsp. baking soda

Combine dates, sugar, water and nuts in saucepan; cook until thick. Set aside to cool.

Cream shortening; beat in brown sugar. Beat in eggs to mix thoroughly.

Sift together dry ingredients; add to creamed mixture and blend well. Chill thoroughly.

Divide dough in half; roll each half in a rectangle ¼″ thick. Spread each with date filling and roll up like a jelly roll. Wrap in waxed paper and chill overnight.

Cut dough in ⅛″ slices and place 1½″ apart on greased baking sheet. Bake in moderate oven (375°) 8 minutes, or until lightly browned. Remove cookies and cool on racks. Makes about 5 dozen.

Pink and White Frosted Diamonds

Pennsylvania Dutch women of Moravian faith invented these cookies and named them Moravian seed cookies. Your fondness for them will depend on how much you enjoy the flavor of caraway.

Tradition requires that you cut the pastry-like dough in diamond shapes, frost them in white and sprinkle on coarse pink sugar.

Diamonds are easy to cut with a knife, although you can use a cookie cutter if you have one. Just roll the dough in a rectangle and cut 2″ diagonal strips one

way, and then the other. And you have no scraps of
dough to reroll and bake.

FROSTED DIAMOND COOKIES

Guaranteed to please caraway fans—
also to dress up the cookie tray

½ c. butter
½ c. sugar
2 eggs
1 tsp. vanilla
3 c. sifted flour
⅛ tsp. salt

1 tsp. caraway seeds
White Mountain Frosting
  (recipe follows)
¼ c. coarse pink decorating
  sugar (about)

Beat butter until light; gradually add sugar and beat
until mixture is fluffy. Beat in eggs and vanilla to blend
thoroughly.

Sift together flour and salt; add to creamed mixture.
Stir in caraway seeds.

Roll dough thin, not more than ⅛″, and cut in 2″
diamonds with sharp knife or cookie cutter. Place ½″
apart on lightly greased baking sheet.

Bake in slow oven (325°) 10 to 12 minutes. Re-
move cookies and cool on racks. Then spread with
White Mountain Frosting and sprinkle with pink sugar.
Makes about 6½ dozen.

White Mountain Frosting: Combine 1 c. sugar, ⅛ tsp.
cream of tartar and ¼ c. water in small saucepan.
Place over heat and stir until sugar dissolves. Continue
cooking syrup to soft ball stage (236°).

Meanwhile, add ⅛ tsp. salt to 1 egg white and beat
until stiff. Pour hot syrup in a fine stream into egg
white, beating constantly until frosting is of spreading
consistency.

DOUBLE CREAM COOKIES

Tea party tidbits—tiny, rich cookies
put together with frosting

1 c. soft butter
⅓ c. heavy cream
2 c. sifted flour

Creamy Frosting (recipe
  follows)

132

Mix together butter, cream and flour; chill thoroughly. Roll ⅛″ thick and cut in 1½″ rounds. Place on waxed paper heavily sprinkled with sugar and turn to coat circles.

Place about 2″ apart on ungreased baking sheet; prick tops with fork in three or four places. Bake in moderate oven (375°) about 8 minutes, until puffy, but not browned. Place cookies on racks to cool. Put together in pairs with Creamy Frosting. Makes about 5 dozen double cookies.

Creamy Frosting: Blend together ¼ c. butter, ¾ c. sifted confectioners sugar, 1 egg yolk and 1 tsp. vanilla or ¼ tsp. almond extract. Beat until smooth.

FIG BARS

The moist fig filling in these butter cookies is not overly sweet

1 c. butter	1 tsp. baking soda
2 c. brown sugar, firmly packed	1 tsp. baking powder
3 eggs	1½ c. ground figs
1 tsp. vanilla	1 c. water
1 tblsp. lemon juice	¾ c. sugar
4 c. sifted flour	3 tblsp. flour
1 tsp. salt	¼ c. chopped walnuts
	2 tblsp. orange juice

To make dough, cream butter and brown sugar. Add eggs, vanilla and lemon juice; beat. Stir together 4 c. flour, salt, baking soda and baking powder; blend into creamed mixture. Chill.

Meanwhile, prepare fig filling. Boil figs in water 5 minutes. Blend sugar and 3 tblsp. flour; stir into figs. Cook over low heat, stirring frequently, until thick. Stir in nuts and orange juice. Cool.

Divide chilled dough in half. Roll each half in a rectangle 18 × 12 × ⅛″ on well-floured pastry cloth. Cut into four 3″ wide strips. Put cooled filling down center of strips. Using a spatula, fold dough over filling. Cut strips in half; transfer strips, seam side down, to ungreased baking sheet, about 2″ apart. Bake in moderate oven (375°) about 15 minutes. Transfer bars to racks to cool. Cut in 2″ bars. Makes about 5 dozen.

FIG/ORANGE-FILLED SQUARES

*Fork tines make decorative edge on two sides
of plump turnovers*

2 c. finely chopped dried figs	1 c. shortening
½ c. white sugar	1 egg
1 c. orange juice	2 tblsp. milk
Dash of salt	1 tsp. vanilla
½ c. sugar	3 c. sifted flour
½ c. brown sugar, firmly	½ tsp. salt
packed	½ tsp. baking soda

To make filling, combine figs, ½ c. white sugar, orange juice and dash of salt in small saucepan. Cook, stirring occasionally, until thick. Set aside to cool. You will have 2 cups.

Cream together ½ c. white sugar, brown sugar and shortening until light and fluffy. Add egg, milk and vanilla; beat well.

Sift together flour, ½ tsp. salt and baking soda; stir into creamed mixture. Chill dough at least 1 hour.

Divide dough into quarters. Roll one quarter at a time on lightly floured board to make a 12 × 8" rectangle. Cut crosswise into 6 strips, each 2" wide. Spread fig filling over half of strips; then top with remaining strips. Press lengthwise edges with floured tines of fork to seal. Cut in 2" lengths. Repeat with remaining portions of dough.

Place 2" apart on ungreased baking sheet and bake in moderate oven (350°) about 10 minutes. Transfer cookies to rack to cool. Makes about 4 dozen.

FINNISH STAR COOKIES

*These decorative cookies are rich like pastry—
with date filling*

1 c. sugar	1 c. butter
1 c. finely cut dates (½ lb.)	½ c. water
1 c. water	1 tblsp. light cream or milk
1½ c. sifted flour	2 tblsp. sugar (for tops)

To make filling, combine 1 c. sugar, dates and 1 c. water in saucepan. Bring to a boil over medium heat;

reduce heat to low and continue cooking and stirring until filling thickens. Set aside to cool.

Blend flour with ½ c. butter with pastry blender as for pie crust. Slowly add ½ c. water; mix well and chill thoroughly.

Roll dough ⅛″ thick. Spread about a third of remaining ½ c. butter over half of dough. Fold buttered half over other half of dough and roll to ⅛″ thickness. Repeat spreading with butter and rolling two more times.

Cut dough in 2½″ squares. Cut 1″ slash in each corner of squares and place about 1 tsp. cooled date filling on center of each square. Fold one point of each slashed corner to center to make pinwheel, and pinch edges to seal. Brush with cream and sprinkle with sugar.

Arrange about 2″ apart on ungreased baking sheet and bake in hot oven (400°) about 10 minutes. Transfer cookies to racks to cool. Makes about 5 dozen.

Fortune Cookies, American Style

Bake fortune cookies for the next social gathering at your house; they're fun for people of all ages. The homemade version tastes better than the Chinese, but differs in shape—flatter, with a smaller center peak.

The recipe for Mom's Fortune Cookies comes from an Illinois woman who has been baking them off and on for more than 10 years. Stored in a covered container and put in a cold place or the freezer, they keep for several months. It's convenient to keep them on hand to bring out on short notice.

The Illinois mother always writes messages to insert in a few cookies she saves especially for her children. That explains the name of the recipe. Her motherly notes run from "I love you" and "It's your turn to feed the cat" to "You're an exceptional child—exceptionally untidy and sweet."

Adult messages are predictions, such as "You'll meet a stranger this week who will bring you happiness" and "If your birthday is between May 1 and August 25, this is your year for exciting travel."

Here's the recipe for the cookies. You'll enjoy using

your imagination when you write the fortunes to enclose in them.

MOM'S FORTUNE COOKIES

These cookies liven up parties;
make them ahead to have on hand

1 c. sugar	⅓ c. milk
⅔ c. shortening	3 c. sifted flour
2 eggs	3 tsp. baking powder
1 tsp. vanilla	½ tsp. salt

Cream sugar and shortening until light and fluffy. Beat in eggs, vanilla and milk to mix thoroughly.

Sift together flour, baking powder and salt. Stir gradually into creamed mixture. Chill well.

Roll dough ⅛" thick and cut with 2" round cutter. Place about 1" apart on ungreased baking sheet.

Type or write your own messages on little slips of paper; fold small and place like tent in center of each cookie on baking sheet. Place another cut-out cookie on top and press edges together to seal.

Bake in hot oven (400°) 10 to 12 minutes. Remove cookies and cool on racks. Makes about 5½ dozen.

FRUIT BLOSSOM COOKIES

Charming as an old-fashioned
flower garden in full bloom

⅔ c. shortening	1½ tsp. baking powder
¾ c. sugar	¼ tsp. salt
1 egg	2 tblsp. milk
½ tsp. vanilla	Citrus/Raisin (or other)
2 c. sifted flour	Filling (recipe follows)

Cream together shortening and sugar. Add egg; beat until light and fluffy. Add vanilla.

Sift together dry ingredients. Add to creamed mixture along with milk. Divide dough in half. Chill 1 hour.

Roll out half of dough; keep the rest chilled. Roll ⅟₁₆ to ⅛" thick. Cut with 2" scalloped cookie cutter. Place about ½ tsp. Citrus/Raisin Filling in centers of half the cookies. Place 1½" apart on greased baking sheet. Cut out centers of remaining half of cookies with

136

1" round cutter; place on filled bottoms and press edges with fork to seal. Repeat this process with remaining half of dough.

Bake in moderate oven (350°) 10 to 12 minutes. Transfer cookies to racks to cool. Makes about 2 dozen.

CITRUS/RAISIN FILLING

Do try the fruity variations—
they add color and taste contrasts

¼ c. chopped seedless raisins	4 tsp. water
½ tsp. grated orange peel	2 tblsp. sugar
1 tblsp. orange juice	½ tsp. flour
½ tsp. lemon juice	⅛ tsp. salt

Combine all ingredients in heavy saucepan. Bring to a boil, stirring constantly. Cook over medium heat about 5 minutes, stirring occasionally. Cool. Makes about ¼ cup.

VARIATIONS

Fig Filling: Substitute chopped dried figs for the raisins.
Apricot Filling: Substitute finely chopped, soft, dried apricots for raisins and add 1½ tsp. orange juice, ¼ tsp. lemon juice, 3 tblsp. water and 1 tsp. flour.
Pineapple Filling: Combine in saucepan ¾ tsp. cornstarch and ¼ c. crushed pineapple, undrained. Cook until clear, stirring constantly. Cool.
Cherry Filling: Mash ¼ c. cherry pie filling. Add a few drops almond extract, if desired.

GINGER COOKIES FOR A CROWD

A big recipe to make when you wish to put
cookies in the freezer

5½ c. sifted flour	1 c. shortening
1 tblsp. baking soda	1 c. sugar
2 tsp. baking powder	1 egg, beaten
1 tsp. salt	½ tsp. vanilla
¾ tsp. ground ginger	1 c. dark molasses
1 tsp. ground cinnamon	½ c. strong coffee

Sift together flour, soda, baking powder, salt, ginger and cinnamon.

Cream shortening; add sugar gradually; beat until light; add egg and vanilla.

Add molasses and coffee, then sifted dry ingredients; mix well; chill.

Roll out on lightly floured board ¼″ thick; cut with round 2″ cutter.

Place about 2″ apart on greased baking sheet. Bake in hot oven (400°) 8 to 10 minutes. Spread on racks to cool. Makes 12 dozen.

Gingerbread Christmas Cookies

Few goodies you make in your kitchen say Merry Christmas more eloquently than gingerbread cookies. You may consider them old-fashioned, but they're as up to date as the carols you sing or the Santa Claus to whom children write such adorable letters. These spicy molasses cookies are especially inviting on Christmas trees, and lend themselves to decorating.

Aside from tradition and tastiness, gingerbread cookies have many qualities that recommend them. You can bake them ahead. They keep satisfactorily for weeks either in the freezer or a cool place. You can cut them in many fancy shapes, such as animals, stars, bells, Christmas trees or whatever forms you wish, including plain and scalloped rounds. And you can decorate them with raisins, currants, candies and white or tinted icing. The dark brown cookie makes an excellent background to show off the trimmings.

Our Gingerbread Christmas Cookies recipe makes cookies that do not break easily. For this reason alone they are a fine choice for Christmas trees. You can hang them on your big tree or a smaller one decorated entirely with cookies. The cookie tree can be a small evergreen. Or cut a flat triangular Christmas tree from a piece of softboard. Cover it with green felt and pin the cookies to the felt, using red and green ribbons you pull through holes made in the cookies before baking.

There are two ways to make the holes in the cookies: 1) Insert 1½″ length of drinking straw into each unbaked cookie in the place you want the hole. Remove the straws before cookies are cool. Pull green and red ribbons through the holes and tie in bows or loops. 2) For each cookie, loop a 5 to 6″ length of string on baking sheet. Press unbaked cookie on a string, leaving at least 1″ overlap to hold cookie securely.

If you have such a hospitality cookie tree, you will need a reserve supply of cookies to replace those your visitors enjoy taking off and eating. Our recipe for Gingerbread Christmas Cookies makes about 12 dozen 2½″ round cookies. It's easy to cut the recipe in half if you want to bake a smaller batch.

GINGERBREAD CHRISTMAS COOKIES

Cookies are sturdy, crisp and hard—
taste like gingerbread. The little pigs with pink icing
curls for tails make a hit with a crowd

½ c. shortening	1 tsp. ground cloves
1 c. brown sugar, firmly packed	1 tsp. ground allspice
	1½ c. dark molasses
2 tsp. baking soda	⅔ c. water
2 tsp. salt	6½ c. sifted flour (about)
1 tsp. ground cinnamon	Ornamental Icing (optional,
1 tsp. ground ginger	see Index)

Cream shortening, sugar, baking soda, salt and spices together until light and fluffy. Beat in molasses. Stir in water.

Gradually stir in enough flour to make a stiff dough (about 6½ c.). Shape dough in ball with hands, wrap in plastic wrap or waxed paper and refrigerate several hours or overnight.

Roll out dough, a small amount at a time, ⅛ to ¼″ thick. Cut with desired cutter; slip a broad spatula under cookie and transfer it to lightly greased baking sheet. Arrange cutouts a short distance apart on baking sheet (they spread very little).

Bake in moderate oven (350°) 10 to 12 minutes, or until cookies are lightly browned. Remove from baking sheet to racks and cool. Decorate with Ornamental Icing, if you wish. Makes about 12 dozen.

Gingerbread Boys: Cut rolled dough for Gingerbread Christmas Cookies with 6″ gingerbread boy cutter. Place them about ½″ apart on lightly greased baking

139

sheet. Place heads of cutout boys on loops of string or insert drinking straws, as described. For each cookie, dip 3 raisins in slightly beaten egg white and press firmly, an equal distance apart, into cookie to represent shirt buttons (you'll need about 12 dozen raisins). For red buttons press in cinnamon candies (red hots) instead of raisins. Carefully move the legs and arms of the boys in different positions to provide animation and variety. Bake cookies, remove drinking straws, if used, and cool on racks. Decorate after cooling, or after freezing or storing. Use Ornamental Icing put through a decorating tube or small plastic bag with small hole cut in one corner. Use to draw faces on gingerbread boys, changing the features to give them a variety of expressions. The recipe for Gingerbread Christmas Cookies makes about 4 dozen 6" Gingerbread Boys.

Gingerbread Pigs: Cut the recipe for Gingerbread Christmas Cookies in half. Roll dough as directed, and cut with pig-shaped cookie cutter. Bake, cool and decorate with Ornamental Icing. You can outline each pig cookie with a thin white line of icing and make icing circles or dots for eyes. Tint a little icing pink with red food color and use it to make a curl on each pig cookie to represent its tail. Makes 64.

NOTE: Children delight in animal cookies. Among their favorites are rooster, hen, rabbit, reindeer and horse cookies.

Old-Fashioned Ginger Creams

Almost everyone cherishes memories of cookies especially enjoyed in childhood. Frosted Ginger Creams are more than a dream. A California homemaker-home economist developed her own recipe for Frosted Ginger Creams, the cookies she ate when a child on visits to an aunt.

She had never acquired the recipe—not written down. But when she had a home of her own, she baked ginger/molasses cookies until she duplicated the favorites of her childhood.

When we tested her recipe, every member of our
140

taste panel gave the cookies an A-1 rating. Bake a batch soon. Your friends and family will rejoice in these old-fashioned treats.

FROSTED GINGER CREAMS

These white-iced ginger cookies are soft, flavorful— and keep well

1 c. shortening
1 c. brown sugar, firmly packed
2 eggs
1 c. dark molasses
2 tblsp. vinegar
5 c. sifted flour (about)
1 tblsp. ground ginger

1 tblsp. baking soda
½ tsp. baking powder
1 tsp. salt
2 tblsp. butter or regular margarine
2 c. sifted confectioners sugar
1 tsp. vanilla
3 tblsp. milk or cream

Cream together shortening and brown sugar until light; beat in eggs, one at a time, beating well to blend. Add molasses and vinegar.

Sift together 4 c. flour, ginger, soda, baking powder and salt; stir into batter. Add additional flour to make a soft dough easy to roll.

Roll dough on lightly floured surface; cut in 2 or 3″ circles. Place about 1″ apart on lightly greased baking sheet.

Bake in moderate oven (375°) 10 to 15 minutes. Remove cookies and cool on wire racks.

Meanwhile, blend butter and confectioners sugar together, add vanilla and milk and beat until smooth. Spread over tops of cooled cookies, leaving a ¼″ rim of brown cookies around the white frosting. Store in airtight containers. Makes 5½ dozen.

GRAPEFRUIT SUGAR COOKIES

These dainty cookies make talk at tea parties—guests ask why they're so good. Candied peel is the secret

1 c. butter
1¼ c. sugar
2 eggs
3 c. sifted flour
2½ tsp. baking powder

½ tsp. salt
¾ c. finely chopped Candied Grapefruit Peel (recipe follows)

141

Cream butter and sugar; add eggs and beat until fluffy.

Sift together dry ingredients; mix in grapefruit peel. Add to creamed mixture. Divide dough in half; place in covered container and chill in refrigerator several hours.

Roll dough about ¼" thick on floured board; cut with floured cutter.

Place 1 to 1½" apart on greased baking sheet and bake in moderate oven (375°) 8 to 10 minutes. Remove cookies and cool on racks. Makes about 5 dozen.

CANDIED GRAPEFRUIT PEEL

Keep this handy—it makes icings and cookies special

Select and wash thick-skinned grapefruit. Cut into quarters and remove pulp. Put peel in saucepan; cover with cold water. Weight down peel with a plate. Let stand several hours or overnight. Drain.

With scissors, cut peel into strips about ¼" wide.

Cover peel with cold water and slowly bring to a simmer (180°) in a saucepan. Remove from heat, cover pan and let stand about 1 hour; drain. Repeat process until peel no longer tastes bitter (about 3 times).

Cover again with water and boil until yellow peel is tender, about 15 minutes. Drain well in colander. Press out water. Pack peel firmly into measuring cup to measure.

Return peel to saucepan. For each cup of peel, add 1 cup of sugar. Place over medium heat; stir until sugar has dissolved (peel forms its own liquid).

Cook peel over medium heat, stirring frequently, until sugar syrup is concentrated; reduce heat to low (syrup should boil gently). Continue cooking until the grapefruit peel is semitransparent and most of the sugar syrup has boiled away.

Drain in colander. Separate pieces of peel on baking sheets and allow to stand until they feel fairly dry. Sprinkle with enough sugar to give a crystalline look.

Store in tightly covered cans, or in plastic bags in the freezer.

HARD-COOKED EGG COOKIES

Cinnamon and nuts splash the tops of the rich, tasty, yellow cookies

1 c. butter or regular margarine	1 tblsp. finely grated lemon peel
1 c. sugar	3 c. sifted flour
1 egg	1 egg, slightly beaten
5 sieved hard-cooked egg yolks (about 1 c.)	1 tsp. sugar
	2 tsp. ground cinnamon
	½ c. chopped nuts

Beat butter, 1 c. sugar and 1 egg to blend thoroughly. Add hard-cooked egg yolks and lemon peel. Stir in flour.

Roll dough about ¼″ thick on lightly floured surface; cut with 2″ round cutter. Place ½″ apart on ungreased baking sheet. Brush tops of cookies with slightly beaten egg.

Combine 1 tsp. sugar and cinnamon; sprinkle with nuts over cookies.

Bake in slow oven (325°) 20 to 25 minutes, or until delicately browned. Remove cookies and cool on racks. Store in container with loose-fitting lid to retain crispness. Makes about 52.

VARIATION

Molded Hard-Cooked Egg Cookies: Instead of rolling dough, shape in 1″ balls. Place 2″ apart on ungreased baking sheet. Flatten by pressing with lightly greased bottom of juice glass. Brush tops with slightly beaten egg, sprinkle with sugar-cinnamon mixture and nuts, and bake like cutout cookies. Makes about 68.

HONEY WAFERS

Honey, spices and bran make these crisp, dainty cookies delicious

½ c. butter	½ tsp. ground cinnamon
½ c. honey	¼ tsp. ground cloves
2 c. sifted flour	¼ tsp. ground allspice
1 tsp. baking soda	¼ c. crushed bran flakes

Cream together butter and honey.

Sift together flour, baking soda, cinnamon, cloves and allspice. Mix with bran flakes.

Combine dry ingredients with honey and butter. Chill 1 hour, or until firm enough to roll easily.

Roll ⅛" thick on lightly floured board. Cut with floured cookie cutter. Place about 2" apart on greased baking sheet; bake in moderate oven (350°) 8 to 10 minutes. Remove cookies and cool on racks. Makes 3 dozen.

EASTER LAMB COOKIES

Stand lambs in green cellophane grass on a tray for a centerpiece

1 c. regular margarine	½ tsp. baking powder
⅔ c. sugar	1 egg, separated
1 egg	1 c. cookie coconut
1 tsp. vanilla	¼ tsp. water
2½ c. sifted flour	2 drops red or blue food color

Beat together margarine and sugar until light and fluffy. Beat in 1 egg and vanilla to blend thoroughly.

Sift together flour and baking powder. Add to creamed mixture. Divide dough in half; wrap each half in waxed paper and chill.

On lightly floured surface, roll half of dough very thin, less than ⅛" if possible. Cut with lamb cookie cutter or pattern.

Beat white from separated egg until foamy. Brush onto unbaked cookies. Sprinkle with half of cookie coconut. Place 1" apart on greased baking sheet.

Bake in moderate oven (350°) 7 to 10 minutes. Place cookies on racks to cool.

Meanwhile, roll second half of dough; cut in same way, but decorate before baking with egg yolk paint: Beat yolk from separated egg with water; add food color. Paint on unbaked cookies; sprinkle with coconut and bake as for first half of cookies. Makes about 76 (38 from each half of dough).

LEMON/ALMOND RICHES

Almond daisies with red centers top these Christmas beauties

1 c. butter or regular
   margarine
1 c. sugar
1 egg, separated
1 tblsp. finely grated lemon
   peel
¼ tsp. salt
2 c. sifted flour

½ c. finely chopped blanched
   almonds
1 tsp. water
2 tblsp. sugar (for tops)
2 c. whole blanched almonds
   (about ¾ lb.)
1 (4 oz.) pkg. candied
   cherries, cut in halves

Beat butter and 1 c. sugar together until light and fluffy. Beat in egg yolk and lemon peel.

Blend together salt and flour and stir into beaten mixture. Stir in chopped almonds. Shape dough in ball, flatten on lightly floured surface and roll ¼" thick. Cut with 2" round cutter.

Slightly beat egg white diluted with water; brush over tops of cookies. Sprinkle lightly with sugar. Press whole almonds around edge of cookies like daisy petals, 5 petals to a cookie. Place a cherry half, rounded side up, in center of each cookie.

Place cookies 1½" apart on lightly greased baking sheet. Bake in slow oven (325°) 15 to 17 minutes, or until cookies brown around edges. Remove cookies and cool on racks. Makes 3½ dozen.

VARIATION

Lemon-Flavored Riches: Omit almond daisy trim, placing a half candied cherry in center of each cookie before baking.

MINCEMEAT/CHEESE COOKIES

Perfect non-sweet addition to cookie tray—taste like mincement pie!

1 c. butter or regular
   margarine
2 c. grated Cheddar cheese
   (½ lb.)

2 c. sifted flour
1 (9 oz.) pkg. prepared
   mincemeat
½ c. water

Cream butter until light; add cheese (at room temperature) and cream until well blended. Stir in flour; mix well and chill.

Meanwhile, cook mincemeat and water until slightly thickened. Set aside to cool.

Roll dough ⅛″ thick on lightly floured surface; cut in 2″ circles. Put half of circles about 1″ apart on lightly greased baking sheet. Place 1 tsp. cooled mincemeat mixture in center of each cookie on baking sheet. Top each with another circle of dough; press edges with fork to seal. Prick cookie tops in several places with tines of kitchen fork.

Bake in moderate oven (350°) 15 minutes, or until lightly browned. Remove cookies to racks to cool. Makes 3½ dozen.

MINCEMEAT-FILLED OATSIES

Substantial and luscious—men especially like this oatmeal cookie

1 c. sifted flour	¾ c. sugar
1 tsp. baking soda	5 c. quick-cooking rolled oats
¼ tsp. salt	1 c. prepared mincemeat
1 tsp. vinegar	1 tsp. lemon juice
½ c. milk	¼ c. water
½ c. butter or regular margarine	6 tblsp. sugar

Sift together flour, baking soda and salt.

Combine vinegar and milk; stir to mix and set aside.

Beat butter until light; gradually beat in ¾ c. sugar. Beat until fluffy.

Add half of flour mixture, the milk and then remaining flour mixture. Mix thoroughly and fold in rolled oats. Chill 4 hours or longer.

Meanwhile, combine mincemeat, lemon juice, water and 6 tblsp. sugar in saucepan. Bring to a boil, stirring constantly. Set aside to cool.

Roll dough, one-third at a time, leaving remaining dough in refrigerator until ready to work with it. Roll dough thin, about ⅛″. Cut with 2½″ round cutter.

Spread 1 tsp. cooled mincemeat mixture on half the cookies. Top with remaining cookies. Place 1″ apart on ungreased baking sheet.

Bake in moderate oven (350°) 10 to 13 minutes. Remove cookies and cool on racks. Makes 3½ dozen.

VARIATION

Date-Filled Oatsies: Substitute 1 c. chopped dates for mincemeat in filling.

COUNTRY MOLASSES COOKIES

Make these cutouts as varied as the shape of your cookie cutters

1 c. sugar
1 c. shortening
1 c. light molasses
1 tblsp. vinegar
6 c. sifted flour
½ tsp. salt

1 tsp. baking soda
½ tsp. baking powder
1 tsp. ground ginger
1 tsp. ground cinnamon
2 eggs, beaten

Combine sugar, shortening, molasses and vinegar in saucepan; bring to boil and cook 2 minutes. Cool.

Sift together flour, salt, soda, baking powder and spices.

Add eggs to cooled molasses mixture. Add dry ingredients and mix well. Chill.

Roll out dough on lightly floured board, about ⅛ to ¼" thick. Cut with cookie cutters of desired shapes; place 1" apart on greased baking sheet.

Bake in moderate oven (375°) 8 to 10 minutes, or until done. Transfer cookies to racks to cool. Makes about 12 dozen.

CRISP MOLASSES COOKIES

Fancy—spread cookies with white frosting, sprinkle with pink sugar

3 c. sifted flour
1 tsp. salt
1 tsp. baking soda
2 tsp. ground cinnamon
2 tsp. ground ginger
⅓ c. sugar

¾ c. shortening
1⅓ c. molasses
Nuts, colored decorating
    sugar or grated orange peel
    (for decorations)

Sift together dry ingredients; cut in shortening.

Heat molasses; add to flour mixture. Chill until stiff enough to roll (3 hours or overnight). Roll very thin, about ⅟₁₆", on lightly floured board. Cut with cookie cutter (leaves, butterflies, gingerbread men or other shapes). Decorate with nuts, colored sugar or orange peel.

Place about 2" apart on lightly greased baking sheets. Bake in hot oven (400°) 7 to 8 minutes, or until lightly browned. Spread on racks to cool. Makes 6 dozen.

NOTE: To make drop cookies, do not chill dough. After mixing, drop from teaspoon about 2" apart onto lightly greased baking sheet. Flatten with bottom of glass; bake as for rolled cookies.

MOLASSES WAGON WHEELS

Children adore these big cookies—with "spokes" of white icing

½ c. shortening	¼ tsp. ground nutmeg
1 c. sugar	¼ tsp. ground allspice
1 c. dark molasses	¼ c. sugar (for tops)
½ c. water	66 raisins (about ⅓ c.)
4 c. sifted flour	1 c. sifted confectioners sugar
1 tsp. baking soda	¼ tsp. salt
1½ tsp. salt	½ tsp. vanilla
1½ tsp. ground ginger	1 tblsp. light cream or dairy
½ tsp. ground cloves	half-and-half

Cream shortening and 1 c. sugar until light and fluffy. Beat in molasses and water to mix thoroughly.

Sift together flour, soda, 1½ tsp. salt and spices; stir into creamed mixture. Chill several hours or overnight.

Roll dough ¼" thick. Press into 3" circles with large glass, or cut with 3" round cutter. Sprinkle tops with sugar. Place ¼ to ½" apart on greased baking sheet. Press 3 large raisins in center of each dough circle.

Bake in moderate oven (350°) about 12 minutes, until almost no imprint remains when touched lightly with finger. Remove from oven, but leave on baking sheet a few minutes before transferring to cooling racks.

Meanwhile, blend confectioners sugar, ¼ tsp. salt, vanilla and cream together until smooth. When cookies are cool, make spokes of wheel with icing put through small plastic bag, with small hole in one corner, and outline raisin center to simulate wheel's hub. Makes about 22.

NEW MOONS

Dainty crisp crescents shine with glaze—
a special-occasion cookie

1 c. butter or regular
  margarine
1¼ c. sugar
2 tsp. grated lemon peel
¼ tsp. salt
1⅓ c. sifted flour

1½ c. grated (not ground)
  blanched almonds
  (½ lb.)
1 tsp. vanilla
2 c. sifted confectioners sugar
2½ tblsp. boiling water
1 tsp. vanilla

Cream butter and sugar until light and fluffy. Add lemon peel, salt, flour, almonds and 1 tsp. vanilla; mix thoroughly. Chill dough.

Roll dough ⅛" thick and cut with crescent cutter. Place about ½" apart on ungreased baking sheet. Bake in moderate oven (375°) 8 to 10 minutes.

Meanwhile, combine confectioners sugar, boiling water and 1 tsp. vanilla. Spread over tops of warm cookies. If glaze gets too thick to spread thinly on cookies, add a few drops of hot water. Place cookies on racks to complete cooling. Makes 10 dozen.

NORWEGIAN HEIRLOOM COOKIES

Cut in squares or diamonds—the granulated sugar
coating sparkles

1 c. butter
½ c. sugar
2 tsp. vanilla

2 c. sifted flour
1 c. finely chopped nuts
¼ c. sugar (for coating)

Cream butter and ½ c. sugar until light and fluffy. Add vanilla and mix well. Stir in flour and nuts. Chill until firm enough to roll.

Roll dough ¼" thick and cut with knife in 2" squares or diamonds. Place ½" apart on ungreased baking sheet.

Bake in moderate oven (375°) 8 to 10 minutes.

While warm roll in sugar. Cool on racks. Makes 5 dozen.

NOTE: Put nuts through nut chopper twice or chop very fine with a knife.

NUT BUTTER COOKIES

Rich cookies—you may want to double recipe for special occasions

1 c. sifted flour
⅓ c. sugar
⅔ c. finely chopped pecans
½ c. butter

¼ c. apricot or red raspberry jam (about)
Viennese Chocolate Frosting (recipe follows)
Pecan halves (about 18)

Sift together flour and sugar; add chopped pecans and mix well. Blend in butter with fork or pastry blender until dough holds together. (Dough will be crumbly.) Chill until easy to handle.

Roll dough on lightly floured surface to ⅛" thickness. Cut in 2" circles and place ½" apart on ungreased baking sheet. Bake in moderate oven (375°) 7 to 10 minutes. Remove from oven and let stand 1 to 2 minutes before removing from baking sheet. Cool completely on racks.

Make sandwich cookies by spreading half the cookies with a thin layer of jam and topping with other half of cookies. Spread Viennese Chocolate Frosting on top of sandwiches and place a pecan half on top of each frosted sandwich. Makes about 1½ dozen.

Viennese Chocolate Frosting: Cream together 2 tblsp. butter and ⅓ c. confectioners sugar until light and creamy. Blend in 1 square unsweetened chocolate, melted and cooled.

Call Them Dishpan or Oatmeal/Molasses Cookies

Big, chewy Oatmeal/Molasses Cookies, made from a recipe that appeared in Farm Journal, are enjoying great popularity in country kitchens. A farm woman in New York State likes to bake the 6 dozen cookies from our recipe in installments because it's easier to find time to get one baking sheet in the oven than several. (Also, her family thinks no cookie can surpass one just out of the oven.) She calls them Dishpan Cookies because the Illinois woman who contributed the recipe to Farm Journal said her grandmother mixed the dough in a dishpan.

Here's the way she makes the cookies in installments: "I shape the dough in rolls 3″ in diameter, wrap them tightly in foil or plastic wrap and store them in the refrigerator or freezer—the freezer if I'm not going to bake them for a week or longer. When I want to bake cookies, I slice the dough ¼″ thick and bake it as the recipe directs."

OATMEAL/MOLASSES COOKIES

A big recipe for big cookies—put some in freezer to have handy

8½ c. sifted flour	2 c. light molasses
1 tblsp. salt	4 eggs, beaten
2 tblsp. baking soda	¼ c. hot water
8 c. quick-cooking rolled oats	3 c. seedless raisins
2½ c. sugar	2 c. ground black walnuts or
1 tblsp. ground ginger	English walnuts
2 c. melted shortening	Sugar (for tops)

Reserve ½ c. flour. Sift together 8 c. flour, salt and baking soda.

In a very large bowl or dishpan, mix rolled oats, sugar and ginger. Stir in shortening, molasses, eggs, hot water, sifted dry ingredients, raisins and nuts. Work dough with hands until well mixed. Add the reserved ½ c. flour if needed to make dough workable.

Roll dough to ¼″ thickness; cut with 3½″ round cutter. Place 2 to 3″ apart on lightly greased baking sheet. Brush with water and sprinkle with sugar.

Bake in moderate oven (375°) 8 to 10 minutes. Remove cookies to racks to cool. Makes 6 dozen.

Open-House Cookies

When it's Christmas time in the Bethlehem, Pennsylvania, area, families visit from one neighbor's home to another to view one another's putz, or Nativity Scene. It's an old Pennsylvania Dutch custom, on these occasions, for the hostess to pass traditional cookies. Many of them are in camel, donkey, star and other fascinating shapes. From women in this community come recipes for three of the favorites, Spiced Christmas Cookies (often called Brown Christmas Cookies), White Christmas Cookies and Pepper Nuts (Pfeffernuesse).

All three recipes make dozens of cookies. And all keep well so you can bake them ahead. Store them in airtight containers or package and freeze. The secret to success in making these treats is to chill the dough overnight before working with it. And do roll Spiced and White Christmas cookies very thin.

SPICED CHRISTMAS COOKIES

Crisp, brown and molasses-flavored cookies to decorate if you wish

1 c. butter	5 c. sifted flour
1½ c. brown sugar, firmly packed	1 tblsp. ground cinnamon
2 c. molasses	1½ tsp. ground ginger
2 tblsp. light cream or dairy half-and-half	½ tsp. ground cloves

Cream butter; gradually add sugar, beating until light and fluffy. Beat in molasses; blend in cream.

Sift together dry ingredients; stir into creamed mixture. Store in covered bowl in refrigerator overnight.

Roll dough thin, using floured pastry cloth on board and rolling pin. Cut in animal shapes.

Place 1 to 1½" apart on greased baking sheet. Bake in moderate oven (350°) 10 to 12 minutes. Remove cookies and cool on racks. Makes 19 dozen.

WHITE CHRISTMAS COOKIES

Sugar, spice and everything nice—cookies are crisp and straw-colored

1 c. butter	4 c. sifted flour
2 c. sugar	⅛ tsp. ground nutmeg
4 eggs, beaten	⅛ tsp. ground cinnamon

Cream butter; gradually add sugar and beat until light and fluffy. Beat in eggs.

Sift together dry ingredients; stir into creamed mixture (dough should be stiff). Store in covered bowl in refrigerator overnight.

Roll dough very thin, using floured pastry cloth on board and rolling pin. Cut in star shapes. Place 1 to 1½" apart on greased baking sheet.

Bake in moderate oven (350°) 10 to 12 minutes, or until crisp and straw-colored. Remove cookies and cool on racks. Makes 16 dozen.

PEPPER NUTS

Store these spicy, hard cookies in airtight containers. You can add a slice of apple to mellow them

3 eggs, beaten	2 tblsp. ground cinnamon
3½ c. brown sugar, firmly packed	1 tblsp. ground cloves
4 c. sifted flour	Ornamental Icing (see Index)
1 tsp. baking powder	Red cinnamon candy (optional)

Combine eggs and sugar; beat well.

Sift together dry ingredients; add gradually to egg-sugar mixture (dough will be very stiff).

Divide dough. Roll with hands on lightly floured board into rolls the thickness of your middle finger. Cut in ½" slices. Place 1 to 1½" apart on greased baking sheet.

Bake in slow oven (300°) 30 minutes. Remove cookies and cool on racks.

Shortly before serving you can top each pepper nut with a dab of Ornamental Icing and a red cinnamon candy (red hots), if you like. Makes 27 dozen.

ORANGE WREATHS

Recipe is from Mexico where cookies accompany hot chocolate

½ c. butter or regular
   margarine
¼ c. sugar
2 tsp. grated orange peel
3 egg yolks, well beaten

2 c. sifted flour
2 tsp. baking powder
1 egg white, beaten until
   foamy

Cream butter, sugar and orange peel together until light and fluffy. Beat in egg yolks and mix well.

Mix and sift together flour and baking powder; add a little at a time to the creamed mixture. Beat after each addition until dough is moderately stiff.

Roll dough on lightly floured surface to ½" thickness. Cut with 2½" doughnut cutter. Place about 2" apart on lightly greased baking sheet. Brush tops of cookies with egg white.

Bake in moderate oven (375°) about 20 minutes, or until golden brown. Remove from baking sheet and cool on racks. Makes about 1 dozen.

NOTE: Gather scraps of dough and centers of rings together in a ball; roll, cut and bake.

PARTY WHIRLS

Pretty pink, brown and cream-colored cookie pinwheels—delicious

1 c. butter
1 c. sugar
2 eggs
½ tsp. vanilla
3 c. sifted flour

½ tsp. salt
½ tsp. ground cinnamon
3 drops red food color
½ square semisweet
   chocolate, melted

Beat together butter and sugar until light and fluffy. Beat in eggs and vanilla to blend well.

Sift together flour, salt and cinnamon; add to creamed mixture. Divide dough in thirds. Tint one-third pink with red food color (stir in food color with a spoon); color the second part brown with melted chocolate, and leave the last third untinted.

Roll each third of dough separately on lightly floured waxed paper into a 13 × 10″ rectangle. Cover baking sheet with waxed paper; hold over untinted dough, invert and remove waxed paper from top of dough on baking sheet. Flip pink rectangle of dough over onto untinted dough and remove waxed paper from it. If edges are not quite even, straighten them by gently rolling with a rolling pin. Then turn chocolate dough onto pink dough and remove waxed paper from it. Straighten edges if necessary. Chill until firm.

Remove dough from refrigerator and roll up tightly as for jelly roll, using waxed paper under dough to help shape the log. Wrap tightly in waxed paper and chill. If you do not want to bake the cookies within three days, cut the long log in half, wrap each log in aluminum foil and store in freezer until ready to bake.

To bake, cut dough in ⅛ to ¼″ slices with sharp knife. Place ½″ apart on ungreased baking sheet and bake in hot oven (400°) about 8 minutes. Remove cookies to cooling racks. Makes about 7 dozen.

AMERICAN SAND TARTS

Crisp cookies, thin as paper, have true buttery flavor, nut trim

1 c. butter	1 egg white, slightly beaten
2¼ s. sugar	Almonds or peanuts
2 eggs	Ground cinnamon
4 c. sifted flour	

Cream butter and sugar until light and fluffy. Beat in eggs, mixing well. Stir in flour. Chill dough thoroughly.

Roll dough very thin and cut with 2½″ round cutter. Brush centers of rounds with egg white and put ½ almond or peanut in center of each cookie. Brush again with egg white and sprinkle nuts with a trace of cinnamon.

Place cookies about ½″ apart on ungreased baking sheet. Bake in hot oven (400°) about 5 minutes. Remove cookies to cooling racks. Makes about 12 dozen.

SCOTCH SHORTBREAD COOKIES

Buttery-rich, extra-good cookies—tint the dough if you like

1 c. butter	2 c. sifted flour
¾ c. confectioners sugar	

Cream butter until light. Add sugar (sift if not smooth) and beat until light and fluffy. Add flour and mix to make a soft dough.

Pat or roll on floured surface to ⅓ to ½″ thickness. Cut with 2½″ cookie cutter or knife. (You can gently flute edges with fingers as for pie crust. Or decorate by pricking cookies with fork.)

Bake on ungreased baking sheet in slow oven (325°) about 20 minutes, until cookies are very delicately browned. Remove cookies and cool on racks. Makes 28 to 30.

STAR COOKIES

Sugar cookies cut in yuletide star shape. Icing will glamorize them

3 c. sifted flour	1¼ c. sugar
2 tsp. baking powder	1 tsp. vanilla
½ tsp. salt	1 egg
½ c. shortening	1 tblsp. milk
½ c. butter or regular margarine	

Sift together flour, baking powder and salt.

Cream shortening and butter with sugar until light and fluffy. Add vanilla, egg and milk; beat thoroughly. Add dry ingredients and mix well. Chill dough 1 hour for easy handling.

Divide dough in fourths; roll out each portion ⅛″ thick. Cut with 2½″ star-shaped cookie cutter. Place 1½ to 2″ apart on greased baking sheet.

Bake in moderate oven (375°) 8 to 10 minutes. Remove cookies and cool on racks. Makes 7 dozen.

Springerle—the Picture Cookie

Springerle is a time-tested, German Christmas cookie with many fans on this side of the Atlantic Ocean. It's one of the first cookies to bake for the yuletide since it needs to mellow from 5 to 8 weeks. Often it's baked and waiting for Christmas even before Thanksgiving.

Traditionally, you sprinkle anise seeds over the surface on which you let the cookie dough stand overnight. You can use oil of anise instead of the seeds if you prefer. Our recipe gives directions for both flavorings.

These are picture cookies. You stamp the designs on the rolled cookie dough either with a board or rolling pin in which designs of birds and flowers are carved. You will find both the boards and rolling pins in housewares departments, especially in late autumn; occasionally you can find interesting old ones in antique shops.

In our tests we discovered it is somewhat easier to use the design board instead of a roller. Certainly this is true for inexperienced springerle bakers. It is important to press the board down firmly on the rolled dough so it leaves a clear print of the design. Lift the board off the dough with steady hands to avoid blurred pictures. If you use the rolling pin, roll it with a little pressure across the sheet of dough *only once*.

Adding too much flour produces a hard cookie. If the dough sticks to board or pin, use care in flouring it. We found chilling the dough 1 hour before rolling helps. Be sure not to roll the dough too thin, for if you do, it's almost impossible to get good imprints.

Making these cookies is a two-day operation because after rolling the dough you let it stand overnight (at least 10 hours) at room temperature before baking. Store the baked cookies in a container with a tight lid and set them in a cool place.

One more pointer: The cookies should not be brown —just a hint of yellow around the edges.

SPRINGERLE

Give these cookies time to mellow—they're well worth waiting for

4 eggs	¼ tsp. salt
2 c. sugar	2 tblsp. melted butter
4 c. sifted cake flour	1 tblsp. anise seeds
1 tsp. baking powder	

Using electric mixer at low speed, beat eggs in large bowl. Gradually add sugar, then beat at medium speed about 10 minutes. (You can use a hand rotary beater, but if you do, increase beating time to 30 minutes.)

Sift together flour, baking powder and salt; blend into egg mixture alternately with butter, mixing well. Cover dough with waxed paper or foil and chill 1 hour.

Dust surface lightly with flour and pat out or roll half of the dough at a time to almost, but not quite, ½" thickness.

Lightly flour springerle board and press it firmly down on dough. Lift board up carefully so as not to mar lines of the design. If board sticks to dough, lightly flour it and the top of the dough. Then brush off flour after removing board. (If you use springerle rolling pin, roll the dough to a flat sheet ½" thick. Then roll over it with springerle rolling pin just once to press in designs.)

Lightly grease baking sheet and sprinkle evenly with anise seeds.

Lift dough carefully to baking sheet, cover loosely with waxed paper and let stand overnight.

When ready to bake, cut dough to cookie size along lines made by springerle board (or rolling pin). Separate on baking sheet by ½" space.

Bake in moderate oven (350°) 5 minutes, then reduce heat to slow (300°) and continue baking about 10 minutes longer. Remove cookies and cool on racks. Makes about 3½ dozen.

NOTE: You can use 6 drops anise oil instead of the anise seeds. Add it to the beaten eggs. Superfine granulated sugar gives the best results in this recipe, but you can use regular granulated sugar.

RAISIN-FILLED COOKIES

Dark fruit filling shows through window in tender, light brown cookies

½ c. shortening	2½ c. sifted flour
1 c. sugar	¼ tsp. baking soda
2 eggs	½ tsp. salt
1 tsp. vanilla	Raisin Filling (recipe follows)

Mix together shortening, sugar and eggs. Stir in vanilla and mix thoroughly.

Sift together flour, soda and salt. Blend into sugar/egg mixture. Chill thoroughly.

Roll dough thin, about ⅟₁₆″, and cut with 2½″ round cutter. (Or use any desired shape cutter.) Place half of cookies 1″ apart on lightly greased baking sheet. Spread a generous teaspoonful of cooled Raisin Filling on each. Cut centers out of other half of cookies, using a small heart, star or other shaped cutter. Place over cookies on baking sheet. Press edges together with floured fork tines or fingers.

Bake in hot oven (400°) 8 to 10 minutes, or until cookies are lightly browned. Spread on racks to cool. Makes about 3½″ dozen.

Raisin Filling: In a small saucepan, combine 2 c. ground or finely cut raisins, ¾ c. sugar and ¾ c. water; cook slowly, stirring constantly, until mixture thickens. Remove from heat; stir in ½ c. chopped walnuts (optional) and 1 tsp. finely grated lemon or orange peel. Cool before using.

VARIATIONS

Prune-Filled Cookies: Cook 2½ c. prunes; drain and mash (you should have 2 c.). Substitute for raisins in Raisin Filling.

Date-Filled Cookies: Substitute 2 c. finely cut-up or ground dates for raisins in Raisin Filling.

Raisin Turnovers: Cut cookie dough in 3″ instead of 2½″ rounds. Place 1 tsp. Raisin Filling on each cookie. Fold over and press edges to seal. Bake like Raisin-Filled Cookies. Makes about 6 dozen.

NOTE: You can use prune or date filling instead of Raisin Filling to make turnovers.

Griddle Cookies—Back in Style

Grandmother used to bake cookies on the griddle to avoid heating the oven in midsummer. Children stopping in her kitchen, hopeful of a handout, remembered how good the warm cookies were with glasses of cold lemonade or bowls of ice cream. No childhood eating experience could be more memorable. So it's good news that the cookies again are coming off griddles to please people of all ages.

Give freezers the thanks. Today's cooks roll and cut the dough and stack the circles with foil between like hamburger patties. As they are wrapped in packages and frozen, it's easy to bring the desired number out. Bake them in your electric skillet—at the table, if that's convenient.

RAISIN GRIDDLE COOKIES

Keep packages of dough in your freezer to bake on short notice

3½ c. sifted flour	1 tsp. ground nutmeg
1 c. sugar	1 c. shortening
1½ tsp. baking powder	1 egg
1 tsp. salt	½ c. milk
½ tsp. baking soda	1¼ c. raisins

Sift dry ingredients together into bowl. Cut in shortening until mixture is mealy.

Beat egg, add milk and blend. Add egg mixture and raisins to flour mixture. Stir until all the ingredients are moistened and dough holds together.

Roll on lightly floured board to ¼″ thickness. Cut with 2″ round cookie cutter.

Heat griddle until a few drops of water dance on it. (Do not overheat griddle.) Oil griddle lightly and place cookies on it. As the bottoms brown, the tops become puffy. Then turn and brown on other side. Serve warm. Makes about 4 dozen.

VARIATION

Lemon Griddle Cookies: Make dough for Raisin Griddle

Cookies, but omit raisins and add 1 tsp. grated lemon peel. Bake as directed.

LEMON SUGAR COOKIES

A time-tested recipe that makes bar, rolled and drop cookies

½ c. butter or regular margarine	1½ tsp. baking powder
1 c. sugar	2 c. sifted flour
1 egg	¼ c. milk
½ tsp. vanilla	1 egg white, slightly beaten (optional)
2 tsp. grated lemon peel	Sugar (optional)
¼ tsp. salt	

Cream butter and sugar thoroughly. Add egg, vanilla and lemon peel. Beat until mixture is light and fluffy.

Sift dry ingredients. Stir into creamed mixture together with milk.

Divide dough in half. Chill 1 hour.

Roll out half of dough on floured board, keeping the other half chilled until ready to use. Roll ¼" thick.

Cut into bars and place about 2" apart on greased baking sheet.

If desired, brush with slightly beaten egg white and sprinkle with sugar. Repeat with remaining dough.

Bake in moderate oven (350°) 12 to 15 minutes. Remove cookies and cool on racks. Makes 2 dozen.

VARIATIONS

Chocolate Chip Cookies: Add ½ c. semisweet chocolate pieces to dough.

Grease and flour two 9" square baking pans. Spread half the dough in each. Bake in moderate oven (350°) 25 minutes, or until light brown.

While still warm cut into 3" squares. Cool in pan on racks. Makes 1½ dozen.

Nut/Sugar Cookies: Mix ½ c. finely chopped nuts into dough. Roll dough and bake as directed.

Coconut Cookies: Add ½ c. shredded coconut. Make drop cookies and place 2" apart on greased baking sheet.

Raisin Cookies: Add ½ c. seedless raisins. Make drop cookies and place 2" apart on greased baking sheet.

Spiced Sugar Cookies: Add ¼ tsp. ground nutmeg and ½ tsp. ground cinnamon to dough, omitting lemon peel. Roll dough. Bake as directed.

SUGAR COOKIES

Sugar-topped, old-fashioned cookies—men say: "Make them bigger"

1 c. shortening	3 c. sifted flour
1 c. sugar	1 tsp. salt
1 c. dairy sour cream	1 tsp. baking powder
3 egg yolks, beaten	½ tsp. baking soda
1 tsp. vanilla	Sugar (for tops)

Cream shortening and sugar thoroughly; add sour cream, egg yolks and vanilla.

Sift together dry ingredients; add to creamed mixture, blending well; chill.

Shape into balls, working with small portions at a time, keeping remaining dough chilled.

Roll out ⅛″ thick on lightly floured surface. Cut with floured 2½″ cutter (sprinkle cutouts with sugar).

Place about 2″ apart on greased baking sheet. Bake in moderate oven (375°) about 15 minutes. Transfer cookies to racks to cool. Makes 6 dozen.

THUMBPRINT COOKIES

Rich and tender rather than sweet—beautiful on tray or plate

¾ c. butter or regular margarine	2 tblsp. sugar
	½ tsp. salt
1 (3 oz.) pkg. cream cheese	¼ tsp. baking powder
2 c. sifted flour	⅓ c. jam or jelly

Cream together butter and cream cheese until light and fluffy.

Sift together flour, sugar, salt and baking powder. Stir into creamed mixture, blending thoroughly.

Roll out on lightly floured surface into a square about ½″ thick. Cut into 1½″ squares.

Place about 1″ apart on ungreased baking sheet. With your thumb make an indentation in center of each cookie. Fill with ½ tsp. jam or jelly.

Bake in a moderate oven (350°) 20 to 25 minutes. Remove cookies and cool on racks. Makes 2½ dozen.

NOTE: For fancy cookies, use jellies or jams of different kinds and colors.

WEDDING RING COOKIES

Gold and silver cookies—ideal for bridal showers, anniversaries

1 c. butter	1 tblsp. water
1¾ c. sifted flour	1 egg white, lightly beaten
1½ tsp. grated lemon peel (optional)	½ c. coarsely chopped blanched almonds
1 tblsp. light cream or dairy half-and-half	½ c. yellow sugar
	Silver dragées

Blend butter and flour with pastry blender until mixture is crumbly. Add lemon peel, cream and water; mix with hands to form a stiff dough. Shape in ball and refrigerate to chill thoroughly.

Divide dough in half; keep one half in refrigerator while working with other half. Roll dough on lightly floured surface to ¼″ thickness. Cut out rings with doughnut cutter. Brush one side of rings with egg white; dip this side of cookies in almonds. Press almonds lightly so they will adhere. Sprinkle with yellow sugar. Repeat with remaining half of dough.

To make double rings, cut one ring and link it through another ring on lightly greased baking sheet. Decorate one of the rings with silver dragées.

Bake 6 double rings at a time in hot oven (425°) about 8 minutes, or until cookies brown around edges. Remove from oven and let cookies cool on baking sheet a few minutes. Transfer with metal spatula to cooling racks. Makes 18 to 19 double rings.

NOTE: You can bake some of the decorated rings singly for guests who like smaller servings than the double rings.

WILD ROSE COOKIES

These cookies are buttery rich, like shortbread, and party pretty

1 c. butter or regular
   margarine
½ c. very fine granulated
   sugar (super fine)
¼ tsp. vanilla

2¼ c. sifted flour
Pink decorating sugar
Yellow decorating sugar, or
   tiny yellow candies

Cream butter with sugar until light and fluffy; beat in vanilla.

Divide flour in thirds. Stir first third into creamed mixture and blend well. Repeat with second third and then with last third. Knead gently until smooth, about 5 minutes. Shape in ball, wrap in clear plastic wrap or waxed paper and chill several hours, or overnight.

Divide dough in fourths. Pat one portion at a time ¼" thick on lightly floured surface. Cut with 2½" round scalloped cutter. Place dough cutouts ½ to 1" apart on ungreased baking sheet. Sprinkle liberally with pink sugar, leaving ¾" circle in center uncovered.

Cut a circle of stiff paper about the same size of cookies and cut out a ¾" circle in center. Lay on cookie and carefully spoon yellow sugar into hole in paper; lift off paper. Or, if you can find small yellow candies, use them for cookie centers.

Bake in slow oven (325°) 12 to 15 minutes, until firm, but do not brown. Transfer cookies to racks and cool. Makes 5 dozen.

NOTE: You can bake the cookies after adding pink sugar, cool them and add dots of frosting, tinted yellow, to make the centers. Use ½ recipe for Ornamental Icing. For dainty teatime cookies, use a 1" round, scalloped cookie cutter.

ORNAMENTAL ICING

Write and draw on cookies with this icing to give them a festive look

1½ to 2 c. confectioners
   sugar

1 to 2 tblsp. slightly beaten
   egg white (about)

Combine confectioners sugar with enough egg white to make an icing you can put through decorating tube or small plastic bag with small hole cut in one corner, but which will have enough consistency to hold its shape on cookies. A second batch of icing can easily be made if needed.

Christmas Cookie Centerpieces

You can bake rolled cookies and put them together to make charming yuletide centerpieces. It takes time to bake the cookies, to build with them and to add decorations, but when you see the way the children and guests of all ages admire your creation, you'll know the minutes were well spent.

The trick is to divide the work. Bake the cookies ahead and freeze them or store them in a cold place. It helps to have them on hand when you are ready to start assembling the scenes.

We give you recipes, patterns and directions for two cookie centerpieces. Take your pick of a country barnyard scene, made with chocolate-flavored cookies, or a Christmas church built with sugar cookies. Snow (frosting) trims both of them.

SUGAR-SYRUP CEMENT

This sweet syrup holds cookies in place when building with them

For Barn: Melt ½ c. sugar in a heavy shallow skillet (at least 12″ across); use lowest heat to melt sugar. For silo, melt another ½ c. sugar.

For Church: Melt 2 c. sugar.

Stir constantly while sugar melts, so that it won't burn. Keep syrup on medium heat while you use it. Be sure to use a wide skillet, so you can dip edges of long cookies into the syrup easily, as you put pieces together.

Work slowly when putting barn or church together. Make sure pieces are "glued" firmly before adding another.

General Directions: Enlarge patterns as indicated (each square equals 1 square inch) and cut from cardboard. Use them to cut cookie pieces.

Dust cardboard patterns with flour and cut around them with a sharp knife.

Bake cookie pieces one day; assemble and decorate cookie scene the next (or store baked cookies in freezer).

Check baked cookies against patterns; trim edges with a sharp knife while cookies are still warm.

GINGER COOKIE CHURCH

Put cookie pieces together with "cement"; arrange trees and fence, build gumdrop bushes and blanket with icing—use diagram as guide

1 c. shortening	1 c. dark corn syrup
1 c. brown sugar, firmly packed	2 eggs, beaten
1 tblsp. grated lemon peel	5½ to 6 c. sifted flour
1 tblsp. ground cinnamon	1 tsp. salt
1 tblsp. ground ginger	1¼ tsp. baking soda

Cream shortening; add brown sugar, lemon peel and spices; blend.

Bring syrup to a boil; pour into creamed mixture; stir until well blended.

Add eggs and blend.

Sift 3 c. flour with salt and baking soda; add to mixture. Stir in 2½ c. flour, a little at a time.

Turn out on lightly floured surface and knead about 10 minutes, using remaining ½ c. flour if necessary.

Chill 1 hour.

Separate dough into several sections. (It is slightly stiffer than ordinary dough. This prevents crumbling.) Roll out each section to ¼" thickness. Transfer to greased baking sheet; smooth out dough with rolling pin. Dust patterns for church pieces with flour; place over dough and cut out with sharp knife. Mark "logs" on doors and sides of church with a two-tined fork or a knife.

Bake in moderate oven (375°) 12 to 15 minutes for large pieces, 5 to 7 for smaller pieces. Remove cookies and cool on racks.

Snow Icing: Place 1 lb. confectioners sugar in mixing bowl. Beat 3 egg whites slightly with a fork; add to confectioners sugar and beat with electric mixer on low

Cut fence pieces and weave together

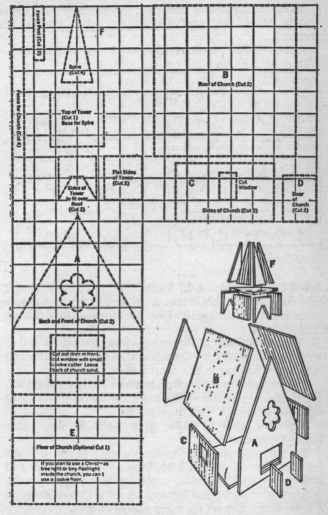

Fence Post (Cut 0)

Fence for Church (Cut 4)

F
Spire
(Cut 4)

Top of Tower
(Cut 1)
Base for Spire

Flat Sides
of Tower
(Cut 2)

Sides of
Tower
to fit over
Roof
(Cut 2)

B
Roof of Church (Cut 2)

C

Cut
Window

Sides of Church (Cut 2)

D
Door
of
Church
(Cut 2)

A

Back and Front of Church (Cut 2)

Cut out door in front,
cut window with small
cookie cutter. Leave
back of church solid.

E
Floor of Church (Optional Cut 1)

If you plan to use a Christmas
tree light or tiny flashlight
inside the church, you can't
use a cookie floor.

Each square = 1 square inch

Each square = 1 square inch

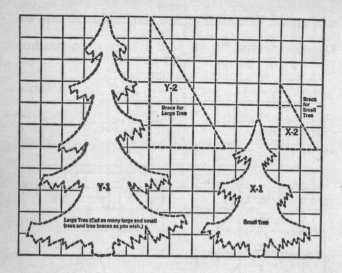

speed for 1 minute. Add 1 tblsp. white vinegar; beat 2 minutes more at high speed, or until stiff and glossy —as for stiff meringue. Use as directed to decorate cookie church.

To Assemble Church: Cover heavy cardboard 20 × 18″ with cotton. Wet your thumb and push a path through the cotton, leading to the church door.

Diagrams show how church and steeple go together. First, fasten colored cellophane or tissue paper over windows of church with flour paste.

Assemble church walls; glue walls to floor with Sugar-Syrup Cement.

To put roof on church, dip slanting edges of walls on one side of church into Sugar-Syrup Cement and quickly set roof in place, carefully lining up top edge with peak of walls and leaving about a 1″ overhang on 3 other sides. Repeat on other side of church.

Add doors, open wide.

Assemble steeple, spire first, then tower; center on top of church roof.

Cookie Trees: To make trees stand up straight, dip the

long, right-angle edge of tree brace (X-2 or Y-2) into Sugar-Syrup Cement and press it at right angle against tree cookie, so bottom of tree and bottom of base are flush.

Gumdrop Bushes: You'll need 1 large green gumdrop and 3 dozen (or more) small green gumdrops for each bush. Break toothpicks into different lengths; use them to attach small gumdrops to large gumdrop base, hiding it completely. Sprinkle with confectioners sugar.

To Decorate Church: Spread Snow Icing liberally on church, trees and fence after they've been put together. Icicles will form naturally if you apply icing from the top.

Sprinkle with confectioners sugar while icing is still moist, for a look of new-fallen snow. Shake sugar through a fine sieve.

COCOA COOKIE BARN

A good "building dough" especially flavored for chocolate lovers

1⅓ c. shortening	1 tsp. baking soda
2 c. sugar	1 tsp. salt
2 eggs	½ c. cocoa
4⅔ c. flour	½ c. milk
2 tsp. baking powder	

Cream shortening and sugar until light and fluffy; add eggs and beat well.

Sift together dry ingredients; add alternately with milk to creamed mixture, mixing well. Chill dough.

Roll out small amount of dough at a time ⅛" thick on lightly floured pastry cloth. Cut desired shapes (see patterns).

Bake on greased baking sheets in slow oven (325°) 10 to 15 minutes. Remove cookies and cool on racks.

White Decorating Frosting: Combine 2 egg whites, 1½ c. sugar, ⅓ c. water, 2 tsp. light corn syrup and ⅛ tsp. salt in top of double boiler; beat 1 minute. Cook over boiling water, beating constantly, until mixture stands in stiff peaks. Remove from heat; transfer to mixing bowl; beat until smooth. Use at once.

Red Decorating Frosting: Beat together 4 c. confectioners sugar, ⅛ tsp. salt, 2½ tsp. red food color, 6 drops yellow food color and 4½ to 5 tblsp. milk until of stiff spreading consistency.

To Assemble Barn Scene: Cover heavy cardboard 30 × 20″ with foil. Set decorated barn and silo at one end. Frost board with another batch of White Decorating Frosting, leaving unfrosted area for pond; swirl frosting for drifts. Don't worry if the roof isn't quite straight—just cover the defects with frosting.

Make pretzel fence. Set decorated animals and trees in frosting snow (prop with toothpicks till frosting dries).

Silo: Cut 30 circles from dough with 2″ cookie cutter. Bake, cool and glue in a stack with Sugar-Syrup Cement.

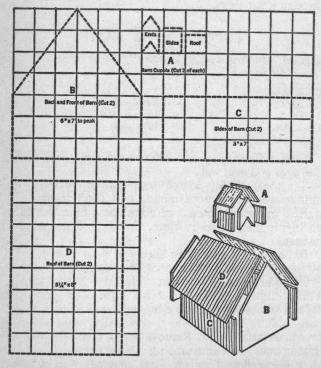

Each square = 1 square inch

170

Animals and Trees: Use any cookie cutters you have, or make your own patterns by tracing from magazines or cards. Give animals character by drawing features (wings, ears, eyes) in dough with toothpick before baking.

To Decorate Barn: Use Red Decorating Frosting for sides of barn and silo. Apply with small-blade spatula to make ridges.

Use 1 batch of White Decorating Frosting for roof of barn, cupola, to make peak of silo and (with decorating tube) for features on animals, trees, barn windows and doors.

Cookie Family in a Christmas House

Cookie dolls all dressed up for the holidays—a whole family of them in a cozy Christmas House—are an ideal gift for children. They will tote this present around until they finally can no longer resist eating them.

Children will sense the love you put into the home-made gift. Most of them will keep the pretty house and store their personal treasures in it.

We give you the recipe and patterns for making the Cookie Family and directions for the Christmas House.

COOKIE FAMILY

It's easiest to bake cookies one day and decorate them the next

⅔ c. shortening	3¼ c. sifted flour
1½ c. sugar	2½ tsp. baking powder
2 eggs	½ tsp. salt
1 tsp. vanilla	**Decorating Frosting**
1 tblsp. milk	

Mix shortening, sugar and eggs. Stir in vanilla and milk.

Sift together flour, baking powder and salt. Blend into creamed mixture. Chill.

Roll out dough ⅛″ thick on floured board or pastry cloth. Dust cardboard patterns with flour. Lay patterns on dough and cut out designs with point of paring knife. Use spatula to move to lightly greased baking sheet. Do not stretch dough.

Before baking Cookie Girl, insert a short piece of paper drinking straw in dough through which to tie hair bow.

Bake in hot oven (400°) 5 to 7 minutes, until lightly browned. Transfer cookies to racks to cool. Cool before frosting. Makes 7 cookie families.

Decorating Frosting:

⅓ c. butter or regular margarine

3 c. sifted confectioners sugar
1½ tblsp. water (about)

PATTERNS FOR THE COOKIE FAMILY
(*Each square = ½ inch*)

Cream butter and sugar thoroughly. Add enough water to make frosting of spreading consistency.

Divide frosting into 7 small dishes and add food color as follows:

White: ⅓ c. for Father's and Boy's shirts, and for dress trimmings.

Brown: Add 2 tsp. cocoa to ¼ c. frosting. For eyes, hair, and for Father's, Mother's and Boy's shoes.

Pink: Add red to ¼ c. frosting. For Mother's dress.

Red: Add red plus small amount of yellow to 2 tblsp. frosting. For Girl's dress, all mouths.

Green: Add green to 2 tblsp. frosting. For Father's and Boy's trousers.

Yellow: Add yellow to 1 tblsp. frosting. For Girl's hair.

Orange: Add yellow plus small amount of red to 2 tblsp. frosting. For Dog.

Let one color frosting dry well before using second on the same cookie.

Spread frosting with narrow spatula. Use paint brush for facial features.

When frosted cookies are completely dry, add white trim on dresses, using decorating tube.

Use narrow red ribbons to tie cookies onto sheet of white cardboard that fits into hosiery-type box.

CHRISTMAS HOUSE

Decorate a hosiery-type box about ¾" to 1" thick to look like a house for the cookie family. Sketch a design to fit box lid (suggestions follow). A red house looks especially festive. To make it, cover lid and bottom of box separately with red wrapping paper. On the lid, paste a roof cut from gray paper; draw shingles on roof. Add a scalloped cornice along roof edge, cut from white paper. Cut a window from yellow paper; cut a Christmas tree from green paper and decorate it with colored signal dots (from stationery store). Paste tree on window and window on house. Add white shutters and white window frame. Cut a white door and paste it in place. Cut dark green bushes and gold lanterns to paste on each side of door. Finally, decorate door with wreath cut from an old Christmas card.

To mount cookies, cut a piece of stiff cardboard to fit inside box. Arrange cookies and mark where holes for ribbon should be made: on both sides of man's neck, both sides of woman's waist, through hair-ribbon hole in girl's head and on opposite side, on both sides of boy's neck and on both sides of dog's neck. Make holes with ice pick or sharp knife. Tie cookies in place with ¼" red ribbon.

Refrigerator Cookies

MAKING REFRIGERATOR cookies is a two-act performance. Act one: mix, shape and freeze or refrigerate the dough; act two: slice and bake. The action may take place days, week or months apart. It's this division of work that elevates refrigerator cookies to first place among summer homemade cookies.

Even if it's hot and humid, you can slice off just enough cookies to meet your immediate needs and bake them quickly without heating the kitchen too much. Country women like to bake the cookies right after breakfast before the sun turns on full heat. Of course the cookies are favorites at all seasons, but summer is their heyday.

You need only a few rules for successful refrigerator cookies. One is to shape the dough in smooth, firm rolls with your hands. Make them the diameter you want your cookies; they spread little in baking. Wrap them tightly in waxed paper, twisting both ends to seal. If you freeze the dough, overwrap with foil. Or wrap them with foil or plastic wrap, taping edges. Most cookie doughs will keep well 3 to 5 days in the refrigerator, 6 months in the freezer.

Use a knife with a long, sharp blade to slice the dough from ⅛ to ¼″ in thickness. The thinner the slices, the crisper the cookies will be. Be sure they are cut to the same thickness so they will bake in the same number of minutes. Bake them until they are lightly browned unless recipe directs otherwise. If you add nuts to the dough, chop them very fine or they will make it difficult to slice cookies neatly.

Refrigerator cookies need no decoration. But for special occasions you can sprinkle waxed paper with decorating sugar or with tiny multicolored candies, finely chopped nuts, chocolate shot (jimmies) or finely crushed stick candy. Turn the roll of cookie dough round and round on the waxed paper to coat it with the decoration. Then wrap and chill or freeze. When baked, the cookies have fancy rims.

You can also tint light-colored dough with food color or press a nut or drop a dab of jelly on cookie slices just before you bake them. Or top ready-to-bake cookies with peaks of meringue, tinted if you like. Our Meringue-Topped Cookies are tasty beauties, especially when you flavor the meringue with peppermint, tint it pink and sprinkle with pink sugar—or coconut or chocolate shot.

Filled refrigerator cookies are so easy to fix. When the slices of dough are on the baking sheet, drop a bit of filling on each one and lay another cookie on top. Try our fruity Mincemeat/Lemon Filling. You can also put *baked* refrigerator cookies together with filling to make sandwiches—to prove that two cookies taste better than one!

For cookies that are on the salty rather than the sweet side, make Old Salts. They're a great snack or appetizer. Our Molasses Almond Cookies are unusual, too—the topping bakes right with the cookies. Our recipe suggests that you shape both the rolls of dough and topping in rolls 1″ in diameter. This produces small cookies which are ideal for tea and other parties. You may prefer to double the recipe and make 2″ rolls.

You'll find recipes for many kinds of refrigerator cookies that are wonderful with ice cream, sherbet, iced or hot tea and coffee, lemonade and other fruit drinks. They also are perfect partners for party punch.

ALMOND REFRIGERATOR COOKIES

A simplified, American version of Chinese cookies—crisp, lacy, rich

1 c. butter or regular
  margarine
2 c. sifted flour
¾ tsp. salt
¾ c. sugar
½ tsp. vanilla

½ tsp. almond extract
1 egg yolk
1 tblsp. water
½ c. blanched almonds, cut
  in halves

176

Cut butter into flour with pastry blender as for pie crust. Work in salt, sugar, vanilla and almond extract with hands. Shape in two long rolls 1 to 1½" in diameter. Wrap tightly in plastic wrap or waxed paper and refrigerate 1 hour, or until firm.

Cut rolls in ¼" slices and place 1" apart on lightly greased baking sheet. Brush top of each cookie sparingly with egg yolk mixed with water. Press an almond half in center of each.

Bake in hot oven (400°) 8 to 10 minutes, or until lightly browned. Cool slightly on baking sheet before removing to cooling rack. (If you do not cool them a little on baking sheet, they will crumble.) Makes about 6½ dozen.

RICH ANISE COOKIES

Keep several rolls in the refrigerator—excellent with ice cream

1 c. butter or regular margarine	½ tsp. vanilla
1 (3 oz.) pkg. cream cheese	2½ c. sifted flour
1 c. sugar	½ tsp. salt
1 egg yolk	2 tsp. anise seeds, crushed

Cream butter, cream cheese and sugar together until light. Add egg yolk and vanilla and beat until light and fluffy.

Combine flour, salt and anise seeds. Blend into creamed mixture until smooth. Shape in two rolls about 2" in diameter on lightly floured waxed paper. Wrap rolls tightly in waxed paper and chill at least 2 hours or overnight.

Cut dough in thin slices, about ⅛" thick; place about 2" apart on ungreased baking sheet. Bake in moderate oven (350°) 10 to 12 minutes, or until cookie edges are browned. Remove cookies and cool on racks. Makes about 6 dozen.

VARIATION

Rich Nutmeg Cookies: Omit anise seeds from Rich Anise Cookies and add 1 tsp. ground nutmeg with the flour.

BUTTERSCOTCH REFRIGERATOR COOKIES

Keep a few cans of dough in freezer to bake on short notice

3½ c. sifted flour
1 tsp. salt
1 tsp. ground cinnamon
1 tsp. baking soda
½ c. shortening
½ c. butter

2 c. brown sugar, firmly packed
2 eggs, well beaten
2 tblsp. warm water
1 tsp. vanilla
1 c. chopped nuts

Sift together flour, salt, cinnamon and soda.

Cream shortening and butter; gradually add sugar; beat until light. Add eggs, water and vanilla; mix well.

Combine dry ingredients and creamed mixture; blend well. Add nuts.

Shape dough into roll 2″ in diameter. Wrap tightly in waxed paper and chill thoroughly—overnight for best results. When ready to bake, cut in ⅛″ slices.

Bake 1½″ apart on ungreased baking sheet in hot oven (400°) 10 to 12 minutes. Spread on racks to cool. Makes 6 dozen.

BLACK WALNUT COOKIES

Descendant of Pennsylvania Dutch slapjacks—cookies taste great

6 c. sifted flour
1 tsp. salt
½ tsp. baking soda
1 tsp. cream of tartar
1¾ c. butter or regular margarine
2¼ c. brown sugar, firmly packed

½ c. sugar
2 eggs, beaten
2 tsp. vanilla
1½ c. black walnuts
1½ c. flaked or shredded coconut

Sift together flour, salt, soda and cream of tartar.

Cream butter; add brown and white sugars gradually and beat until fluffy. Add eggs and vanilla; mix well.

Grind nuts and coconut together in food chopper using medium blade, or use blender. Add to creamed mixture. Add sifted dry ingredients and blend well. Chill.

Shape dough in four rolls about 2" in diameter. Wrap tightly in waxed paper and chill thoroughly.

Cut rolls in ⅛" slices; place about 1" apart on ungreased baking sheet. Bake in moderate oven (350°) 10 to 12 minutes. Remove cookies and cool on racks. Makes 8 to 9 dozen.

BLUSHING REFRIGERATOR COOKIES

The pink glow of cookies contrasts charmingly with their gay red tops

1 c. butter	5 drops red food color
½ c. sugar	2¾ c. sifted flour
½ c. brown sugar, firmly packed	½ tsp. baking soda
	½ tsp. salt
2 eggs	Red decorating sugar
1 tsp. vanilla	(for tops)

Combine butter, sugars, eggs and vanilla; beat until very light. Add food color.

Sift together flour, baking soda and salt. Stir into first mixture. Mix with hands until dough is smooth. Shape in two rolls, each 2" in diameter and about 9½" long. Wrap tightly in waxed paper, twisting ends. Chill in refrigerator overnight or a couple of days, or freeze.

When ready to bake, cut dough in thin slices, about ⅛" thick, with a sharp knife. Arrange ½" apart on ungreased baking sheet. Sprinkle tops with red sugar.

Bake in hot oven (400°) 6 to 8 minutes. Remove from baking sheet and cool on racks. Makes 8 dozen.

VARIATIONS

Chocolate Wafers: Make like Blushing Refrigerator Cookies, only omit food color and red decorating sugar, and add 2 squares unsweetened chocolate, melted and cooled, to butter. Sprinkle tops of wafers before baking with finely chopped nuts or green decorating sugar, or decorate them, when cool, with Ornamental Icing (see Index).

Filled Refrigerator Cookies: Make half of recipe for Blushing Refrigerator Cookies, but omit food color and red decorating sugar. Place half of the cookies on baking sheet; top each with ½ tsp. Mincemeat/Lemon

179

Filling, then top with another cookie and bake as directed. Makes 2 dozen.

Mincemeat/Lemon Filling: Stir together ¼ c. prepared mincemeat, 2 tblsp. chopped walnuts and 2 tsp. grated lemon peel.

CHOCOLATE COOKIE SANDWICHES

Fill with pastel pink and green frosting
for a festive party tray

½ c. shortening	1¾ c. sifted flour
½ c. sugar	1 tsp. salt
1 egg	½ tsp. baking powder
3 tblsp. milk	Peppermint Frosting (recipe
2 squares unsweetened	follows)
chocolate, melted and cooled	

Cream shortening and sugar until fluffy; beat in egg, milk and chocolate.

Sift together flour, salt and baking powder. Stir into creamed mixture. Shape dough in two smooth rolls about 2" in diameter, 6" long. Wrap each in waxed paper and chill several hours until firm, or overnight.

Slice rolls thin, about ⅛", with sharp knife. Place 1½" apart on lightly greased baking sheet. Bake in moderate oven (375°) 7 to 10 minutes (watch carefully). Remove cookies and cool on racks. Spread half the cookies with Peppermint Frosting. Top with remaining cookies. Makes 2½ dozen.

Peppermint Frosting: Combine 2 c. sifted confectioners sugar, 1½ tblsp. butter and 2½ tblsp. dairy half-and-half or light cream. Beat until smooth. Add 3 to 4 drops peppermint extract. Divide in half; to one part add 3 drops red food color, to the other, 2 drops green food color.

CHOCOLATE FILLED COOKIES

Partially melted chocolate candy wafers
form the luscious filling

1 c. butter	2½ c. sifted flour
1 c. sugar	¼ tsp. cream of tartar
1 egg	40 thin round chocolate
1 tsp. vanilla	candy wafers

Cream butter and sugar until light and fluffy. Add egg and vanilla. Beat well.

Sift flour and cream of tartar; add to creamed mixture and beat until blended. Chill until dough is firm enough to handle. Then shape dough in two rolls, each about 10″ long. Wrap tightly in waxed paper or plastic wrap and chill overnight.

Cut one roll of dough in ⅛″ slices. Place 20 rounds 1 to 1½″ apart on ungreased baking sheet. Place a chocolate wafer on each. Top with 20 more rounds of dough. Press dough circles together, completely covering chocolate wafers. Repeat with other roll of dough.

Bake in moderate oven (375°) about 10 minutes, or until cookies are delicately browned. Transfer cookies to racks to cool. Makes 40.

NOTE: Work with half of dough at a time, keeping the remaining dough in refrigerator.

CHOCOLATE MINT WAFERS

Chocolate/mint flavors complement each other in these thin cookies

¼ c. heavy cream	⅛ tsp. peppermint extract
1 tblsp. vinegar	2 c. sifted flour
½ c. shortening	¾ c. cocoa
1 c. sugar	½ tsp. baking soda
1 egg	¼ tsp. salt

Combine heavy cream and vinegar in measuring cup; set aside.

Cream together shortening and sugar; stir in egg and peppermint extract.

Sift together remaining dry ingredients; add alternately with heavy cream to creamed mixture. Mix thoroughly. Divide dough in half and shape into two rolls. Wrap tightly in waxed paper and chill several hours in refrigerator.

Cut dough in ⅛″ slices with sharp knife; place 1½″ apart on ungreased baking sheet. Bake in moderate oven (350°) 15 minutes. Remove cookies and cool on racks. Makes 3 dozen.

EASY DATE FILL-UPS

*For crisper cookies refrigerate filling
and add just before serving*

½ c. butter
½ c. lard
½ c. dairy sour cream
¾ c. brown sugar, firmly
   packed
2 tsp. baking soda
1 tsp. salt

1 tsp. vanilla
2½ c. sifted flour
2 c. quick-cooking rolled oats
1¼ c. halved dates (8 oz.)
½ c. sugar
¼ c. water

Blend together butter, lard, dairy sour cream, brown sugar, baking soda, salt and vanilla. Add flour and oats and mix well.

Divide dough in half. Shape each part in a roll 2″ in diameter. Wrap in foil or waxed paper and refrigerate overnight, or at least 8 hours. (For faster chilling place in freezer.)

To bake, cut dough in ⅛″ slices; place about 1″ apart on ungreased baking sheet. Bake in moderate oven (350°) 8 to 12 minutes, or until light golden brown. Remove cookies and cool on racks.

To make filling, combine dates, white sugar and water in saucepan. Cook over medium heat until thick and smooth, stirring constantly. Cool until lukewarm.

At serving time, spread half of cooled cookies on bottom sides with date filling; top with remaining cookies. Makes about 4 dozen.

VARIATION

Austrian Cookie Rounds: Omit the date filling. Melt together in custard cup, set in hot water, ½ c. semisweet chocolate pieces and 1 tblsp. shortening. Spread on half of cookies while still slightly warm to coat them with a glaze. Let harden. Before serving, spread a thin layer of currant or other red jelly on the unglazed cookies and top with a glazed cookie, glazed side up.

FINNISH SHORTBREAD COOKIES

*Rich cookies, a treat from Finnish kitchens—
we give you variations*

2 c. butter   ⅛ tsp. salt
1 c. sugar   Chopped almonds
4 c. sifted flour   Sugar (for tops)

Cream butter and 1 c. sugar thoroughly. Add flour and salt. Shape in long, slender rolls 1″ in diameter. Wrap rolls tightly in waxed paper and chill thoroughly.

Cut dough in ½″ slices; place ½ to 1″ apart on ungreased baking sheet. Press each circle down with your thumb. Sprinkle with almonds, then with sugar.

Bake in hot oven (400°) 7 to 10 minutes. (Cookies should not brown.) Remove cookies and cool on racks. Makes about 14 dozen.

NOTE: You can take the dough from the refrigerator and bake cookies whenever convenient. It's a good idea to chill the dough at least 24 hours.

VARIATIONS

Easter Shortbreads: Prepare dough for Finnish Shortbread Cookies; chill thoroughly (do not form in rolls). Divide chilled dough in thirds, and work with one part at a time. Roll dough ⅓″ thick on lightly floured surface. Cut first third of dough with Easter bunny cookie cutter; arrange ½″ apart on ungreased baking sheet. Do not sprinkle with almonds. Bake in hot oven (400°) 8 minutes. Remove cookies and cool on racks. Repeat with second third of dough, but cut with chicken cookie cutter. Then roll and cut last portion of dough with an Easter cross cookie cutter. (All cutters are from 2 to 2½″ at longest or widest place.)

When all cookies are cool, frost tops with Tinted Frosting. Use pink dragées to decorate each cross (one dragée centered in each extension of the cross). Spread frosted cookies out in tight container with waxed paper between layers if they are to be held a few hours or a couple of days before serving. Set in a cold place. Cookies are especially handsome served on a purple or black lacquer or a silver tray. Makes 5 dozen.

Tinted Frosting: Beat together until smooth 2 c. sifted confectioners sugar, 1 tsp. vanilla and 3 to 4 tblsp. milk, enough to make a frosting of spreading consistency. Divide in thirds. To one part, add 1 drop of red food color to make a delicate pink frosting for the bunnies; to the second part, add 2 drops yellow food color to make frosting for chickens; and to the last third, add 1 drop green food color to make a pale green frosting for the crosses.

FRESH LEMON COCONUT COOKIES

Lemon peel provides a fresh citrus taste
that's wonderful with coconut

¼ c. butter	¾ c. shredded coconut
¼ c. shortening	1¾ c. sifted flour
1 c. sugar	½ tsp. salt
1 egg	2 tsp. baking powder
2 tsp. grated lemon peel	

Cream together butter, shortening and sugar. Add egg and beat until light and fluffy. Add lemon peel and coconut; stir to blend.

Sift together dry ingredients; stir into creamed mixture. Divide dough in half and shape into rolls. Wrap tightly in waxed paper and store in refrigerator at least several hours.

Cut dough in thin slices with sharp knife; place 1½″ apart on ungreased baking sheet. Bake in hot oven (400°) 10 minutes. Remove cookies and cool on racks. Makes about 4 dozen.

LEMON THINS

Just right to escort ice cream, sherbet,
light puddings and fruits

1 c. butter or regular margarine	½ tsp. baking powder
½ c. sugar	⅛ tsp. salt
1 egg, beaten	1 tblsp. lemon juice
2 c. sifted flour	½ tsp. grated lemon peel

Cream together butter and sugar; add egg; mix well.

Sift together flour, baking powder and salt; combine with sugar mixture. Add lemon juice and peel.

Form into rolls 1½ to 2″ in diameter; wrap tightly in waxed paper and chill.

Slice very thin. Bake 1½″ apart on ungreased baking

sheet in moderate oven (375°) 8 to 10 minutes. Remove cookies and cool on racks. Makes 5 to 6 dozen.

MERINGUE-TOPPED COOKIES

Beauties—pink, peppermint-flavored
meringue with pink sugar trim

1 c. butter or regular margarine	¼ tsp. salt
1½ c. sugar	½ tsp. cream of tartar
3 eggs, separated	¼ tsp. almond extract
2 tsp. grated orange peel	Colored decorating sugar, decorating candies or
3 c. sifted flour	flaked coconut (optional)

Beat butter until light. Add ¾ c. sugar and beat until light and fluffy. Beat in egg yolks and orange peel to blend well.

Stir together flour and salt; add to creamed mixture. Shape in two rolls 1½" in diameter. Wrap tightly in waxed paper, twisting ends, and refrigerate overnight.

Cut dough in ¼" slices. Place about 1" apart on ungreased baking sheet.

Beat egg whites with cream of tartar until foamy. Gradually add remaining ¾ c. sugar and beat until stiff, but not dry. Fold in almond extract. Drop by teaspoonfuls onto cookie slices. Sprinkle top of meringue with colored sugar, decorating candies or flaked coconut.

Bake in moderate oven (350°) 10 to 12 minutes, or just until delicately browned. Remove cookies to cooling rack. Makes about 5 dozen.

NOTE: For fascinating holiday cookies, tint meringue with food color; omit almond extract and flavor with other extracts. Use peppermint extract for pink or green meringues, lemon extract for yellow meringues and orange extract for orange-colored meringues (mixture of red and yellow food color makes orange). Sprinkle tops of meringues with colored sugar to match color of meringue, or with decorating candies, silver or other colored dragées, flaked coconut or chocolate shot (jimmies). A tray of these handsome, buttery rich cookies provides decorative and delicious hospitality for a party or open house.

MINCEMEAT REFRIGERATOR COOKIES

Mincemeat is the seasoning in this big recipe—
makes 9 dozen

¾ c. butter
1 c. sugar
1 egg
½ tsp. vanilla
1 tsp. finely grated lemon peel
¾ c. prepared mincemeat

3 c. sifted flour
½ tsp. baking soda
½ tsp. salt
1 tsp. ground cinnamon
½ c. chopped walnuts

Cream together butter and sugar until light and fluffy.
Beat in egg, vanilla and lemon peel. Stir in mincemeat.

Sift together flour, baking soda, salt and cinnamon;
gradually add to creamed mixture, mixing well. Stir in
nuts.

Divide dough in half. Place each part on a lightly
floured sheet of waxed paper and form in a roll 1½″
in diameter, about 12″ long. (Sprinkling waxed paper
with a little flour helps you to shape smooth rolls.)
Wrap rolls in waxed paper and refrigerate several hours,
overnight or 2 or 3 days.

With sharp knife, cut dough in ⅛″ slices; place 1½″
apart on ungreased baking sheet. Bake in moderate
oven (375°) about 10 minutes. Remove cookies to
cooling racks at once. Makes 9 dozen.

MOCHA NUT COOKIES

Chocolate and coffee combine in these
distinctive cookies

½ c. shortening
1 c. sugar
1 egg
2 squares unsweetened
  chocolate, melted

½ c. chopped walnuts or
  pecans
1 c. sifted flour
¼ tsp. salt
1 tsp. baking powder
2 tsp. instant coffee powder

Cream together shortening and sugar. Add egg and
beat until light and fluffy. Stir in chocolate and nuts.

Sift together dry ingredients and add to creamed
mixture; blend thoroughly. Divide dough in half and
shape into rolls. Wrap tightly in waxed paper; chill
in refrigerator at least several hours.

Cut dough in ⅛″ slices; place 1½″ apart on ungreased baking sheet. Bake in moderate oven (375°) 15 minutes. Remove cookies and cool on racks. Makes about 6 dozen.

MOLASSES/ALMOND COOKIES

Little coffee-flavored molasses cookies
with a baked-on topping

½ c. shortening	¼ tsp. salt
3 tblsp. light molasses	¼ tsp. baking soda
1 tsp. instant coffee powder	½ c. butter
½ tsp. vanilla	½ c. confectioners sugar
1½ c. sifted flour	½ c. chopped almonds

Beat shortening until light. Gradually beat in molasses. Stir in coffee powder and vanilla.

Sift together flour, salt and baking soda. Add to molasses mixture. Form dough into a roll 1″ in diameter, about 13″ long. Wrap tightly in waxed paper, twisting ends, and chill in refrigerator 2 hours or overnight.

Combine butter, confectioners sugar and almonds. Shape in roll 1″ in diameter; wrap tightly in waxed paper, twisting ends. Chill 2 hours or overnight.

To bake, cut each roll in ¼″ slices; place dough slices about 1″ apart on ungreased baking sheet and top with almond slices. Bake in moderate oven (350°) 10 to 12 minutes. Remove cookies and cool on racks. Makes about 4 dozen.

OATMEAL/MAPLE COOKIES

Whole wheat flour and maple flavoring
give the cookies distinction

1 c. soft butter	1½ c. whole wheat flour
1 c. brown sugar, firmly packed	1 c. quick-cooking rolled oats
1 tsp. maple flavoring	¼ c. chocolate shot (jimmies)
	¼ c. finely chopped walnuts

Cream butter, brown sugar and flavoring together until fluffy. Stir in flour and oats; mix until blended.

Divide dough in half. Shape each half into a roll 1½″ in diameter. Roll one roll in chocolate shot and the other in nuts. Wrap tightly in waxed paper; chill several hours or overnight.

Cut ¼″ slices and place 1½″ apart on ungreased

187

baking sheet. Bake in moderate oven (350°) 12 to 15 minutes. Cool on baking sheet until firm before removing to cooling rack. Makes 6 dozen.

OLD SALTS

Perfect snack—hide or they'll disappear.
Salted tops, sweet inside

1 c. shortening	¼ tsp. salt
1 c. sugar	½ tsp. baking powder
1 egg	½ tsp. baking soda
1 tsp. vanilla	3 c. quick-cooking rolled oats
1¼ c. sifted flour	Salt (for tops)

Cream shortening and sugar until light and fluffy. Beat in egg and vanilla to mix thoroughly.

Sift together flour, ¼ tsp. salt, baking powder and soda; add to creamed mixture. Stir in rolled oats.

Divide dough in quarters and place each part on sheet of lightly floured waxed paper. Shape in roll 1" in diameter and about 12" long. Wrap in waxed paper and chill several hours or overnight. (It's easier to shape soft dough on waxed paper lightly floured.)

Cut in ¼" slices (dough will be crumbly and cannot be cut thinner). Sprinkle tops lightly with salt. Place about 1" apart on greased baking sheet.

Bake in moderate oven (375°) 10 to 12 minutes. Let stand a couple of minutes before removing from baking sheet to rack for cooling. Makes about 12 dozen.

SIX-IN-ONE REFRIGERATOR COOKIES

You make 18 dozen cookies of six flavors
from one batch of dough

2 c. butter	½ c. shredded coconut
1 c. sugar	½ c. finely chopped pecans
1 c. light brown sugar, firmly packed	½ tsp. ground nutmeg
2 eggs, beaten	1 tsp. ground cinnamon
1 tsp. vanilla	1 square unsweetened chocolate, melted
4 c. flour	¼ c. finely chopped candied cherries
1 tsp. baking soda	
½ tsp. salt	

Cream butter. Gradually add sugars; cream until light and fluffy.

Add eggs and vanilla; mix well.

Sift together flour, soda and salt; gradually add to creamed mixture, beating well after each addition.

Divide dough in six parts. Add coconut to one part; pecans to second; nutmeg and cinnamon to third; melted chocolate to fourth; and candied cherries to fifth. Leave the last portion plain. Chill 30 minutes, or longer.

Shape dough into six rolls about 1¾" in diameter. Wrap tightly in plastic wrap or waxed paper and refrigerate overnight, or freeze.

When ready to use, slice with sharp knife in ⅛" slices. (If frozen, thaw just enough to slice.) Place on lightly greased baking sheet.

Bake in moderate oven (375°) 10 to 12 minutes, until lightly browned. Remove cookies and cool on racks. Makes 18 dozen.

Molded Cookies

CHRISTMAS CANE Cookies tied with red ribbons . . . two-color cookie snails, or Swirls . . . Chocolate Bonbon Cookies with shiny pink Peppermint Glaze . . . Mexican Fiesta Balls dotted with cherries and fragrant with coffee—these will give you an idea of charming cookies you can make with recipes in this section.

Our molded cookies come in many sizes and shapes. Among the tasty tidbits are Spanish Wedding Cakes made from lemon-flavored cookie dough wrapped around almonds. Frosted Yule Logs resemble short, fat pencils coated with nuts. And Honeyed Yo-Yos are big, plump cookies sweetened and flavored with honey and brown sugar. Put together in pairs with apricot or other jam between, they really look like yo-yos. Men especially think they're right, both in size and taste.

This cookbook contains several superior recipes for sugar cookies. But our Molded Sugar Cookies take second place to none of them. They won several blue ribbons at fairs for the woman who shares the recipe with you. If you like sugar cookies that are golden and crisp on the outside and soft within, this recipe is for you.

Molded cookies especially delight women who like to create beautiful food and who like to shape dough with their hands. The technique can give you the same sort of satisfaction an artist experiences from molding clay.

Though fascinating, these cookies are not difficult to make, nor unduly time consuming. But do plan to spend enough time to achieve artistic results.

Rules are few—it's imaginative work and defies many

cut-and-dried regulations. The dough has to be right. If it's too soft, chill it until you can easily handle it.

Balls of dough are the beginning of many molded cookies. Some of them retain their spherical shape during the baking, while others, such as Snickerdoodles, flatten. Some cookies are flattened before you put them in the oven. Use the bottom of a glass tumbler, greased lightly every time you press it on the dough. Some recipes recommend that you dip the glass lightly in flour or in sugar. And you flatten some cookies with the floured tines of a fork, pressed crosswise and then lengthwise to make a design.

Gather cheer, if you're new at this baking art, by reminding yourself that the more cookies you mold, the faster you'll do it well. Mothers report that some children excel in shaping cookie dough. Give them an opportunity to participate.

ALMOND BUTTERBALLS

Right for teas, parties, receptions—
a hostess favorite

1 c. butter or regular margarine	2 c. sifted flour
¼ c. confectioners sugar	1 c. chopped almonds
1 tsp. vanilla	Confectioners sugar (for coating)
⅛ tsp. almond extract	

Cream butter and ¼ c. confectioners sugar until light and fluffy; add flavorings.

Stir in flour and almonds; blend well.

Form dough into tiny balls; place about 1″ apart on ungreased baking sheet. Bake in moderate oven (350°) about 20 minutes.

Roll cookies in confectioners sugar while warm. Cool on racks. Makes about 6 dozen.

BLACK WALNUT CRESCENTS

Serve these with applesauce
for a great winter supper dessert

½ c. butter
½ c. shortening
⅓ c. sugar
2 tsp. water
2 tsp. vanilla

2 c. sifted flour
½ c. chopped black walnuts
Confectioners sugar (for dipping)

Cream butter and shortening until light; add sugar, cream until light and fluffy. Beat in water, vanilla, flour and nuts. Chill 4 hours, or overnight.

Shape dough in rolls about 15″ long and ½″ in diameter; then cut in 3″ lengths. Shape in crescents.

Place about ½″ apart on ungreased baking sheet, and bake in slow oven (325°) 12 to 15 minutes. Do not let cookies brown. Cool slightly on baking sheet, then remove from baking sheet and dip in confectioners sugar. Place on racks to cool. Makes about 44.

NOTE: Black walnuts have a pronounced flavor. If you wish to decrease it, put 2 tblsp. chopped black walnuts in a ½ c. measure and fill with chopped walnuts, English-type.

CHRISTMAS CANE COOKIES

There's a hint of peppermint in these entwined
red and creamy white butter cookie strips,
shaped like canes for the yuletide

1 c. butter or regular margarine
1 c. sifted confectioners sugar
1 egg
1½ tsp. vanilla
½ tsp. almond extract

2½ c. sifted flour
½ tsp. salt
½ tsp. red food color
¼ c. crushed red and white peppermint candy
¼ c. sugar

Beat butter and confectioners sugar until mixture is light and fluffy. Beat in egg, vanilla and almond extract to blend well.

Mix flour and salt and stir into creamed mixture. Divide in half. Blend food color into one half. Work with ¼ plain dough and ¼ tinted dough. Keep remainder of dough in refrigerator until you are ready to use it.

Take 1 tsp. plain dough and roll with hands into a strip 4″ long. Then roll 1 tsp. tinted dough into a strip the same length. Lay the two strips side by side and twist together, holding both ends of strips, to make a red and white striped rope. Place the rope on ungreased baking sheet and curve one end to make the cane's handle. Repeat, making one cane at a time so the dough will not dry out and be difficult to twist and shape. Place canes about 1" apart on baking sheet (12 will fit on one baking sheet). Then repeat with remaining portions of dough.

Bake in moderate oven (375°) about 10 minutes. Remove from baking sheet at once. Combine candy and white sugar; sprinkle on hot cookies. Cool on racks. Makes about 4 dozen.

EASY CANE COOKIES

Cookies are dappled with red flakes
of peppermint candy—tie the canes with
Christmas ribbons for a festive look

1 c. butter or regular margarine	2½ c. sifted flour
1 c. confectioners sugar	½ tsp. salt
1 egg	½ c. crushed red and white peppermint candy
1 tsp. vanilla	2 tblsp. sugar
¼ tsp. peppermint extract	

Beat together butter and confectioners sugar until light and fluffy. Beat in egg, vanilla and peppermint extract to blend well.

Combine flour and salt and stir into creamed mixture. Wrap dough in waxed paper and chill at least 1 hour.

When ready to shape, mix crushed candy with white sugar. Roll 1 level measuring tablespoonful of dough on surface sprinkled with small amount of crushed candy mixture to make a 6" rope. Place on greased baking sheet. Curve one end down to form handle of cane. Repeat until all the crushed candy mixture and dough have been used.

Bake in moderate oven (375°) about 12 minutes, until lightly browned. Remove at once from baking sheet and cool on racks. Makes about 3½ dozen.

NOTE: You can use stick candy of different colors and different extracts instead of the peppermint candy.

CHOCOLATE BONBON COOKIES

Tiny cookies with a shiny red peppermint glaze—
for holiday parties

2 c. sifted flour
½ tsp. baking powder
½ tsp. salt
½ c. butter or regular margarine
½ c. sugar
1 egg

1 square unsweetened chocolate, melted
1 tsp. vanilla
Peppermint Glaze (recipe follows)
Silver dragées, nuts or canned frostings (for decorations)

Sift together flour, baking powder and salt.

Cream butter and sugar together until light and fluffy. Beat in egg, melted chocolate and vanilla. Stir in flour mixture, a third at a time, blending well. The dough will be stiff.

Roll rounded teaspoonfuls of dough, one at a time, into balls between hands. Place balls about 2″ apart on lightly greased baking sheet.

Bake in moderate oven (350°) about 12 minutes, until firm. Remove from baking sheet to wire racks. Repeat until all dough is baked. Cool thoroughly.

To glaze cookies, arrange at least 1″ apart on racks over waxed paper. Spoon Peppermint Glaze over to cover cookies completely (scrape glaze that drips onto waxed paper back into bowl). Spoon a second coating of glaze over the cookies; let cool. Trim with silver dragées, nuts or frostings from pressurized cans. Makes about 31.

NOTE: For Christmas holidays, use green frosting to make holly leaves, dots of red frosting for holly berries.

PEPPERMINT GLAZE

Perfect for chocolate cookies;
tint glaze pink or green if you wish

3 c. sifted confectioners sugar
2 to 3 tblsp. water

¼ tsp. red food color (optional)
¼ tsp. peppermint extract

Combine all ingredients and beat until smooth. The glaze should be thin enough to pour from a spoon. If it gets too thick while working with it, add a few drops of water and beat until smooth. Makes about 1 cup.

Vanilla Glaze: Omit peppermint extract and red food color; add ½ tsp. vanilla and make glaze as directed.

CAPE COD CHOCOLATE CHIP COOKIES

A great 20th century cookie that rates
among the all-time champions

1 c. butter or regular margarine	2¼ c. sifted flour
¾ c. brown sugar, firmly packed	1 tsp. baking soda
	1 tsp. salt
¾ c. sugar	1 (6 oz.) pkg. semisweet chocolate pieces
2 eggs	
1 tsp. vanilla	½ c. chopped walnuts

Cream butter until fluffy; gradually add sugars and beat until light and fluffy. Beat in eggs and vanilla, mixing well.

Sift together flour, baking powder and salt; add to creamed mixture and blend. Stir in chocolate pieces and nuts. Chill dough several hours or overnight.

Roll dough by teaspoonfuls between palms of hands and place 2″ apart on greased baking sheet. Flatten balls with fingertips to make flat rounds. Bake in moderate oven (350°) 10 to 12 minutes, or until light golden brown. Cool a few minutes on baking sheets before removing to racks to cool. Makes about 6½ dozen.

HOSTESS CINNAMON BALLS

Cookie balls wear cinnamon-walnut-sugar
coating—they're special

½ c. butter or regular margarine	1 tsp. baking powder
	¼ tsp. salt
1 c. sugar	½ c. finely chopped nuts
1 egg, unbeaten	1 tblsp. ground cinnamon
1 tsp. vanilla	1 tblsp. sugar
1¼ c. sifted flour	

Cream butter and 1 c. sugar. Add egg and vanilla; beat well for 2 minutes with electric mixer at medium speed.

Sift together flour, baking powder and salt; add to creamed mixture; chill.

Mix nuts, cinnamon and 1 tblsp. sugar.

Mold dough into walnut-size balls; roll each in nut mixture.

Place balls 2½" apart on greased baking sheet. Bake in moderate oven (350°) 12 to 15 minutes. Remove cookies and cool on racks. Makes about 20.

CHOCOLATE CRACKLES

Use confectioners sugar to put designs on these
soft chocolate party cookie balls. The tops crackle
in baking—a hostess favorite

2 eggs
1 c. sugar
1 tsp. vanilla
3 squares unsweetened chocolate, grated
2 c. finely grated (chopped very fine) pecans (7½ oz.)

¼ c. finely ground dry bread crumbs
2 tblsp. flour
¾ tsp. ground cinnamon
⅛ tsp. salt
¼ c. confectioners sugar (for coating)

Beat eggs with sugar and vanilla to blend well. With spoon, mix in chocolate, pecans, bread crumbs, flour, cinnamon and salt. Chill dough until easy to handle.

Shape part of dough at a time in 1" balls, leaving remaining dough in refrigerator until ready to work with it. Roll balls in confectioners sugar and arrange 1" apart on greased baking sheet.

Bake in slow oven (325°) 12 to 15 minutes (they will be soft and crackled on top). Remove cookies and cool on racks. Store in tightly covered container. Makes about 3½ dozen.

EASY CHOCOLATE CRACKLES

These cookies made with cake mix have a moist,
fudge-like center

1 (1 lb. 2½ oz.) pkg. devil's food cake mix
2 eggs, slightly beaten
1 tblsp. water

½ c. shortening
Confectioners sugar (for coating)

Combine cake mix, eggs, water and shortening. Mix with a spoon until well blended.

Shape dough into balls the size of walnuts. Roll in confectioners sugar.

Place 1½" apart on greased baking sheet. Bake in moderate oven (375°) 8 to 10 minutes. Remove cookies and cool on racks. Makes 4 dozen.

CHOCOLATE MACAROONS

If you like chocolate and chewy cookies, these will please you

½ c. shortening
4 squares unsweetened chocolate
2 c. sifted flour
2 tsp. baking powder
½ tsp. salt

2 c. sugar
4 eggs
2 tsp. vanilla
Confectioners sugar (for coating)

Melt together shortening and chocolate.

Sift together flour, baking powder and salt.

Add sugar to chocolate, stirring until smooth. Add eggs singly, beating well after each; add vanilla.

Add flour mixture; blend thoroughly.

Chill dough 2 to 3 hours.

Dip out rounded teaspoons of dough; form it into small balls. Roll each in confectioners sugar. Place about 2" apart on lightly greased baking sheet.

Bake in moderate oven (375°) about 10 minutes. (Do not overbake. Cookies should be soft when taken from oven.) Remove cookies and cool on rack. Makes 5 to 6 dozen.

COCONUT CRISPIES

Crisp cookies with crinkled tops— perfect with ice cream

½ c. regular margarine
½ c. sugar
½ c. brown sugar, firmly packed
1 egg
½ tsp. vanilla

1 c. sifted flour
½ tsp. baking soda
½ tsp. salt
½ c. crushed corn flakes
½ c. flaked coconut

Beat together margarine and white and brown sugars until light and fluffy. Beat in egg and vanilla to blend well.

Sift together flour, baking soda and salt. Stir into creamed mixture. Fold in corn flakes and coconut. Chill until dough can easily be shaped in balls.

Shape dough by teaspoonfuls in little balls; place 2" apart on lightly greased baking sheet. Bake in moderate oven (350°) about 10 minutes, or until cookies are lightly browned. Remove at once from baking sheet to racks to cool. Store these thin crisp cookies in container with loose-fitting lid. Makes 50.

NOTE: You'll need 2 c. corn flakes to make about ½ c. crushed.

VIENNESE CRESCENTS

Use almonds in crescents for the Vienna version;
or use pecans, shape in balls and you have
Mexican Wedding Cakes

1 c. butter	1 c. ground almonds (or
¾ c. sugar	pecans)
1½ tsp. vanilla	Confectioners sugar (for
2½ c. sifted flour	coating)

Cream butter until light; gradually add sugar and beat until light and fluffy. Beat in vanilla.

Gradually blend in flour and nuts. Chill dough thoroughly so it will handle easily.

Form teaspoonfuls of dough into crescents; place ¾" apart on ungreased baking sheet. Bake in moderate oven (350°) 12 to 15 minutes, or until lightly browned. Cool slightly; remove from baking sheet and, while warm, roll in confectioners sugar. Cool on racks. Makes about 7½ dozen.

CRISSCROSS COOKIES

A winner because it has that wonderful
lemon/brown sugar taste

4 c. sifted flour	2½ c. brown sugar, firmly
1½ tsp. baking soda	packed
2 tsp. cream of tartar	1½ tsp. vanilla
1 tsp. salt	1 tsp. lemon extract
1⅓ c. shortening	3 eggs, beaten

Sift together flour, soda, cream of tartar and salt.

Cream shortening; add brown sugar gradually. Add vanilla, lemon extract and eggs; beat until light and fluffy. Add sifted dry ingredients and mix until smooth. Chill several hours.

Roll level tablespoons of dough into balls the size of a small walnut. Place about 1" apart on greased baking sheet. Press lightly with tines of fork, making a crisscross pattern.

Bake in moderate oven (375°) 8 to 10 minutes. Remove cookies and cool on racks. Makes 8 dozen.

HEIRLOOM DANISH COOKIES

A rich version of sugar cookies;
dress them up for the holidays

½ c. shortening	2 c. sifted flour
½ c. regular margarine	½ tsp. baking soda
1 c. sugar	½ tsp. cream of tartar
1 egg	2 to 3 tblsp. sugar (for tops)
1 tsp. vanilla	

Cream together shortening, margarine, 1 c. sugar, egg and vanilla until light and fluffy.

Sift together flour, baking soda and cream of tartar. Gradually stir into creamed mixture to make a smooth dough. Chill thoroughly.

Roll dough in ¾" balls; place 1½" apart on ungreased baking sheet and flatten with fork. Sprinkle with sugar.

Bake in slow oven (325°) 12 to 15 minutes. Remove cookies to racks to cool. Makes about 6 dozen.

NOTE: You can tint cookie dough and sprinkle with colored sugar to match. A few red and green cookies are pretty in a Christmas gift package.

DOUBLE TREAT COOKIES

Cookies full of children's favorites—
better make a triple batch

2 c. sifted flour	2 eggs
2 tsp. baking soda	1 tsp. vanilla
½ tsp. salt	1 c. peanut butter
1 c. shortening	1 c. chopped salted peanuts
1 c. sugar	1 (6 oz.) pkg. semisweet
1 c. brown sugar, firmly	chocolate pieces
packed	

Sift together flour, baking soda and salt.

Beat together shortening, white and brown sugars, eggs and vanilla until fluffy. Blend in peanut butter. Add sifted dry ingredients. Stir in peanuts and chocolate pieces.

Shape batter into small balls and place about 2" apart on ungreased baking sheet. Flatten with a drinking glass dipped in sugar. Bake in moderate oven (350°) 8 minutes, or until brown. Transfer cookies to racks to cool. Makes 7 dozen.

GREEK EASTER COOKIES

Excellent with coffee! These cookies are rich,
but not very sweet

½ c. butter	7 c. sifted flour
1 c. sugar	3½ tsp. baking powder
½ c. salad oil	1 tsp. salt
½ c. melted shortening	1 egg yolk
⅔ c. milk	2 tblsp. milk
2 eggs	2½ tblsp. sesame seeds
1 tsp. vanilla	

Cream butter until light and fluffy; gradually beat in sugar, salad oil, melted shortening and milk. Beat in 2 eggs and vanilla.

Sift together flour, baking powder and salt, and gradually add to creamed mixture to make a soft dough.

Shape in 1½" balls and work each ball under fingers on lightly floured surface to make a rope 7 to 8" in length. Twist each strip of dough and shape in double twist, making 2 loops like a figure 8 with ends overlapping slightly. Place about ½" apart on ungreased baking sheet.

Combine egg yolk and milk; brush on cookies. Sprinkle with sesame seeds.

Bake in moderate oven (350°) about 20 minutes, or until golden. Cool slightly on baking sheet on rack; then remove from baking sheet and cool completely on racks. Makes about 5 dozen.

Four-from-One Angel Cookies

This cookie cookbook contains many favorite recipes from Farm Journal readers, among them these Angel Cookies. An upstate New York woman says: "They are our best-liked cookies. It's a big recipe that makes about nine dozen so I make four different kinds.

"I divide the dough in quarters and bake the first portion plain. I roll the balls of dough from the second portion in flaked or cookie coconut. To the third, I add ½ c. semisweet chocolate pieces, to the fourth, ½ c. chopped salted peanuts."

You may think of other ways to introduce variety and interest to the cookie plate or tray.

ANGEL COOKIES

*Keep a supply in your freezer ready
to serve with coffee or tea*

1 c. butter or regular margarine	2 tsp. vanilla
1 c. lard	4½ c. sifted flour
1 c. sugar	2 tsp. baking soda
1 c. brown sugar, firmly packed	2 tsp. cream of tartar
2 eggs	2 tsp. salt
	1 c. chopped nuts
	White sugar (for dipping)

Cream together butter, lard and white and brown sugars. Beat in eggs, one at a time, to mix thoroughly. Add vanilla.

Sift together flour, baking soda, cream of tartar and salt. Add to creamed mixture. Stir in nuts. Chill dough until it is easy to handle.

Shape dough in balls the size of walnuts; dip tops in sugar. Arrange about 2" apart on lightly greased baking sheet. Sprinkle several drops of water on each cookie.

Bake in moderate oven (350°) 15 minutes. Remove cookies and cool on racks. Makes 9 dozen.

NOTE: You can divide the ingredients in half to bake 4½ dozen cookies.

GINGER BLOSSOM COOKIES

Nuts make cream-colored centers
for brown cookies—attractive

¾ c. shortening	1 tsp. ground ginger
1 c. brown sugar, firmly packed	1 tsp. ground cinnamon
¼ c. light molasses	½ tsp. ground cloves
1 egg, beaten	2 tsp. baking soda
2¼ c. sifted flour	¼ tsp. salt
	25 blanched almonds

Cream shortening and sugar; add molasses and egg; blend well.

Sift dry ingredients; add to creamed mixture; mix well.

Roll into balls about 1½" in diameter; place 2½" apart on greased baking sheet. Flatten slightly; press almond in center of each.

Bake in moderate oven (350°) 12 to 15 minutes. Remove cookies and cool on racks. Makes 25.

CRACKLE-TOP GINGER COOKIES

To make cookie tops glisten,
sprinkle with sugar before baking

1 c. shortening	½ tsp. salt
2 c. brown sugar, firmly packed	2 tsp. baking soda
1 egg, well beaten	2 tsp. ground ginger
1 c. molasses	1 tsp. vanilla
4 c. sifted flour	1 tsp. lemon extract
	Sugar (for tops)

Cream shortening; gradually add brown sugar. Blend in egg and molasses; beat until light and fluffy.

Sift together dry ingredients; gradually blend into creamed mixture. (Dough should be soft but not sticky, or tops won't crackle.)

Add vanilla and lemon extract. Chill about 4 hours,

or until dough can be handled with light dusting of flour on hands and board.

Shape dough into balls about 1½″ in diameter. Place 3″ apart on greased baking sheet. (Do not flatten.)

Bake in moderate oven (350°) 12 to 15 minutes, or until brown. Sprinkle with sugar, then remove from baking sheet with pancake turner. Spread on racks to cool. Makes about 30.

HONEY/NUT COOKIES

Good keepers if you hide them—
rich and crisp but not too sweet

1 c. butter or regular margarine	1 tsp. ground cinnamon
¼ c. honey	1 c. chopped walnuts
2 c. sifted flour	Confectioners sugar (for tops)

Cream butter until light; add honey and beat to mix thoroughly. Sift flour and cinnamon together; beat into creamed mixture. Stir in nuts.

Shape in 1½″ balls; place about 2″ apart on lightly greased baking sheet. Flatten with bottom of drinking glass dipped in flour. Bake in slow oven (325°) 15 minutes, or until lightly browned. Cool on baking sheet a few minutes; place on racks and while still warm, dust with confectioners sugar. Makes about 5 dozen.

HONEYED YO-YOS

Put flat sides together with jam—
big sandwiches resemble yo-yos

1 c. shortening	1 tsp. vanilla
1 c. brown sugar, firmly packed	3½ c. sifted flour
3 eggs	2 tsp. baking soda
⅓ c. honey	¼ tsp. salt
	¾ c. apricot jam

Cream together shortening and brown sugar until light and fluffy. Beat in eggs. Add honey and vanilla and beat to mix thoroughly.

Sift together flour, baking soda and salt. Add to

creamed mixture. Chill overnight, or several hours until firm.

Shape dough in balls the size of large walnuts. Place 2" apart on ungreased baking sheet. Bake in moderate oven (350°) 10 to 12 minutes, until almost no imprint remains when you press cookie lightly with finger. Transfer cookies to racks and cool.

Put flat bottom sides of cookies together in pairs with apricot jam (or other fruit jam) between. Makes about 2½ dozen.

JELLY DIAGONALS

Use jelly, jam or preserves of another color for half the batch for contrast—try apricot and grape preserves for interesting effect

¾ c. butter	½ tsp. baking powder
⅔ c. sugar	½ tsp. ground nutmeg
1 egg	¼ tsp. salt
2 tsp. vanilla	¼ c. apricot jam or preserves,
2 c. sifted flour	or currant jelly

Cream butter until light; add sugar and beat until fluffy. Beat in egg and vanilla to mix thoroughly.

Sift together flour, baking powder, nutmeg and salt. Stir into creamed mixture; mix thoroughly.

Divide dough in quarters. Form each part into a roll about 12" long, ¾" in diameter. Place two rolls at a time 4" apart on ungreased baking sheet; have the rolls at least 2" from edges of baking sheet. Make a depression about ⅓" deep lengthwise down the center of each roll. You can do this with a knife handle. Fill the cavity with jam, preserves or jelly (you'll need about 1 tblsp. for each roll).

Bake in moderate oven (350°) 15 to 20 minutes, until lightly browned around edges. While warm, cut in diagonal slices, about 10 to a roll. Cool cookies on racks. Makes 40.

BRAZILIAN LACE-EDGED COOKIES

Lacy edges give these cookies a gay look— nice for entertaining

¼ c. soft butter or regular	2 tblsp. water
margarine	1 c. sifted flour
1½ c. brown sugar, firmly	1 tsp. ground cinnamon
packed	1 c. chopped Brazil nuts

Cream butter; add sugar gradually and cream until light and fluffy. Blend in water.

Sift flour and cinnamon; add nuts. Combine mixtures. Shape dough in small balls, about 1". Place 2" apart on greased baking sheet.

Bake in slow oven (325°) about 15 minutes.

Remove from oven; let stand about 30 seconds before lifting from baking sheet with wide spatula. (If cookies get too crisp to come off smoothly, return to oven and heat about a minute to resoften.) Remove cookies and cool on racks. Makes about 5 dozen.

LEMON ANGEL COOKIES

*Lemon-filled meringue tops these lovely
hostess specials*

⅔ c. shortening	1 tsp. salt
1 c. brown sugar, firmly	1 tsp. baking soda
packed	3 egg whites
2 eggs	¾ c. sugar
1 tsp. vanilla	Lemon Filling (recipe follows)
2 c. sifted flour	

Beat shortening with brown sugar until light and fluffy. Beat in the 2 eggs, one at a time, and vanilla to mix well.

Sift together flour, salt and baking soda and add to creamed mixture. Chill dough 1 hour.

Beat egg whites until foamy; add sugar gradually and beat until stiff peaks form. Set aside.

Shape chilled dough into balls, using 1 tsp. dough for each ball. Place 2" apart on ungreased baking sheet. Flatten to ⅛" thickness with bottom of 2" juice glass.

Top each cookie with 1 tsp. meringue. With the spoon, make a hollow in center of meringue on cookie. Bake in slow oven (325°) 10 to 12 minutes, or until cookies are cream-colored. Cool cookies on racks, then fill depressions in meringue on top of cookies with lukewarm Lemon Filling. Store cookies in refrigerator until time to serve them. Makes 4 dozen.

NOTE: You can fill these cookies with other fillings, jelly or jam or whipped cream just before serving.

LEMON FILLING

Filling on meringue-topped cookies
will have a dull, yellow look

1 c. sugar	3 egg yolks
2 tblsp. cornstarch	¼ c. lemon juice
¼ tsp. salt	1 tsp. grated lemon peel
¼ c. water	1 tblsp. butter

Combine ½ c. sugar, cornstarch and salt in small saucepan, mixing well. Stir in water. Cook over low heat, stirring constantly, until mixture thickens (it will not be clear).

Beat together egg yolks and ½ c. sugar. Blend a little of the hot mixture into egg yolks, then add to mixture in saucepan. Cook over low heat, stirring constantly, about 2 minutes, or until mixture thickens; remove from heat.

Stir in lemon juice, lemon peel and butter. Cool until lukewarm.

LEMON SNOWBALLS

A great hostess favorite—pure white cookies
accented with lemon

½ c. shortening or butter	¼ tsp. cream of tartar
⅔ c. sugar	3 tblsp. lemon juice
2 tsp. grated lemon peel	1 tblsp. water
1 egg	½ c. chopped nuts
1¾ c. sifted flour	Confectioners sugar (for
½ tsp. baking soda	coating)

Cream together shortening, sugar and lemon peel until light and fluffy. Add egg; beat until smooth.

Sift together flour, baking soda and cream of tartar. Add to creamed mixture alternately with lemon juice and water.

Stir in nuts. Chill dough.

With floured hands, form dough into small balls and

place 1″ apart on ungreased baking sheet. Bake in moderate oven (350°) 8 to 10 minutes. Remove from sheet and roll immediately in confectioners sugar. Cool on racks. Makes 3½ dozen.

VARIATION

Orange Snowballs: Omit lemon peel and lemon juice. Substitute grated orange peel and orange juice. Use pecans for nuts.

MEXICAN FIESTA BALLS

Chocolate, coffee and maraschino flavors
blend in these gala cookies

1 c. butter	½ tsp. salt
½ c. sugar	1 c. finely chopped nuts
2 tsp. vanilla	½ c. chopped drained
2 c. sifted flour	maraschino cherries
¼ c. cocoa	1 c. confectioners sugar (for
1 tblsp. instant coffee powder	coating)

Beat butter until light; gradually add sugar. Beat until light and fluffy. Add vanilla and beat to blend well.

Sift together flour, cocoa, coffee powder and salt; gradually add to creamed mixture. Blend in nuts and cherries; chill until easy to handle.

Shape dough into balls 1″ in diameter and place 1″ apart on ungreased baking sheet. Bake in slow oven (325°) 20 minutes. Remove cookies to cooling racks and, while warm, roll in confectioners sugar. Makes 5 dozen.

MEXICAN SEED COOKIES

Anise and sesame seeds give these thin
sugar cookies a new taste

1 tblsp. whole anise seeds	1 egg
2 tblsp. boiling water	2 c. sifted flour
⅔ c. sugar	1 egg, lightly beaten
¾ c. butter or regular	⅓ c. Toasted Sesame Seeds
margarine	(see Index)
⅛ tsp. baking soda	

Combine anise seeds and boiling water and let stand.

207

Beat together sugar and butter until fluffy. Beat in soda and 1 egg. Drain anise seeds and add to mixture.

Stir in flour, a little at a time, and mix well. Wrap dough in waxed paper and chill overnight.

When ready to bake, roll dough in ½″ balls. Place about 3″ apart on ungreased baking sheets. Flatten to ¹⁄₁₆″ thickness with the bottom of a glass. Brush tops with lightly beaten egg. Sprinkle each with toasted sesame seeds.

Bake in hot oven (400°) 7 to 8 minutes, or until lightly browned. Remove cookies and cool on racks. Makes 6 dozen.

MEXICAN THUMBPRINTS

*The custard filling bakes in these rich
and luscious party cookies*

1 egg yolk	½ c. sugar
1 tblsp. sugar	2 egg yolks
1 tblsp. flour	1 tsp. vanilla
¼ tsp. vanilla	2¼ c. sifted flour
Dash of salt	1 tsp. baking powder
½ c. heavy cream	⅛ tsp. salt
1 c. butter	

To make filling, blend 1 egg yolk with 1 tblsp. sugar, 1 tblsp. flour, ¼ tsp. vanilla and dash of salt in top of double boiler. Add the cream gradually and blend well. Cook over water, stirring constantly, until custard is thick and smooth. Cover surface of custard with waxed paper or plastic wrap. Chill thoroughly.

To make cookies, beat butter until light; gradually add ½ c. sugar and beat until fluffy. Beat in 2 egg yolks and 1 tsp. vanilla to blend well.

Sift together 2¼ c. flour, baking powder and ⅛ tsp. salt. Mix into egg yolk mixture to blend thoroughly. Chill dough until easy to handle, at least 1 hour.

Shape heaping teaspoonfuls of dough into balls; place 1″ apart on ungreased baking sheet. With thumb, press medium-size indentations in each dough ball. Put ¼ tsp. filling in each.

Bake in moderate oven (350°) 13 to 15 minutes, or until light brown. Remove cookies and cool on racks. Makes 4½ dozen.

MOLASSES BUTTERBALLS

Easy to make and really delicious—
brown cookies in white dress

1 c. butter or regular margarine	½ tsp. salt
¼ c. molasses	2 c. finely chopped walnuts
2 c. sifted flour	Confectioners sugar (for coating)

Cream butter; add molasses.

Sift flour and salt; stir in nuts.

Add flour mixture to creamed mixture; blend well. Shape dough into small balls, about 1″ in diameter.

Place about 1″ apart on ungreased baking sheet. Bake in moderate oven (350°) 25 minutes, or until lightly browned. Roll in confectioners sugar while warm. Cool cookies on racks. Makes about 4 dozen.

SPICY MOLASSES BALLS

Brown sugar adds to the tastiness of these spicy,
country specials

¾ c. shortening	¼ tsp. salt
1 c. brown sugar, firmly packed	2 tsp. baking soda
1 egg	1 tsp. ground cinnamon
¼ c. molasses	1 tsp. ground ginger
2½ c. sifted flour	½ tsp. ground cloves
	Sugar (for dipping)

Cream shortening and brown sugar; blend in egg and molasses.

Sift together remaining ingredients, except sugar; stir into creamed mixture; mix well. Shape into ¾″ balls; dip tops in sugar. Place 2″ apart on greased baking sheet.

Bake in moderate oven (350°) 12 to 15 minutes. Remove cookies and cool on racks. Makes about 4 dozen.

PARTY PINKS

Crisp cookies with pink tops bring glamor
to festive entertaining

¾ c. butter or regular
  margarine
1½ c. sifted confectioners
  sugar
1 tsp. vanilla
3 drops red food color (about)

1 egg yolk
1½ c. sifted flour
¼ tsp. salt
1 egg white, slightly beaten
1 c. finely chopped pecans

Cream butter, sugar and vanilla until light and fluffy. Add food color to make a delicate pink. Take out ¼ c. mixture and refrigerate.

To remainder of creamed mixture add egg yolk, flour and salt; mix thoroughly. Shape in balls about 1" in diameter. Dip in egg white, then in nuts.

Place 1½" apart on ungreased baking sheet. Bake in moderate oven (350°) 10 minutes. Remove from oven and quickly make indentation in each cookie by pressing with back of ¼ tsp. measuring spoon (round bowl). Return to oven and bake about 7 minutes longer.

Transfer from baking sheet to racks. When cool, place ¼ tsp. reserved pink creamed mixture in the center of each cookie. Makes 3 dozen.

PEANUT/APPLE COOKIES

Apple gives these cookies their moistness,
peanut butter, the flavor

½ c. shortening
½ c. smooth peanut butter
½ c. sugar
½ c. brown sugar, firmly
  packed
1 egg

½ tsp. vanilla
½ c. grated peeled apple
1½ c. sifted flour
½ tsp. baking soda
½ tsp. salt
½ tsp. ground cinnamon

Cream together shortening, peanut butter and sugars until light and fluffy. Beat in egg, vanilla and apple to mix well.

Sift together remaining dry ingredients; stir into creamed mixture to blend well. Chill several hours.

Work with a fourth of dough at a time, leaving remaining dough in refrigerator until ready to use. Shape in 1" balls and place 1½" apart on greased baking sheet. Flatten balls with a fork moistened in cold water.

Bake in moderate oven (350°) 12 to 15 minutes. Remove cookies and cool on racks. Makes about 5 dozen.

PEANUT BLOSSOM COOKIES

*Chocolate stars make pretty centers
and make cookies look festive*

1 c. shortening
1 c. sugar
1 c. brown sugar, firmly
  packed
2 eggs
1 c. peanut butter
3½ c. sifted flour

2 tsp. baking soda
1 tsp. salt
2 tblsp. milk
½ c. sugar (for dipping)
Chocolate candy stars for
  centers (about 1 lb.)

Cream shortening, 1 c. white sugar and brown sugar together until light and fluffy. Beat in eggs and peanut butter.

Sift together flour, baking soda and salt and stir into creamed mixture. Add milk and mix.

Shape in 1 to 1½" balls with hands; dip in ½ c. sugar and arrange 2 to 3" apart on lightly greased baking sheet. Bake in moderate oven (350°) 7 minutes. Remove from oven and quickly press a small chocolate candy star in center of each cookie. (Candy will fall off cookie when cooled unless it is pressed in before cookie is completely baked.) Return to oven and bake 5 to 7 minutes longer.

Remove from baking sheet to racks and cool. Makes about 10 dozen.

PEANUT DROPS

*These cookies have crisp, ragged tops
with flashes of red cherries*

¼ c. butter or regular
  margarine
½ c. peanut butter
½ c. brown sugar, firmly
  packed
½ c. sugar
1 egg
1¼ c. sifted flour
¼ tsp. baking soda

¼ tsp. salt
¼ c. butter
⅓ c. sugar
1 egg
½ c. chopped salted peanuts
3 c. corn flakes
¼ c. chopped drained
  maraschino cherries

To make cookie dough, beat ¼ c. butter and peanut butter together; gradually add brown sugar and ½ c.

211

white sugar and beat until light and fluffy. Beat in 1 egg to mix thoroughly.

Sift together flour, baking soda and salt. Add to first mixture; mix well.

Make topping by creaming together ¼ c. butter and ⅓ c. white sugar. Add remaining ingredients and beat well.

Shape cookie dough into 1″ balls; place 2″ apart on lightly greased baking sheet and flatten with a fork. Top each cookie with about 2 tblsp. topping.

Bake in moderate oven (375°) 12 to 15 minutes. Transfer cookies to racks to cool. Makes 34.

PECAN BONBONS AND LOGS

For variety bake part of dough in logs—
bonbons are very pretty

2 c. sifted flour	2 tsp. vanilla
¼ c. sugar	2½ c. finely chopped pecans
½ tsp. salt	Confectioners sugar (for
1 c. butter or regular	coating)
margarine	

Sift flour, sugar and salt into mixing bowl. Blend in butter and vanilla with pastry blender. Add 2 c. nuts.

Shape half the dough into ½″ balls. Roll in remaining nuts. Place about 1½″ apart on greased baking sheet and bake in moderate oven (350°) 15 to 20 minutes. Cool cookies on racks.

Roll remaining dough into logs; bake. While warm, roll in confectioners sugar. Makes 4 dozen.

PECAN COOKIES

Jewel-like centers make these a pretty
addition to the party tray

2 c. ground pecans	⅓ c. strawberry preserves
⅔ c. sugar	18 candied or maraschino
½ tsp. salt	cherries, cut in halves
2 egg whites	

Combine pecans and sugar. Add salt and egg whites and mix until mixture is completely moistened.

Form into small balls (mixture will be moist). Place

about 2" apart on ungreased baking sheet. Press a small hole in center of each ball with your fingertip. Fill with strawberry preserves. Top with cherry halves, cut side down.

Bake in moderate oven (350°) about 15 minutes. Remove from baking sheet at once to prevent sticking. Cool on racks. Makes 3 dozen.

PECAN DROPS

The brown beauties with red-cherry trim are perfect for Christmas

1 c. butter or regular margarine	1 tblsp. vanilla
½ tsp. salt	2 c. sifted flour
½ c. sifted confectioners sugar	1 c. finely chopped pecans
	Candied cherries, cut in sixths

Blend together butter, salt, sugar and vanilla. Add flour and pecans; mix well; chill.

Shape into small balls; place about 2" apart on lightly greased baking sheet. Press small hole in center of each ball with fingertip; insert piece of cherry in each. Bake in moderate oven (350°) about 15 minutes. Remove cookies and cool on racks. Makes 5 dozen.

PECAN FINGER COOKIES

Pecan halves in cookie jackets—a tasty addition to the teatime tray

1 c. butter	¼ tsp. salt
½ c. sugar	1 c. pecan halves
2 tsp. vanilla	¼ c. confectioners sugar (for coating)
2 c. sifted flour	

Beat butter until light; add sugar and vanilla and beat until mixture is fluffy.

Blend together flour and salt; stir into creamed mixture and mix well. With the fingers, shape rounded teaspoonfuls of dough around each pecan half. If dough is soft, chill before using. Cut pecan halves in two if necessary.

Place about 1" apart on lightly greased baking sheet; bake in moderate oven (350°) 15 to 18 minutes, or until a light brown. While cookies are still warm, roll in confectioners sugar. Cool on racks. Makes about 4½ dozen.

Coconut/Pecan Finger Cookies: Before baking cookies, dip them in 1 egg white beaten lightly with 1 tblsp. water and roll in ¾ c. flaked coconut.

PECAN PUFFS

Pecan cookie balls are snowy white
with confectioners sugar coating

½ c. butter	2 c. sifted flour
½ c. regular margarine	1 c. finely chopped pecans
6 tblsp. confectioners sugar	¾ c. confectioners sugar (for
6 tblsp. water	coating)
2 tsp. vanilla	

Place butter, margarine, 6 tblsp. confectioners sugar, water, vanilla, flour and nuts in bowl. Mix with electric mixer at medium speed. Chill dough briefly, about 1 hour.

Pinch off pieces of dough about the size of walnuts. Roll between hands to form balls. Place 1½" apart on ungreased baking sheet. Bake in moderate oven (350°) 18 to 20 minutes. While warm, roll in confectioners sugar. Cool on racks. For a heavier coating, roll again in confectioners sugar when cool. Makes 4 dozen.

PEPPARKAKOR

Black pepper gives "bite" to these Swedish
gingersnaps

1 c. sugar	1 tblsp. ground ginger
1 c. butter or lard	½ tsp. black pepper
1 c. light molasses	3½ c. sifted flour
1 tsp. baking soda	Sugar (for dipping)
1 tsp. salt	

Cream sugar and butter until light and fluffy. Beat in molasses.

Sift together baking soda, salt, ginger, pepper and flour; add to creamed mixture and beat to mix well. Chill dough until easy to handle.

214

Shape dough with hands into balls the size of large marbles. Dip in sugar before baking. Place 1½" apart on lightly greased baking sheet.

Bake in moderate oven (350°) 12 to 15 minutes, or until lightly browned. Cool on baking sheet 1 minute, then transfer to rack to cool completely. Makes about 7 dozen.

PRETZEL COOKIES

Pretzel shape adds charm to a tray of assorted cookies—rich-tasting

⅔ c. butter	⅛ tsp. salt
½ c. sugar	3 c. sifted flour
½ tsp. vanilla	½ c. sugar (for dipping)
3 eggs	½ c. finely chopped walnuts

Cream butter with ½ c. sugar until light and fluffy. Beat in vanilla and 2 eggs to mix thoroughly. Combine salt and flour; add to creamed mixture. Knead dough until smooth. Set aside for 1 hour or longer.

Take up small portions of dough (the size of large walnuts) and roll under hands on pastry cloth or board into 7" lengths with the diameter of a pencil. Form in pretzel shapes. Brush with remaining egg, slightly beaten, then dip tops in remaining ½ c. sugar and nuts.

Place about 1" apart on ungreased baking sheet; bake in slow oven (325°) about 25 minutes, or until cookies are a very light brown. Remove cookies and cool on racks. Makes about 40.

RIBBON COOKIES

Colorful cookies for your party—serve them with steaming hot coffee

1 c. butter or regular margarine	¼ c. chopped candied red cherries
1½ c. sugar	¼ c. chopped candied green cherries
1 egg	
1 tsp. vanilla	⅓ c. semisweet chocolate pieces, melted over hot, not boiling, water
2½ c. sifted flour	
1½ tsp. baking powder	
½ tsp. salt	¼ c. chopped pecans

Cream butter and sugar until light and fluffy. Add egg and vanilla; beat.

Sift together flour, baking powder and salt; blend half into butter-sugar mixture; stir in remaining flour mixture until blended.

Divide dough in three parts. Add red cherries to one, green cherries to second and chocolate and pecans to the third part.

Line bottom and sides of 9 × 5 × 3" loaf pan with foil. Pat red cherry dough into bottom of pan; pat chocolate dough over this; pat green cherry dough over top. Press each layer down firmly. Cover and refrigerate for several hours.

Turn out of pan. Cut in half lengthwise. Slice each bar in ⅛" thick slices. Place 1½" apart on ungreased baking sheet. Bake in hot oven (400°) 10 to 12 minutes. Remove cookies and cool on racks. Makes 8 dozen.

SANDBAKELSER

In Sweden these fragile sand tarts are served upside down on blue plates—or fill upright tarts with whipped cream at serving time

⅓ c. blanched almonds	1 egg white
½ c. butter	1 tsp. vanilla
½ c. sugar	1¼ c. sifted flour

Put almonds through fine blade of food chopper twice. Set aside.

Mix together well butter, sugar, unbeaten egg white and vanilla. Stir in flour and almonds. Cover and chill 2 hours or longer.

With lightly floured fingers, press dough over bottom and sides of sandbakelser molds (they're like tiny fluted tart pans). Press dough as thin as possible, or about ⅛" thick. Set on ungreased baking sheet.

Bake in moderate oven (350°) about 12 minutes, or until very delicately browned. Cool 3 minutes or until molds are cool enough to handle. Tap molds lightly on table to loosen cookies. Cool on racks. Makes 2½ to 3 dozen, depending on size of molds and thinness of cookies.

SAND BALLS

Honey enhances flavor; roll twice in sugar for snowy white coating

1 c. butter	1 tsp. vanilla
½ c. confectioners sugar	¾ c. chopped walnuts
2 tblsp. honey	Confectioners sugar (for
2¼ c. sifted flour	coating)
¼ tsp. salt	

Cream butter, confectioners sugar and honey together thoroughly. Add flour, salt, vanilla and nuts. Mix with hands, if necessary, to blend well.

Form into balls 1″ in diameter and chill thoroughly.

To bake, place cookie balls 2½″ apart on greased baking sheet. Bake in moderate oven (375°) 14 to 17 minutes. While still warm, roll in confectioners sugar. Cool cookies on racks. Then roll in confectioners sugar again. Makes 4 dozen.

Snickerdoodles

Generations of boys and girls have returned home from school happy to find the kitchen fragrant with cinnamon-sugar and the cookie jar filled with freshly baked Snickerdoodles. These cookies are just as popular today as they were long ago. The Pennsylvania Dutch proudly claim them as their invention, but the cookies were not strangers in New England homes, for most of the very old regional cookbooks with age-yellowed pages include the recipe, as do later editions. Good recipes always have journeyed from one section of the country to another because women like to share their favorites. Evidence of this is the thousands of recipes they sent to FARM JOURNAL for possible use in this cookbook.

Recipes undergo changes with the years. Originally, Snickerdoodles often were either rolled or drop cookies, sprinkled with sugar and cinnamon. Many women today prefer to shape the dough in small, even-sized balls and to roll them in a cinnamon-sugar mixture, the true Cape Cod way. The molded cookies come from the oven in almost perfect rounds. Our recipe is for this kind.

SNICKERDOODLES

The crisp cookies with crinkly sugar-cinnamon tops always please

½ c. butter or regular margarine	2⅔ c. sifted flour
½ c. lard	2 tsp. cream of tartar
1½ c. sugar	1 tsp. baking soda
2 eggs	¼ tsp. salt
1 tsp. vanilla	2 tblsp. sugar
	1 tsp. ground cinnamon

Beat butter and lard until light; add 1½ c. sugar and beat until fluffy. Beat in eggs and vanilla.

Sift together flour, cream of tartar, baking soda and salt; add to beaten mixture.

Combine 2 tblsp. sugar and cinnamon.

Shape dough in small balls, about 1", and roll in sugar-cinnamon mixture. Place 2" apart on ungreased baking sheet. Bake in hot oven (400°) 8 to 10 minutes. (Cookies flatten during baking.) Remove cookies and cool on racks. Makes about 6 dozen.

SWIRLS

These decorative, two-color cookies will provide party conversation

1 c. butter or regular margarine	¼ tsp. salt
½ c. sifted confectioners sugar	½ tsp. vanilla
	¼ tsp. almond extract
2¼ c. sifted flour	3 drops red food color
	12 drops yellow food color

Beat butter until light; add confectioners sugar and beat until fluffy.

Sift together flour and salt and blend well into creamed mixture. Divide dough in half. Leave one half plain and blend vanilla into it with electric mixer on low speed. To remaining half add almond extract and food colors to produce an orange-colored dough. Chill thoroughly.

Take 1 teaspoonful plain dough and shape into a pencil-like roll 6" long. Repeat with tinted dough. (If dough gets warm while working with it and sticks to surface, lightly flour surface.) Lay the two rolls side by side on ungreased baking sheet and coil them. Repeat with remaining dough, leaving 1″ between coils.

Bake in hot oven (400°) about 8 minutes, or until cookies are set but not browned. Remove cookies and cool on racks. Makes 3 dozen.

CRACKLED SUGAR COOKIES

An old-fashioned cookie: subtle lemon flavor, pretty, crinkled top

1 c. shortening (part butter)	¼ c. sugar
1½ c. sugar	1 tsp. grated orange peel
6 egg yolks, or 3 eggs, beaten	½ tsp. grated lemon peel
1 tsp. vanilla	2 tblsp. finely chopped black
½ tsp. lemon extract	walnuts
½ tsp. orange extract	½ tsp. ground nutmeg
2½ c. flour	1 tblsp. brown sugar
1 tsp. baking soda	2 tblsp. sugar
1 tsp. cream of tartar	¼ c. chocolate shot (jimmies)

Cream shortening and 1½ c. sugar until fluffy. Add yolks and flavorings; beat.

Combine flour, baking soda and cream of tartar; add to creamed mixture. Shape in 1″ balls. Divide balls in thirds.

Combine ¼ c. sugar with orange and lemon peels; roll one-third of balls in mixture.

Roll second third of balls in mixture of nuts, nutmeg, brown sugar and 2 tblsp. sugar.

Roll remaining balls in chocolate decorations (jimmies).

Place cookie balls about 2″ apart on ungreased baking sheet. Bake in moderate oven (350°) 12 to 15 minutes. Remove cookies and cool on racks. Makes about 5 dozen.

JUMBO SUGAR COOKIES

Extra-crisp, big, thin cookies with crinkled tops sell fast at bazaars

2 c. sugar	1 tsp. baking soda
1 c. shortening	1 tsp. salt
2 eggs	1 tsp. ground cinnamon
2 c. sifted flour	(for tops)
2 tsp. cream of tartar	2 tblsp. sugar (for tops)

Beat together 2 c. sugar and shortening until light and fluffy. Beat in eggs to mix thoroughly.

Sift together flour, cream of tartar, baking soda and salt. Stir into creamed mixture. On lightly floured waxed paper, form dough into four rolls, each about 12″ long and 1 to 1¼″ in diameter. Cut in 1″ slices. Dip tops of cookies in mixture of cinnamon and 2 tblsp. sugar. Place 3″ apart, cinnamon-sugar sides up, on greased baking sheet.

Bake in moderate oven (375°) about 12 minutes. Let stand on baking sheet 1 minute before removing to cooling racks. Makes 4 dozen.

MOLDED SUGAR COOKIES

Have won blue ribbons in baking contests—crisp crust, soft interior

2½ c. sifted flour	1 c. butter
2 tsp. cream of tartar	1 tsp. vanilla
1 tsp. baking soda	1 c. sugar
½ tsp. salt	2 eggs, beaten

Sift together flour, cream of tartar, baking soda and salt.

Cream butter, vanilla and sugar until light and fluffy. Add eggs and beat well. Add sifted dry ingredients, a fourth at a time, stirring to mix thoroughly. Chill 1 hour.

Shape dough in 1″ balls and place 2½″ apart on greased baking sheet. Flatten by pressing with bottom of drinking glass coated with sugar. (Dip bottom of glass in sugar before flattening each cookie.)

Bake in moderate oven (375°) 8 minutes, or until golden. Remove cookies to racks to cool. Makes about 5½ dozen.

DOUBLE VANILLA BARS

These cookies, twice flavored with vanilla, win praise and disappear fast. Keep Vanilla Sugar on hand for a gourmet touch in baking

5 egg yolks	3¾ c. sifted flour
1 c. plus 2 tblsp. sugar	⅛ tsp. salt
2 tsp. vanilla	Vanilla Sugar (recipe follows)
1 c. butter	

Beat egg yolks until light. Gradually beat in sugar, beating after each addition. Then beat 3 minutes longer. Beat in vanilla.

With pastry blender, cut butter into flour mixed with salt until particles are fine. Add to egg mixture and blend. Then knead with hands until dough is smooth. Chill 1 hour.

Pinch off dough, about 1 tblsp. at a time; flour hands and roll into strips about 2″ long and ½″ thick. Place 1″ apart on ungreased baking sheet.

Bake in moderate oven (350°) 12 to 15 minutes, or until golden brown. Cool about 3 minutes before removing from baking sheet to racks. Carefully dip each cookie while warm into Vanilla Sugar to coat completely. Cool, then dip again in Vanilla Sugar. (If you wish, you can use sifted confectioners sugar instead of the Vanilla Sugar.) Makes about 5½ dozen.

Vanilla Sugar: Sift 1 (1 lb.) pkg. confectioners sugar into a container with a tight-fitting lid. Split a vanilla bean (available at many spice and flavoring counters) lengthwise; cut up and add to container of sugar. Cover and let stand 3 days or longer before using. Sugar will keep for months if tightly covered. You will need about half of it to coat these cookies.

SPANISH WEDDING CAKES

You wrap these cookies with lemon flavor around almonds

1 c. butter
¼ c. sifted confectioners
   sugar
1 tblsp. grated lemon peel
1 tblsp. water
2½ c. sifted flour

¼ tsp. salt
½ c. whole blanched almonds
   (about)
¾ c. confectioners sugar (for
   coating)

Cream butter until light and fluffy. Stir in ¼ c. confectioners sugar, lemon peel and water.

Mix flour with salt; beat into butter mixture. Knead with hands until dough is light.

Pinch off 1 heaping teaspoonful of dough at a time; press it flat and then press it around a whole almond to cover completely. Shape like a little loaf. Place about 1″ apart on lightly greased baking sheet.

Bake in moderate oven (350°) about 15 minutes, or until cookies start to brown around bottom. Take care not to overbake. Remove from baking sheets and cool 2 or 3 minutes on racks, then roll in confectioners sugar. Cool completely and then roll again in confectioners sugar. Store in airtight container. Makes about 4 dozen.

FROSTED YULE LOGS

Shape of yule logs adds interest to Christmas cookie tray or box

1 c. butter or regular
   margarine
¾ c. sugar
1 egg
1 tsp. vanilla

3 c. sifted flour
½ tsp. ground nutmeg
¼ c. sugar
1 c. finely chopped pecans
1 egg white

Beat butter until light; add ¾ c. sugar and beat until light and fluffy. Beat in egg and vanilla to blend well.

Sift together flour and nutmeg; stir into creamed mixture. Shape dough into fat pencil-shaped rolls, each about 2″ long, to represent yule logs.

Combine remaining ¼ c. sugar and pecans. Beat egg white slightly. Dip yule logs into egg white and then roll in nut mixture. Place 1″ apart on lightly greased baking sheet.

Bake in moderate oven (375°) about 10 minutes, until browned. Remove cookies and cool on racks. Makes 6 dozen.

Pressed Cookies

GIVE A cookie press to a woman who likes to bake and turn her loose in her kitchen. Sweet things happen—like tender-crisp, buttery-rich cookies in many designs. Spritz, the highly revered Swedish pressed cookies, are the kind most frequently made, but different forms or shapes, flavors and decorations result in great variety. It seems incredible that so many delicacies can come from the same dough until you start using a press.

Among the designs in spritz that attract attention are the letter cookies. You'll find two recipes for them in this section, Lindsborg Letter Spritz, from a Swedish-American community in Kansas, and Lemon Cookie Letters.

You'll want to try our Royal Crowns, a splendid pressed cookie in which hard-cooked egg yolks are an ingredient.

As the term "pressed" suggests, you put the dough through a cookie press with one of a variety of plates inserted to produce cookies of the shape desired. Women who bake this kind of cookie consider it easy and quick.

The beauty of pressed cookies is partly in their design or shape. They all taste wonderful. Serve them undecorated or fancied up as you wish. You can top them, before baking, with bits of candied fruits, raisins, currants or chopped nuts. Or you can add decorations after baking, arranging them in designs and securing them to the cookie with drops of corn syrup or egg white. Use coarse colored sugar, multicolored tiny candies, dragées or tiny red cinnamon candies for the trims. And if you're in the mood, tint the dough with food color before you put it in the press.

The dough for pressed cookies needs to be right. Butter is the first choice of fats, but you can use regular margarine or shortening. Be sure to have the fat at room temperature before you start to mix the dough. Beat it with the electric mixer at medium speed until soft, or beat it with a spoon. Gradually add the sugar, beating all the time, and continue beating until the mixture is light and fluffy, but do not overbeat.

When the dough is ready, test it by pressing a small amount through the press. It should be pliable and soft, but not crumbly. Unless the dough is soft or the recipe directs that you chill it, work with it at room temperature. Dough that's too cold crumbles. When the dough seems too soft, add 1 to 2 tblsp. flour; if too stiff, add 1 egg yolk.

Put about one-fourth of the dough in the press at a time. Hold the press so it rests on the baking sheet unless you are using a star or bar plate. Press dough onto a cool baking sheet; if it is warm, the fat in the dough melts and the cookies will not adhere to the sheet when you lift off the press. Do not remove press until the dough forms a well-defined design. You may need to wait a few seconds to give it time to cling to the baking sheet. You will not need to exert pressure on the press or the handle if the dough is right.

Pressed cookies are rich. Bake them on an ungreased baking sheet until they are set. You bake some pressed cookies until lightly browned around the edges, while others are not browned at all.

ORANGE/CHEESE COOKIES

Rows of ridges on cookies make them look like little washboards

1 c. butter or regular margarine	1 tblsp. grated orange peel
1 (3 oz.) pkg. cream cheese	1 tblsp. orange juice
1 c. sugar	2½ c. sifted flour
1 egg	1 tsp. baking powder
	Dash of salt

Combine butter and cream cheese; beat until light. Gradually add sugar, beating until mixture is fluffy. Beat in egg, orange peel and juice to blend thoroughly.

Sift together flour, baking powder and salt. Add to creamed mixture, blending well.

Put plate with narrow slit in cookie press. Put a fourth of dough into press at a time and press rows of strips of dough about 1″ apart onto ungreased baking sheet. With knife, mark strips in 2″ lengths.

Bake in moderate oven (375°) 8 to 10 minutes, until very delicately browned. Immediately cut strips into pieces on knife marks. Remove cookies and cool on racks. Makes about 12½ dozen.

NOTE: Sprinkle some of the cookies before baking with chocolate shot (jimmies) for a tasty, interesting touch.

PEANUT BUTTER PRESSED COOKIES

Glamorize peanut butter cookies by shaping them with cookie press

¾ c. butter or regular margarine	½ tsp. vanilla or almond extract
3 tblsp. peanut butter	1¾ c. sifted flour
½ c. sugar	¼ tsp. salt
1 egg yolk	

Beat together butter and peanut butter until light. Gradually beat in sugar, beating until light and fluffy. Beat in egg yolk and vanilla to blend thoroughly.

Sift together flour and salt. Add to creamed mixture; mix to a smooth dough.

Fit desired plate into cookie press. Put one-fourth of the dough in cookie press at a time. Force cookies 1″ apart onto ungreased baking sheet. Bake in moderate oven (375°) 8 to 10 minutes, or until delicately brown. Remove cookies and cool on racks. Makes about 3 dozen.

ROYAL CROWNS

A tasty, unusual, regal addition to the holiday cookie collection

4 hard-cooked egg yolks	⅔ c. sugar
½ tsp. salt	½ tsp. almond extract
1 c. butter or regular margarine	2½ c. sifted flour
	Red or green candied cherries

Force egg yolks through a coarse sieve with back of spoon. Add salt and mix.

Cream together butter and sugar until light and fluffy. Add almond extract and egg yolks. Add flour and mix well.

Place dough in cookie press. Force dough through crown design 1 to 2″ apart onto lightly greased baking sheet. Decorate with bits of candied cherries.

Bake in moderate oven (375°) 7 to 10 minutes. Remove cookies and cool on racks. Makes 6 dozen.

SPRITZ

Change shape of these tender cookies with different press plates

1 c. butter	1 tsp. almond extract, vanilla
2/3 c. confectioners sugar	or 1/4 c. grated almonds
1 egg	2 1/2 c. sifted flour
1 egg yolk	

Combine butter, sugar, egg, egg yolk and almond extract. Work in flour.

Use a fourth of the dough at a time; force it through cookie press 1″ apart onto ungreased baking sheet in desired shapes. Bake in hot oven (400°) 7 to 10 minutes, or until set but not browned. Remove cookies and cool on racks. Makes 4 to 6 dozen, depending on size.

CHOCOLATE SPRITZ

The potent chocolate flavor of these crisp cookies delights many. They add charming contrast to a tray of light-colored spritz

1 c. butter or regular	3 egg yolks
margarine	1 tsp. vanilla, or 3/4 tsp.
2/3 c. sugar	almond extract
1 1/2 squares unsweetened	1/8 tsp. salt
chocolate, melted	2 1/2 c. sifted flour

Cream butter with sugar until light and fluffy. Beat in chocolate, egg yolks and vanilla. Stir salt into flour to mix thoroughly. Work into creamed mixture, a little at a time.

Divide dough into fourths and put each part through

cookie press ½ to 1" apart on ungreased baking sheet. (Use whatever shaped disk in press you like.)

Bake in hot oven (400°) 7 to 10 minutes, until cookies are set, but do not brown. Remove at once to racks to cool. Makes about 7 dozen.

NOTE: See recipe in Index for Date/Nut Kisses if you want to use leftover egg whites in a delicious treat.

SPRITZ CHOCOLATE SANDWICHES

Pretty-as-a-picture, special-occasion spritz taste simply great—slender cookies with chocolate filling and chocolate-nut ends

1 c. butter or regular margarine	2½ c. sifted flour
	½ tsp. salt
1¼ c. sifted confectioners sugar	Buttery Chocolate Frosting (recipe follows)
1 egg	1 c. chopped walnuts
1 tsp. vanilla	

Beat butter until light; gradually add sugar, beating after each addition. Beat until light and fluffy. Beat in egg and vanilla to blend well.

Sift together flour and salt. Gradually add to creamed mixture, mixing well.

Put star plate in cookie press. Place a fourth of dough in press at a time. Press out to make 2½" strips about 1" apart on ungreased baking sheet.

Bake in hot oven (400°) 6 to 8 minutes, or until very delicately browned. Place cookies at once on cooling rack. When cool, put cookies together in pairs with Buttery Chocolate Frosting between. Dip ends of sandwiches in the frosting and then in chopped nuts. Makes 69 sandwiches.

Buttery Chocolate Frosting: Beat 3 tblsp. butter until light and fluffy. Add 1½ squares unsweetened chocolate, melted. Beat in ¾ tsp. vanilla, ⅛ tsp. salt, 3½ c. sifted confectioners sugar and enough dairy half-and-half or light cream (about 6 tblsp.) to make frosting of spreading consistency.

227

PINEAPPLE SPRITZ

Decorate them with silver or colored dragées for special occasions

1½ c. butter or regular margarine
1 c. sugar
1 egg
2 tblsp. thawed frozen pineapple juice concentrate

4½ c. sifted flour
1 tsp. baking powder
Dash of salt
Silver and colored dragées (optional)

Beat together butter and sugar until light and fluffy. Beat in egg and pineapple juice concentrate to blend thoroughly.

Sift together flour, baking powder and salt. Add to creamed mixture, blending well. (Dough will be stiff.)

Put rosette or other plate into cookie press. Put a fourth of dough in press at a time. Press out dough designs about 1″ apart onto ungreased baking sheet. Decorate with silver and colored dragées.

Bake in moderate oven (375°) 8 to 10 minutes, until firm but not brown. Remove at once from baking sheet to cooling racks. Makes 9 dozen.

SCANDINAVIAN SPRITZ

Crisp, buttery-tasting, fragile—serve with fruit punch or coffee

2¼ c. sifted flour
½ tsp. baking powder
¼ tsp. salt
1 c. butter or regular margarine

¾ c. sugar
3 egg yolks, beaten
1 tsp. almond extract, or ¼ c. grated almonds

Sift together flour, baking powder and salt.

Cream butter; add sugar gradually and beat until light. Add egg yolks and almond extract. Add dry ingredients; work with hands if dough seems crumbly.

Using a fourth of dough at a time, force it through cookie press 1 to 2″ apart onto ungreased baking sheet in desired shapes. Bake in hot oven (400°) 7 to 10 minutes, until set but not brown. Remove cookies and cool on racks. Makes about 6 dozen.

LEMON COOKIE LETTERS

Cookie initials will honor a guest, a school team or any occasion

1 c. butter or regular margarine	1 tblsp. lemon juice
½ c. sugar	1 egg
½ c. brown sugar, firmly packed	2½ c. sifted flour
1 tsp. grated lemon peel	¼ tsp. baking soda
	⅛ tsp. salt

Beat butter until light; beat in sugars until light and fluffy. Beat in lemon peel and juice and egg to blend thoroughly.

Sift together flour, baking soda and salt. Add to creamed mixture, blending well.

Fill press with a fourth of dough at a time. Press letters about 1″ apart on ungreased baking sheet. Bake in moderate oven (375°) 10 to 12 minutes, until light brown on edges. Remove from baking sheet to cooling racks. Makes about 8½ dozen.

LINDSBORG LETTER SPRITZ

A Kansas version of Swedish spritz—they always start conversation

1 c. butter or regular margarine	¾ tsp. almond extract or vanilla
¾ c. sugar	2 c. sifted flour
1 egg yolk	1 tsp. baking powder
	⅛ tsp. salt

Cream butter with sugar until light and fluffy. Beat in egg yolk and almond extract. Beat until very fluffy.

Sift together flour, baking powder and salt; gradually add to creamed mixture, beating with mixer on low speed. Beat just enough to blend. Shape dough in ball, wrap in waxed paper and chill several hours or overnight.

Let dough warm slightly before using (very cold dough does not easily leave press). Using cookie press with star-shaped disk, press out dough in long, straight strips on cold, ungreased baking sheet.

Cut each strip in 4″ pieces and shape in letters such

229

as S, R, A, B, Y, U and O (or shape as desired). You will need to add pieces of dough to form some letters. Place ½ to 1″ apart on ungreased baking sheet.

Bake in moderate oven (350°) 8 to 10 minutes, or until edges of cookies are a golden brown. Remove cookies to wire racks and cool. Makes about 6 dozen.

NOTE: To store, pack in containers in layers with waxed paper between. Freeze or keep in a cool place.

Meringue Cookies

THE OLD-FASHIONED name for these small, airy clouds of flavorful sweetness we call meringue cookies is "kisses." By whatever name, they're delicious. Serve them with red-ripe strawberries or juicy sliced peaches and cream or ice cream. Or garnish ice cream sundaes with our little puffs, Miniature Meringues. And if wondering what dessert to take to the picnic, consider non-gooey meringues as the companion to fruit to eat from the hand—grapes, sweet cherries or pears.

Meringues are versatile—you can use your ingenuity to add charm and flavor to them. For a Valentine luncheon or party, bake our Jeweled Meringues, dotted with tiny red cinnamon candies, in heart shape. Add chopped dates and nuts to meringue cookies and you have our Date/Nut Kisses, which enhance any assortment of holiday or special-occasion cookies.

Tint meringue in pastel shades with food colors before baking for color-schemed effects at showers and receptions. Sprinkle coarse red sugar over meringue rosettes and you'll have our Holiday Party Kisses. They look like lovely red and white roses on the cookie tray at open houses and inspire word bouquets to the hostess.

Meringues are easy to make. Beat the egg whites with the electric mixer at medium speed until foamy. Continue to beat while you gradually add the sugar. Then beat until mixture is stiff and glossy. Drop it from a teaspoon to form peaks or put it through a pastry tube with the rosette or one of the other tips. Space the meringues about 1″ apart on greased baking sheets or on brown paper spread on baking sheets. Bake until set; then remove from baking sheet and cool

231

on racks in a place free of drafts. Notice the time for baking listed in the recipe you are using. Some meringue cookies come from the oven white, while others take on a delicate beige around the edges.

Thrifty women to this day think meringue cookies are the best way to use leftover egg whites.

COCONUT KISSES

If you like macaroons you'll enjoy these chewy, moist cookies

¼ tsp. salt	½ tsp. vanilla or almond
½ c. egg whites (4 medium)	extract
1¾ c. sugar	2½ c. shredded coconut

Add salt to egg whites and beat until foamy. Gradually beat in sugar. Continue beating until mixture stands in stiff peaks and is glossy. Fold in vanilla and coconut.

Drop by heaping teaspoonfuls 2″ apart onto greased baking sheet. Bake in slow oven (325°) 20 minutes, or until delicately browned and set. Remove from baking sheet and cool on racks. Makes about 3 dozen.

VARIATIONS

Walnut Kisses: Substitute finely chopped walnuts for the coconut in recipe for Coconut Kisses.
Chocolate/Coconut Kisses: Follow directions for making Coconut Kisses, but stir in 1 square unsweetened chocolate, melted and cooled until lukewarm, before folding in coconut.

CORN FLAKE KISSES

An inexpensive sweet to serve with apples or grapes for dessert

¼ tsp. salt	1 tsp. grated orange peel or
2 egg whites	vanilla
1 c. sugar	3 c. corn flakes

Add salt to egg whites and beat until foamy. Gradually beat in sugar. Continue beating until mixture stands in peaks and is glossy. Fold in orange peel and corn flakes.

Drop by teaspoonfuls 2″ apart onto greased baking

sheet. Bake in moderate oven (350°) 15 to 18 minutes, or until set and delicately browned. Remove from baking sheet and cool on racks. Makes about 3 dozen.

DATE/NUT KISSES

You can depend on these easy-to-make party treats to please

3 egg whites	1 tsp. vanilla
1 c. sugar	¾ c. chopped walnuts
¼ tsp. salt	¾ c. chopped dates

Put egg whites, sugar, salt and vanilla in top of double boiler; stir to blend. Place over boiling water and beat with rotary beater until mixture stands in peaks. (To prevent meringues from being lumpy, scrape bottom and sides of pan occasionally with rubber scraper.) Stir in nuts and dates at once.

Drop heaping teaspoonfuls of mixture about 2″ apart onto lightly greased baking sheets (let one sheet wait while you bake the other).

Bake in slow oven (300°) 12 to 15 minutes, or until very lightly browned. Remove from baking sheet immediately and cool on racks. Makes about 40.

NOTE: Date/Nut Kisses offer an ideal way to use the 3 leftover egg whites when you make Chocolate Spritz (see Index).

HOLIDAY PARTY KISSES

Red and green rosettes—the small meringues are perfect for Christmas

3 egg whites	¾ c. sugar
⅛ tsp. salt	Red and green decorating
⅛ tsp. cream of tartar	sugar

Beat egg whites with electric mixer at medium speed until froth starts to appear. Add salt and cream of tartar. Continue beating for 5 minutes, or until soft peaks form. Gradually add half the white sugar, beating constantly; then beat 5 minutes. Add remaining half of white sugar in the same way. After beating for 5 minutes, continue beating until the sugar is completely dissolved.

Remove beater and place the meringue mixture in a pastry tube with rosette end. Press it out to make rosettes 1″ apart on brown paper spread over a baking sheet. (Or drop mixture from teaspoon.) Sprinkle half the meringues with red sugar, the other half with green sugar.

Bake in very slow oven (250°) 1 hour, or until meringues are firm, but not browned. (When done, meringues should lift off paper easily.) Remove from paper and cool on racks. Makes 26.

NOTE: When making meringues or kisses, or anything that uses only egg whites, slip the leftover yolks into a wire sieve immersed in a pan of simmering water. Simmer for 5 minutes. Remove and dry, then press the yolks through the sieve. Use to garnish salads, cooked buttered vegetables, creamed vegetables, soups and other dishes. One wonderful way to salvage egg yolks is to make Hard-Cooked Egg Cookies or Royal Crowns (see Index).

DEBBIE'S PEPPERMINT KISSES

A 12-year-old Hoosier girl bakes these for her mother's parties

4 egg whites	1½ c. brown sugar, firmly
¼ tsp. salt	packed
¼ tsp. cream of tartar	1 (12 oz.) pkg. semisweet
1 tsp. peppermint extract	chocolate pieces

Beat egg whites, salt, cream of tartar and peppermint extract together until soft peaks form.

Add brown sugar gradually, beating all the time. Beat until stiff peaks form.

Set aside 48 chocolate pieces and fold remainder into egg white mixture.

Drop teaspoonfuls 1″ apart onto plain paper spread on baking sheet. Top each with a chocolate piece.

Bake in slow oven (300°) 20 to 25 minutes, or until set and slightly brown. Remove from paper while slightly warm, this way: Remove paper from baking sheet, spread a wet towel on the hot baking sheet and place the paper of kisses on top. Let stand only 1 minute.

The steam will loosen the kisses and they will slip off easily on a spatula. Makes about 4 dozen.

NOTE: Instead of plain paper, you can line the baking sheet with waxed paper.

PINK KISSES

These lovely pink meringues are chewy like coconut macaroons

1 (3 oz.) pkg. strawberry flavor gelatin	⅔ c. egg whites (about 5 to 7)
1 c. sugar	¾ tsp. almond extract
¼ tsp. salt	1 (3½ oz.) can flaked coconut

Combine gelatin, sugar and salt.

Beat egg whites at high speed on electric mixer, gradually adding gelatin-sugar mixture. Add almond extract and continue beating until glossy and stiff peaks form. Stir in coconut.

Place brown paper on baking sheet. Drop mixture by heaping teaspoonfuls about 1" apart onto paper. Bake in very slow oven (275°) 35 to 40 minutes. Remove from paper and cool on racks. Makes 62.

VARIATION

Pink Raspberry Kisses: Substitute raspberry flavor gelatin for the strawberry, and bake as directed.

Jeweled Meringues for Entertaining

These cookies have an easy-do aspect: You put the meringues in the oven in the evening, turn off the heat and forget them until morning when they'll be baked. Place them in a container, cover loosely with waxed paper and set in a cool place.

If you wish, you can freeze them. Wrap each meringue in plastic wrap and place in a plastic bag, or wrap with heavy-duty aluminum foil. They'll stay in good condition up to a month. To use, take meringues from bag or remove foil and let stand at room temperature in their individual wraps for 4 to 6 hours. Then unwrap and serve.

The cinnamon candies do not melt during baking. In addition to contributing flashes of bright color to the snowy-white meringues, and a texture contrast, they provide a taste of cinnamon. They're especially appropriate for the yuletide season and for Valentine parties, when touches of red in food are so inviting. Many hostesses like to serve the meringues with ice cream.

JEWELED MERINGUES

Especially pretty for a Valentine special—if shaped like hearts

2 egg whites	½ tsp. vanilla
⅛ tsp. salt	½ c. red cinnamon candies
½ tsp. cream of tartar	(red hots)
¾ c. sugar	

Beat egg whites until foamy. Add salt and cream of tartar. Beat until stiff peaks form. Add sugar, 1 tblsp. at a time, beating after each addition. Stir in vanilla. Fold in candies.

Drop mixture by teaspoonfuls 1 to 1½″ apart onto lightly greased baking sheet. Place in moderate oven (350°); turn off heat. Leave in oven overnight. (Do not open oven door before at least 2 hours have passed.) Meringues do not brown. Remove from baking sheet and cool on racks. Makes 25.

MERINGUES À LA BELLE

Crackers give these crunchy, crisp kisses a faint salty taste

3 egg whites	1 tsp. vanilla
¾ c. sugar	⅔ c. crushed saltine crackers
½ tsp. baking powder	½ c. chopped nuts

Beat egg whites until frothy. Gradually add sugar, beating until meringue stands in soft peaks; scrape bottom and sides of bowl occasionally with rubber spatula. Blend in baking powder and vanilla. Fold in crackers and nuts.

Drop mixture by rounded teaspoonfuls 1″ apart onto two lightly greased baking sheets. Bake one sheet at a time in slow oven (300°) about 20 minutes. Remove from baking sheets at once and cool on racks. Makes about 3 dozen.

MINIATURE MERINGUES

Serve these atop or alongside fruit, chocolate or other sundaes

1 large egg white	⅓ c. very fine granulated
Few grains salt	sugar (superfine)
	¼ tsp. vanilla

With electric mixer at medium speed, beat egg white and salt until mixture stands in soft, tilted peaks. Beat in sugar, 1 tblsp. at a time; continue beating until sugar is dissolved. (Rub a little of mixture between thumb and forefinger to determine if grains of sugar are dissolved.) Stir in vanilla.

Drop by rounded teaspoonfuls 1″ apart onto well-greased baking sheet. Bake in very slow oven (250°) 45 minutes, until firm and crisp, but not browned. Remove with metal spatula to wire racks to cool. Store in container with loose-fitting lid, or freeze in tightly covered container. Use to garnish ice cream or as an accompaniment to it. Makes 20 to 24.

BIT O' NUT SWEETS

Meringue cookies that taste like candy. So little work and so good

2 egg whites	½ c. chopped dates
2 c. brown sugar, firmly	½ c. chopped candied lemon
packed	peel, or other candied fruit
2 c. sliced Brazil nuts	

Beat egg whites until stiff. Beat in brown sugar gradually. Work in nuts, dates and lemon peel. Drop by teaspoonfuls 1″ apart onto greased baking sheet.

Bake in very slow oven (250°) 30 minutes. Remove from baking sheet immediately and cool on racks. Makes about 5 dozen.

VARIATION

Double Date Sweets: Omit candied lemon peel, and increase amount of chopped dates to 1 c.

237

Cookie Confections

TO MAKE cookie confections is to cook young. They're short on work, long on good eating.

No need to get out your electric mixer to make cookie confections. Nor will you have to heat the oven for some of them. Holiday Fruit Bars, for instance. Full of good things, such as dates, candied cherries, nuts and vanilla wafers, the bars are "No-Bake." Chocolate/Peanut Crunchers also skip the oven.

Another characteristic of many cookie confections is the absence of flour from the ingredient list. Substituting for it often are foods made with flour or from grains, such as graham crackers, whole or in crumbs, vanilla wafers, rolled oats and other cereal representatives from supermarket shelves.

All cookie confections are a cross between cookies and candy; those that contain no food made with flour or cereals are more candy-like. Date/Coconut Balls and Carnival Candy Cookies are two tasty examples. It's this union of cookie and candy qualities that makes them "confections."

Look at the recipe for Basic Graham Cracker Mix and the intriguing cookies in which it appears. You press the mix into a pan, spread or pour on something luscious, bake, cool and cut it into bars. For example, an easy chocolate filling makes Fudgies distinctive; the refreshing lemon tang in Lemon-Filled Bars explains why hostesses like to serve them with fruit salads.

You'll find great variety in our cookie confections. In some—Swedish Almond Creams, for instance—you lay graham crackers over the bottom of the pan, top with filling and bake. You take a couple more steps with Graham Cracker Bars: Top the filling with a layer of graham crackers and spread on frosting. These are make-ahead specials; you refrigerate them overnight before cutting in bars and serving. You get them ready the day before your party.

The adaptability of cookie confections deserves as much credit for their astonishing success as the ease with which you fix them. They're the answer to so many occasions. For snacking they have few equals and Potpourri Cookies are outstanding in this category. To make them you melt together chocolate pieces, marshmallows and butter and pour the mixture over crisp, oven-toasted rice cereal, salted peanuts and broken pretzel sticks. Your friends will enjoy nibbling on them while watching television with you.

Today's youngsters like quick results and turn to confection-making—easier to make than candy, and the results are foolproof. Join the ranks of up-to-date cooks and build up your repertoire of cookie confections from the recipes that follow.

BASIC GRAHAM CRACKER MIX

This is the starting point for any of the four recipes that follow

2¼ c. graham cracker crumbs   ⅓ c. sugar
½ c. melted butter

Combine all ingredients, and use as directed.

COCONUT CARAMEL BARS

With the basic mix on hand, you can have cookies in 20 minutes

Basic Graham Cracker Mix   ⅓ c. light or heavy cream
28 caramels (½ lb.)   1 c. flaked coconut

Press two-thirds Basic Graham Cracker Mix over bottom of 13 × 9 × 2″ pan.

Melt caramels with cream over hot water. Stir in coconut. Spoon here and there over crumbs in pan. Spread carefully to cover crumbs. Sprinkle with remaining third of graham cracker mix; press down firmly.

Bake in moderate oven (375°) 15 minutes. Cool partially in pan set on rack; then cut in 3 × 1″ bars, or any desired size. Makes 39.

VARIATION

Nut Caramel Bars: Substitute 1 c. chopped nuts for coconut in Coconut Caramel Bars.

FUDGIES

*The easy-to-make fudge filling makes these
chocolate-delicious*

Basic Graham Cracker Mix
**1 (15 oz.) can sweetened
condensed milk (not
evaporated)**

**1 (6 oz.) pkg. semisweet
chocolate pieces**
½ c. chopped nuts

Press two-thirds Graham Cracker Mix over bottom of 13 × 9 × 2″ pan.

Heat sweetened condensed milk in saucepan. Blend in chocolate pieces and stir until mixture thickens. Stir in nuts. Pour evenly over mix in pan. Sprinkle with remaining third of mix. Press down firmly.

Bake in moderate oven (375°) 15 minutes. Cool slightly in pan set on rack; then cut in 2″ squares, or desired size. Makes 2 dozen.

LEMON-FILLED BARS

*Serve these tangy lemon bars with dessert fruit cups
and salads*

Basic Graham Cracker Mix
2 eggs, slightly beaten
½ c. water
1 c. sugar

3 tblsp. lemon juice
2 tsp. grated lemon peel
2 tblsp. butter

Press all but 1 c. Graham Cracker Mix over bottom of 13 × 9 × 2″ pan.

Combine remaining ingredients, except mix, in saucepan. Cook over low heat, stirring constantly, until very thick and clear. Pour over basic mix in pan. Sprinkle on remaining mix; press down.

Bake in moderate oven (375°) 20 minutes. Partially

cool in pan set on rack; then cut in 3 × 1″ bars, or desired size. Makes 39.

MATRIMONIAL GRAHAM BARS

You'll like the happy marriage of date and graham cracker flavors

Basic Graham Cracker Mix	**⅔ c. water**
1½ c. halved pitted dates	**¼ c. sugar**

Press two-thirds of Basic Graham Cracker Mix over bottom of 13 × 9 × 2″ pan.

Cook dates, water and sugar together until thick and smooth, stirring frequently. Spoon here and there over crumbs in pan; spread carefully to cover. Sprinkle remaining third of basic mix over date filling; press down firmly.

Bake in moderate oven (375°) 15 minutes. Partially cool in pan set on rack; then cut in 3 × 1″ bars, or desired size. Makes 39.

CANDY BAR COOKIES

Here's the top favorite new recipe from an experienced cookie baker

½ c. butter or regular margarine	**1 (6 oz.) pkg. butterscotch pieces**
1 c. fine graham cracker crumbs	**1 c. flaked coconut**
	1 c. broken nuts
1 (6 oz.) pkg. semisweet chocolate pieces	**1 (15 oz.) can sweetened condensed milk (not evaporated)**

Melt butter in 13 × 9 × 2″ pan. Sprinkle graham cracker crumbs evenly over bottom of pan. Then sprinkle on chocolate pieces. Next sprinkle on butterscotch pieces, then the coconut. Sprinkle on nuts. Dribble sweetened condensed milk over top.

Bake in moderate oven (375°) about 25 minutes. Set pan on rack and cut in 3 × 1″ bars when partly cooled, but while still warm. Remove from pan when cool. Makes 39 bars.

CHOCOLATE/COCONUT BARS

Many popular cookies contain graham crackers—here's a good one

2 c. crushed graham crackers
¼ c. sugar
½ c. melted butter or regular margarine

1 (15 oz.) can sweetened condensed milk (not evaporated)
2 c. flaked coconut
1 (6 oz.) pkg. semisweet chocolate pieces

Combine graham crackers, sugar and butter. Mix well and pat into ungreased 13 × 9 × 2″ pan. Bake in moderate oven (350°) 15 minutes.

Combine sweetened milk and coconut. Spread on baked layer. Return to oven and bake 15 minutes longer.

Melt chocolate pieces and spread over baked layers. Cool in pan set on rack, then cut in 2½ × 1¼″ bars. Makes about 3 dozen.

DATE MALLOW CHEWS

Three sure-fire goodies in these bars: dates, nuts and marshmallows

½ c. butter
1 (10½ oz.) pkg. miniature marshmallows
1¼ c. cut-up dates
2 c. graham cracker crumbs

½ c. chopped nuts
1 square semisweet chocolate
2 tblsp. milk
1 tblsp. butter
1 c. confectioners sugar

Melt ½ c. butter in 3-qt. saucepan. Add marshmallows and cook over low heat until melted, stirring constantly. Stir in dates, graham cracker crumbs and nuts. Press into buttered 9″ square pan.

Combine chocolate, milk and 1 tblsp. butter in small saucepan over low heat; stir constantly until chocolate and butter are melted. Stir in confectioners sugar. Spread over mixture in pan. Let stand in pan until set, then cut in 1½″ squares. Makes 3 dozen.

DATE/MARSHMALLOW BALLS

Skip-the-oven cookies, sweet and rich—a real confection treat

1½ c. chopped dates	3½ c. graham cracker
1¼ c. chopped nuts	crumbs
2 c. miniature marshmallows	1 (6½ oz.) pkg. fluffy white frosting mix

Combine dates, 1 c. nuts, marshmallows and 2½ c. graham cracker crumbs. Mix thoroughly.

Prepare frosting mix as directed on package. Add to the date mixture and mix until completely moistened.

Combine remaining ¼ c. nuts and 1 c. graham cracker crumbs in small bowl.

Form date mixture into 1½" balls. Roll in graham cracker crumbs and nuts. Store in covered container at least 12 hours to mellow. Makes 3 dozen.

FRUITCAKE SQUARES

This holiday bar cookie was rated "yummy" by taste-testers

6 tblsp. butter or regular margarine	1 c. dates
1½ c. graham cracker crumbs	Flour
1 c. shredded coconut	1 c. coarsely chopped walnuts or pecans
2 c. cut-up mixed candied fruit	1 (15 oz.) can sweetened condensed milk (not evaporated)

Melt butter in 15½ × 10½ × 1" jelly roll pan. Sprinkle on crumbs; tap sides of pan to distribute crumbs evenly. Sprinkle on coconut. Distribute candied fruit as evenly as possible over coconut.

Cut dates into a small amount of flour so they won't stick together. Distribute dates over candied fruit. Sprinkle on nuts. Press mixture lightly with hands to level it in pan. Pour sweetened condensed milk evenly over top.

Bake in moderate oven (350°) 25 to 30 minutes. Cool completely in pan on rack before cutting in 1½" squares. Remove from pan. Makes 70.

GRAHAM CRACKER BARS

Simple start with graham crackers ends up with elegant cookies

30 graham crackers	1 c. flaked coconut
1 c. brown sugar, firmly packed	1 c. graham cracker crumbs
½ c. butter or regular margarine	2 c. confectioners sugar
	5 tblsp. melted butter
½ c. milk	3 tblsp. dairy half-and-half
	½ tsp. vanilla

Line bottom of greased 13 × 9 × 2" pan with 15 graham crackers.

In saucepan, combine brown sugar, ½ c. butter, milk, coconut and graham cracker crumbs. Bring to a boil and cook, stirring constantly, until thick, about 10 minutes. (Mixture burns easily.) Spread evenly on top of whole graham crackers in pan. Top with remaining 15 graham crackers to cover.

Beat together confectioners sugar, melted butter, dairy half-and-half and vanilla until mixture is smooth. Spread on top of graham crackers in pan.

Cover with waxed paper and let stand in refrigerator overnight before cutting in 3 × 1" bars. Makes 39.

JIFFY CANDY COOKIES

Children like to make these cookies that taste like candy bars

18 graham crackers, broken into small pieces	1 (6 oz.) pkg. semisweet chocolate pieces
1 (15 oz.) can sweetened condensed milk (not evaporated)	½ c. chopped pecans
	½ c. flaked coconut

Combine all ingredients. Pour into greased 8" square pan. Bake in moderate oven (350°) 35 minutes.

While warm, cut in 1½" squares and place on cooling rack. Makes about 25.

NOTE: These cookies will firm when cool.

MAGIC COOKIE BARS

Cut bars to fit appetites—these cookies are almost like candy

½ c. regular margarine, melted
1½ c. graham cracker crumbs
1 c. chopped nuts
1 (6 oz.) pkg. semisweet chocolate pieces
1 (6 oz.) pkg. butterscotch pieces
1½ c. flaked coconut
1 (15 oz.) can sweetened condensed milk (not evaporated)

Cover bottom of 13 × 9 × 2″ pan with melted margarine. Sprinkle evenly with graham cracker crumbs.

Sprinkle nuts, then chocolate pieces, butterscotch morsels and coconut over crumbs. Pour sweetened condensed milk over coconut.

Bake in moderate oven (350°) 25 to 30 minutes, until lightly browned. Cool in pan set on rack 15 minutes, then cut in 3 × 1½″ bars. Lift from pan with spatula and complete cooling on rack. Makes 2 dozen.

PRALINE COOKIES

"Child pleasers" . . . these candy-like cookies are made in minutes

24 graham crackers
1 c. light brown sugar, firmly packed
¼ c. butter or regular margarine
1 c. chopped pecans

Line the bottom of a greased 15 × 10½ × 1″ jelly roll pan with graham crackers.

Place brown sugar and butter in small saucepan; bring to a rolling boil over medium heat and cook 1½ minutes. Remove from heat. When mixture has stopped bubbling, stir in nuts. Spoon it on and spread over graham crackers.

Bake in moderate oven (350°) 10 minutes. Cool in pan on rack, then cut in 2 × 1″ bars. Makes about 48.

SEVEN-LAYER BARS

Just layer ingredients in pan—easy and delicious

¼ c. butter or regular margarine
1 c. graham cracker crumbs
1 c. shredded coconut
1 (6 oz.) pkg. semisweet chocolate pieces
1 (6 oz.) pkg. butterscotch pieces
1 (15 oz.) can sweetened condensed milk (not evaporated)
1 c. chopped nuts

Melt butter in 13 × 9 × 2″ pan. Sprinkle crumbs evenly over butter; tap sides of pan to distribute crumbs evenly. Sprinkle on coconut, chocolate and butterscotch pieces.

Pour sweetened condensed milk (not evaporated) evenly over top. Sprinkle on nuts and press lightly into pan.

Bake in moderate oven (350°) 30 minutes. Cool in pan on rack, then cut in 2 × 1″ bars. Makes about 40.

SWEDISH ALMOND CREAMS

Creamy almond candy on crisp graham crackers— wonderful taste

15 graham crackers	½ c. butter
¼ c. light or heavy cream	¾ c. sliced almonds
¾ c. sugar	¼ tsp. almond extract
¼ c. light corn syrup	

Arrange graham crackers to cover bottom of heavily buttered 13 × 9 × 2″ pan.

Combine cream, sugar, corn syrup and butter in small saucepan; boil 3 minutes. Stir in almond slices and extract. Pour over crackers in pan.

Bake in moderate oven (375°) 10 minutes, or until lightly browned. Partially cool on rack, then cut in 3 × 1″ bars. Makes 39.

THREE-LAYER CHOCOLATE SQUARES

The cookies to make when your oven is busy—they taste wonderful

½ c. butter or regular margarine	¼ c. butter or regular margarine
¼ c. cocoa	1 tsp. cornstarch
½ c. sifted confectioners sugar	2 tsp. sugar
1 egg, slightly beaten	3 tblsp. light cream or evaporated milk
2 tsp. vanilla	1 tsp. vanilla
3 c. graham cracker crumbs	2 c. sifted confectioners sugar
½ c. chopped pecans	1 (9¾ oz.) sweet chocolate candy bar

Melt ½ c. butter. Add the following ingredients, one at a time, stirring after each addition: cocoa, ½ c.

confectioners sugar, egg, 2 tsp. vanilla, cracker crumbs and pecans. Stir until mixture is well blended, then press it into lightly greased 13 × 9 × 2″ pan.

Melt ¼ c. butter. Combine cornstarch and 2 tsp. sugar; add to butter and blend thoroughly. Add cream; cook, stirring constantly, until thick and smooth. Cool; add 1 tsp. vanilla and 2 c. confectioners sugar. Blend well and spread over first layer. (Drop by teaspoonfuls and spread carefully—this is a stiff mixture.)

Melt chocolate bar over hot water; spread it over the cream filling. Cool in pan on rack, and cut in 1″ squares before chocolate sets completely. Makes about 9 dozen.

HALLOWEEN TREATS

Let your youngsters make these cookies for trick or treat visitors

2 c. sugar
⅔ c. milk
6 tblsp. peanut butter

1 tsp. vanilla
1¼ c. crumbled soda crackers
(40 squares)

Heat together sugar and milk in 2-qt. saucepan; boil 3 minutes. Remove from heat; add peanut butter. Then add vanilla and crackers. Mix well. Cool, then form into 1″ balls. Makes 34.

COCONUT/CORN FLAKE CRISPIES

Chocolate topknots help to make party cookies out of the cereal base

3 egg whites
¼ tsp. salt
1 c. sugar
1 tsp. vanilla

2 c. crushed corn flakes
1⅓ c. flaked coconut
½ c. chopped pecans

Beat egg whites until frothy; add salt and gradually beat in sugar. Continue beating until very stiff and glossy. Stir in vanilla, corn flakes, coconut and pecans.

Drop heaping teaspoonfuls of dough 2″ apart onto ungreased brown wrapping paper covering baking sheet.

Bake in slow oven (325°) 15 to 18 minutes, until set and delicately browned. Remove from oven and lift off paper holding cookies; lay wet towel on hot baking sheet. Place paper of cookies on towel; let stand 1 minute (steam will loosen cookies). Lift cookies with spatula to cooling rack. Makes 40.

VARIATIONS

Chocolate/Coconut Crispies: Make like Coconut/Corn Flake Crispies, but stir 2 squares unsweetened chocolate, melted and slightly cooled, into batter. Bake as directed.

Chocolate-Topped Crispies: Melt together over hot water 1 (6 oz.) pkg. milk chocolate pieces, 2 tblsp. shortening and 2 tblsp. shaved paraffin. Hold the baked cookies, one at a time, in the hand and dip tops in mixture.

PEANUT CHEWS

Peanut butter fans will like these crunchy cookies—fine for snacks

9 c. corn flakes
1½ c. sugar
¼ tsp. salt
¾ c. light corn syrup

¼ c. butter or regular
   margarine
¾ c. water
2 tsp. vanilla
½ c. crunchy peanut buttter

Place corn flakes in a bowl.

Combine sugar, salt, corn syrup, butter and water in saucepan. Bring to a boil and reduce heat. Continue to cook to the hard ball stage (250°), using care not to overcook.

Remove from heat and stir in vanilla and peanut butter. Pour mixture over corn flakes.

Toss with a fork to cover corn flakes with syrup completely. Work quickly.

Drop in clusters onto waxed paper. Makes about 40.

PEANUT BUTTER DROPS

A quick confection; nutritious too—children like these

1 c. sugar
1 c. light corn syrup
½ c. peanut butter

4 c. ready-to-eat high protein
   cereal
1 c. thin pretzel sticks, broken
   in 1" lengths

Mix sugar and syrup in large saucepan. Bring to a boil over medium heat; cook about 30 seconds. Remove from heat and add peanut butter. Stir until smooth. Stir in cereal and pretzel sticks.

Drop by tablespoonfuls onto waxed paper. Makes about 4½ dozen.

DATE/COCONUT BALLS

Snowy coconut decorates these baked-in-a-skillet date cookies

2 tblsp. butter	½ c. chopped nuts
1 c. sugar	2 c. oven-toasted rice cereal
2 eggs, beaten	1 c. flaked coconut
1 c. chopped dates	

Put butter in heavy skillet with sugar, eggs and dates. Cook over medium-low heat, stirring constantly, until mixture leaves sides of skillet. (Mixture burns easily.)

Remove from heat; add nuts and cereal. Shape in 1″ balls with hands; roll in coconut. Store in tightly covered container (cookies are good keepers). Makes 38.

COCONUT CRISPS

Cookie bars, luscious with dates, nuts and snowy coconut topknots

6 c. oven-toasted rice cereal	¼ tsp. salt
1 c. chopped walnuts	1 c. chopped dates
¾ c. butter or regular margarine	1 tblsp. vanilla
	2 tblsp. lemon juice
1¼ c. sugar	1 (3½ oz.) can flaked coconut
2 tblsp. milk	

Combine cereal and walnuts in greased 13 × 9 × 2″ pan.

Combine butter, sugar, milk, salt and dates in saucepan. Cook to the soft ball stage (240°); stir occasionally. Remove from heat and add vanilla and lemon juice.

Pour hot syrup over cereal/nut mixture; stir lightly

to coat cereal. Spread mixture evenly in pan. Sprinkle coconut over top and press mixture firmly into pan. Let set 4 hours or longer.

When firm, cut in 3 × 1¼" bars. Makes 2½ dozen.

POTPOURRI COOKIES

Perfect snack to munch on while watching television or visiting

1 (6 oz.) pkg. semisweet
  chocolate pieces
½ c. butter or regular
  margarine
1 (10 oz.) pkg. marshmallows

4 c. oven-toasted rice cereal
2 c. salted Spanish peanuts
2 c. raisins
2 c. broken pretzel sticks
  (about ½" lengths)

Melt chocolate pieces, butter and marshmallows in top of double boiler over simmering water. Stir to blend.

Combine rice cereal, peanuts, raisins and broken pretzel sticks in a greased large bowl. Pour melted chocolate mixture over and stir to coat all pieces. With two teaspoons form into clusters; drop onto greased baking sheets. Cool until set. Makes 5 dozen.

PUFFED-UP RICE FINGERS

Candied fruits add color and flavor to these crunchy cereal bars

5 c. puffed rice
¼ c. diced mixed candied
  fruit
½ c. coarsely chopped nuts
½ c. sugar

¾ c. dark corn syrup
⅓ c. water
½ tsp. salt
1 tblsp. butter or regular
  margarine

Spread puffed rice in shallow pan and heat in moderate oven (350°) about 10 minutes. Then turn into a greased large bowl. Stir in fruit and nuts.

In medium-size saucepan stir together sugar, corn syrup, water and salt. Cook over medium heat to soft ball stage (236° on candy thermometer). Stir in butter.

Stir hot syrup mixture into puffed rice until evenly coated. Using greased hands, pack mixture firmly into greased 13 × 9 × 2" pan. Cut in 3 × 1" bars. Makes 39.

CHOCOLATE OATSIES

Shortcut to hospitality—make these fast-fix,
candy-good cookies

2 c. sugar
½ c. milk
¼ c. butter or regular
  margarine
⅓ c. cocoa

3 c. quick-cooking rolled oats
½ c. flaked or shredded
  coconut
½ c. peanut butter
1 tsp. vanilla

Combine sugar, milk, butter and cocoa in saucepan.
Boil 1 minute. Remove from heat.

Mix in rest of ingredients.

Drop by teaspoonfuls onto waxed paper. Makes 30.

FARMHOUSE CHOCOLATE CRUNCH

These chewy cookies containing black walnuts are
cousins of candy

⅔ c. butter or regular
  margarine
½ c. light corn syrup
1 tsp. salt
3 tsp. vanilla

1 c. brown sugar, firmly
  packed
4 c. quick-cooking rolled oats
2 (6 oz.) pkgs. semisweet
  chocolate pieces
½ c. chopped black walnuts

Melt butter in a large saucepan. Add syrup, salt, vanilla, brown sugar and rolled oats; mix well. Press into a well-greased 15½ × 10½ × 1″ jelly roll pan.

Bake in hot oven (425°) 12 minutes. During the last 2 minutes of baking, sprinkle on chocolate pieces. When they melt, remove pan from oven and spread chocolate evenly to cover top. Sprinkle with chopped nuts. Cut in 1½″ squares while still warm. Cool in pan on rack. Recut when cool. Makes about 70.

PEANUT CANDY-BAR COOKIES

Chewy, toffee-like bars topped with tasty
peanut-chocolate

251

2 c. quick-cooking rolled oats	¼ tsp. baking soda
1 c. graham cracker crumbs	1 tsp. vanilla
¾ c. brown sugar, firmly packed	½ c. salted peanuts
½ c. melted butter	1 (6 oz.) pkg. semisweet chocolate pieces
½ c. dark corn syrup	½ c. peanut butter

Combine all ingredients, except chocolate pieces and peanut butter. Spread or press into greased 13 × 9 × 2" pan. Bake in moderate oven (375°) 15 to 20 minutes, or until light golden brown.

Meanwhile, melt together chocolate pieces and peanut butter over hot water. Spread over baked cookie while warm. Cool slightly in pan set on rack, then cut in 3 × 1" bars. Makes 39.

CEREAL SLICES

These crunchy confection cookies really rate high with youngsters

½ c. butter	4 c. assorted bite-size shredded cereal biscuits (wheat, rice and corn)
1 (10½ oz.) pkg. miniature marshmallows	
2 c. salted peanuts	

Melt butter in 3-qt. saucepan. Add marshmallows and cook over low heat, stirring constantly, until melted. Stir in nuts and cereals (oat puffs are good included in this combination).

Divide mixture in half on sheets of foil or waxed paper. Shape each half in a 15" long roll, using fork and side of foil or waxed paper to aid in the shaping. Wrap rolls tightly and refrigerate until firm. To serve, cut in ½" slices. Makes 5 dozen.

CHOCOLATE/PEANUT CRUNCHERS

Chocolate-marshmallow mix covers salted peanuts and crisp cereals

¼ c. butter	1½ c. salted peanuts
1 (6 oz.) pkg. semisweet chocolate pieces	2 c. assorted bite-size shredded cereal biscuits (wheat, corn and rice)
1 (10½ oz.) pkg. miniature marshmallows	

Melt butter in 3-qt. saucepan over low heat. Add chocolate pieces and marshmallows; cook and stir constantly until melted, smooth and syrupy. Stir in peanuts and cereal (oat puffs are good included in assortment).

Spread in buttered 9" square pan, using 2 forks to spread evenly. When firm, cut in 1½" squares. Makes 3 dozen.

SPICY CRUNCH

If you want a snack guests rave about, here's the recipe to use

3 c. puffed oat cereal
2 c. shredded rice, bite-size biscuits
2 c. shredded corn, bite-size biscuits
2 c. shredded wheat, bite-size biscuits
1 c. raisins

1 c. pecan halves
½ c. butter or regular margarine
1⅓ c. brown sugar, firmly packed
¼ c. light corn syrup
2 tsp. ground cinnamon
½ tsp. salt

Butter a large bowl and toss cereals, raisins and pecans in it to mix.

Combine butter, brown sugar, corn syrup, cinnamon and salt in a heavy skillet. Stir constantly over medium heat until boiling. Boil 3 minutes.

Pour the hot syrup over cereal mixture in the bowl; stir to coat thoroughly.

Spread on two buttered baking sheets. Cool. When firm, break into pieces. Makes about 2½ quarts.

APRICOT/COCONUT BALLS

The refreshing tart-sweet flavor of apricots pleases everyone

1 c. apricot preserves
2 tblsp. butter
2½ c. vanilla wafer crumbs
2 c. flaked coconut

¼ c. currants (optional)
½ tsp. rum flavoring (optional)

Combine apricot preserves and butter in saucepan. Bring to a boil. Stir in vanilla wafer crumbs, ½ c. coconut, currants and rum flavoring.

Place remaining 1½ c. coconut in shallow dish. Drop teaspoonfuls of apricot mixture into coconut and roll to coat thoroughly. Shape into balls. Place on waxed paper. Makes 3½ dozen.

HOLIDAY FRUIT BARS

Ideal no-bake fruit cookies for Christmas celebrations and gifts

½ c. butter
1 (10½ oz.) pkg. miniature marshmallows
¾ c. chopped nuts

1 c. candied cherries, cut in halves
1 c. dates, cut in halves
1½ c. vanilla wafer crumbs

Melt butter in 3-qt. saucepan. Add marshmallows; cook over low heat, stirring constantly, until melted. Add remaining ingredients; mix thoroughly.

Spread mixture in buttered 9″ square pan, using fork to spread evenly. When ready to serve, cut in 1½″ squares. Makes 3 dozen.

VARIATION

Cereal Christmas Fruit Bars: Substitute 1½ c. oven-toasted rice cereal for vanilla wafer crumbs.

ALMOND BARS

These skip-the-oven cookies are so easy to make and so good to eat

¾ c. blanched almonds
¼ c. candied cherries
¼ c. toasted flaked or shredded coconut
1 tblsp. butter or regular margarine

1½ tblsp. honey
¼ tsp. almond extract
1 (4 oz.) pkg. sweet cooking chocolate

Grind almonds and cherries together. Add coconut.

Cream butter, honey and almond extract together; add ground mixture; mix well. Shape into large rectangle on waxed paper.

Melt chocolate; spread over top; chill until firm. Cut in 2½ × 2″ bars. Makes 18 to 20.

ALMOND BONBONS

This new almond Christmas special adds distinction to the cookie tray

3 c. finely chopped blanched
   almonds (1 lb.)
3 egg whites, stiffly beaten
1 tblsp. heavy cream
1 tsp. almond extract
2 c. sifted confectioners sugar
1 tsp. water

1 tblsp. lemon-flavored iced
   tea mix
Chocolate pieces or nuts
   (for centers)
Sugar or tiny multicolored
   decorating candies

Combine almonds, stiffly beaten egg whites, heavy cream, almond extract, confectioners sugar, water and tea mix. Stir until ingredients are well blended.

Butter hands lightly (mixture is somewhat sticky) and form in 1″ balls around chocolate pieces or nuts (one in each ball). Roll half of balls in sugar, the other half in colored candies. Makes about 5 dozen.

CARNIVAL CANDY COOKIES

Colored marshmallows give a festive look to these chocolate drops

1 (6 oz.) pkg. semisweet
   chocolate pieces
¼ c. peanut butter
2 tblsp. light corn syrup

2 tblsp. shortening
1 c. salted peanuts
1 c. colored miniature
   marshmallows

Melt together in saucepan over low heat chocolate pieces, peanut butter, corn syrup and shortening. Stir until smooth. Cool slightly, then stir in peanuts and marshmallows; avoid overstirring.

Drop by teaspoonfuls onto waxed paper. Let set until firm. Makes about 2 dozen.

VARIATION

Peanut/Cereal Candy Cookies: Use ½ c. salted peanuts and ½ c. oat puffs (cereal circles) in Carnival Candy Cookies instead of 1 c. salted peanuts.

Casserole Cookies

A Missouri school teacher contributed this recipe. She says she makes the confection cookies every yuletide season. The teachers take turns providing candy daily for their lounge the week before the holiday vacation. Casserole Cookies disappear quickly, which is adequate proof of their popularity.

You bake the cookie mixture in a casserole. A crust forms on top, but it disappears when you stir the hot cookies with a spoon. When mixture cools, you shape the cookies in 1″ balls and roll them in granulated sugar. The white sugar granules glisten on the dark cookie balls.

CASSEROLE COOKIES

A cookie-candy hybrid, baked in a casserole—inviting and rewarding

2 eggs	1 c. flaked coconut
1 c. sugar	1 tsp. vanilla
1 c. chopped walnuts	¼ tsp. almond extract
1 c. chopped dates	¼ c. sugar (for coating)

Beat eggs well; gradually add 1 c. sugar, beating until mixture is light and fluffy. Stir in nuts, dates, coconut, vanilla and almond extract. Turn into ungreased 2-qt. casserole.

Bake in moderate oven (350°) 30 minutes. Remove from oven and while still hot, stir well with wooden spoon. Let cool, then form into 1″ balls. Roll in ¼ c. sugar. Makes about 34.

COCONUT/DATE MARBLES

These attractive cookie marbles taste like date bars—party fare

1 egg	1 c. finely cut dates (8 oz.)
½ c. sugar	1 (7 oz.) pkg. cookie coconut
1 tsp. vanilla	½ c. finely chopped pecans
⅛ tsp. salt	4 drops red food color

Beat egg until foamy; gradually beat in sugar, vanilla and salt. Beat until fluffy. Stir in dates, ¾ c. coconut and pecans. Spread in greased 9" square pan.

Bake in slow oven (300°) about 30 minutes, or until golden. (Test by pressing lightly with fingertip. If cookie springs back, it is done.)

Set pan on rack to cool. Cut in 1½ × 1" bars. Roll each bar in hands to make a 1" ball. Tint half of the remaining coconut pink with red food color. Roll half the cookie balls in pink coconut, the other half in white. Makes about 4 dozen.

CHOCOLATE/PEANUT CLUSTERS

They'll remind you of candy, but you bake them like cookies—good

⅓ c. sifted flour	2 squares unsweetened
⅔ c. sugar	chocolate, melted
½ tsp. salt	2 tsp. light corn syrup
⅓ c. shortening	1 tsp. vanilla
1 egg	2½ c. unsalted peanuts

Sift flour, sugar and salt into bowl. Add shortening, egg, chocolate, corn syrup and vanilla; mix well. Add nuts.

Drop teaspoonfuls of dough 1" apart, onto greased baking sheet. Bake in moderate oven (350°) 8 minutes.

Cool cookies before removing to wire rack—they're very tender when hot! Makes 3 dozen.

VARIATIONS

Chocolate/Raisin Clusters: Use only 1½ c. peanuts and add 1 c. raisins.
Chocolate/Date Clusters: Use 1½ c. chopped walnuts instead of peanuts and 1 c. chopped dates.

DATE/NUT MACAROONS

They're moist, chewy, tasty and so easy to make. Try them soon

⅔ c. sweetened condensed
   milk (not evaporated)
1 c. flaked or shredded
   coconut

1 c. chopped nuts
1 c. chopped, pitted dates
1 tsp. vanilla

Mix together all ingredients. Shape into balls and place about 1″ apart on greased baking sheet.

Bake in moderate oven (350°) 10 to 12 minutes, until golden brown. Remove cookies and cool on racks. Makes about 2 dozen.

ROCKY ROAD FUDGE BARS

They're dual purpose—serve these treats as cookies or candy

½ c. light corn syrup
½ c. sugar
1 (6 oz.) pkg. semisweet
   chocolate pieces

¼ c. peanut butter
½ c. chopped nuts
2 c. miniature marshmallows

Combine corn syrup and sugar in saucepan; bring to a boil and boil 2 minutes. Stir in chocolate pieces and peanut butter; cool slightly. Add nuts and marshmallows, stirring just enough to distribute.

Spread evenly in buttered 9″ square pan. To serve, cut in 1½″ squares. Makes 3 dozen.

VARIATIONS

Rocky Road Fudge Slices: If desired, shape Rocky Road Fudge Bars mixture into two 10″ rolls. (Mixture is somewhat soft and is a little difficult to handle, but slices are very attractive.) Wrap rolls tightly in aluminum foil or waxed paper and refrigerate until firm. To serve, cut in ¼ to ½″ slices.

Cereal Rocky Road Fudge Slices: Make like Rocky Road Fudge Slices, but substitute 2 c. oat puffs (cereal circles) for the marshmallows.

SOUTHERN CANDY-COOKIES

Luscious butterscotch mix coats raisins, nuts and marshmallows

½ c. light corn syrup
½ c. brown sugar, firmly
  packed
½ c. peanut butter

1 (6 oz.) pkg. butterscotch
  pieces
2 c. light raisins (seeded)
½ c. chopped pecans
2 c. miniature marshmallows

Bring to a boil corn syrup and brown sugar; boil 2 minutes. Remove from heat; blend in peanut butter and butterscotch pieces. Stir in raisins, pecans and marshmallows, using care not to overmix.

Drop by rounded teaspoonfuls onto waxed paper. To hasten setting, place in refrigerator. Makes about 3½ dozen.

COCONUT MARZIPANS

Fruit flavor gelatin contributes color and zip to these cookies

1 (3 oz.) pkg. fruit flavor
  gelatin
2⅓ c. flaked or cookie
  coconut (7 to 8 oz. pkg.)
½ c. sweetened condensed
  milk (not evaporated)

¼ c. heavy or light cream
¼ c. sugar
¼ c. butter
1 c. confectioners sugar

Set aside 1 tblsp. gelatin to use in glaze. Combine coconut, sweetened condensed milk and remaining gelatin (strawberry, cherry, lemon, lime or orange). Mix thoroughly.

Form mixture into cookies in shape of berries or fruit to correspond to flavor of gelatin; let stand a few minutes.

Meanwhile, make glaze: Combine cream, sugar, butter and reserved gelatin in small saucepan. Boil 2 minutes; stir in confectioners sugar. Drop shaped cookies, one at a time, into glaze to coat. Lift out of glaze with fork, allowing excess to drip off. Place on waxed paper. (If necessary, thin glaze with a little milk while coating cookies.) Makes about 2½ dozen.

Pie-Bar Dessert Cookies

OUR PIE-BAR dessert cookies, inspired by popular pies, prove there is something new under the sun—something mighty good to eat. The idea for this cross between cookies and pies came about through concern about calories.

Many Americans in this diet-conscious age try to skip dessert yet long for at least a few bites of delicious sweetness to top off the meal or to enjoy with coffee at evening social affairs. Our food editors in their travels around the country asked: "What is your favorite dessert? What would you choose if you were not counting calories?" Men promptly replied: Pies. And a surprising number of women gave the same answer.

With this in mind when we were working on this cookie book, some creative Test Kitchen work evolved our recipes for small cookies that taste like pies. We call them pie-bar dessert cookies. Taste-testers rated them as tasty as the pies from which they descend. We knew from that moment we had the right rich, satisfying miniature desserts.

The cookies, with the exception of Pumpkin Pie Squares, are finger food. It's easier to eat the spicy, pumpkin cookies with a fork. But there's nothing wrong about serving any of these pie-bar cookies on a small plate with a fork and coffee alongside.

Neither is there any reason why you can't cut these cookies a little larger, although if much bigger, you defeat the major reason for them—cookies small enough to please weight-watchers and permit them to have dessert without feeling guilty.

Which pie-bars taste best? Is it Sour Cream/Raisin, Golden Lemon, Brownie or Chess? Or are Pecan and

French Apple Pie-Bars even better? Try all 16 of these exciting cookies and the variations before you decide.

CRAN/APPLE PIE-BARS

Sugar glistens on lattice top over cranberry-orange filling

2 c. sifted flour
½ tsp. salt
⅔ c. shortening
2 tblsp. butter or regular margarine
5 to 6 tblsp. water

1 (10 oz.) pkg. frozen cranberry-orange relish, thawed
1 c. finely chopped apple
⅓ c. sugar
Sugar (for top)

To make crust, combine flour and salt; cut in shortening and butter until particles are the size of small peas. Add water gradually, while stirring with a fork, until mixture is moist enough to hold together. Reserve ⅓ of dough to use for topping.

Roll remaining ⅔ of dough on floured surface to make a 14 × 9″ rectangle. Place on ungreased baking sheet.

To make filling, combine cranberry-orange relish, apple and ⅓ c. sugar. Spread over pastry, leaving a ½″ margin on all sides.

Roll out remaining ⅓ of dough. Cut in strips about ½″ wide, half of them 14″ long, the other half 9″ long. Crisscross over filling to make a lattice top; fold lower crust up over. Sprinkle with sugar.

Bake in hot oven (400°) 30 to 35 minutes, or until pastry is golden brown. Cool in pan on rack. Cut in 2 × 1½″ bars. Makes about 3½ dozen.

NOTE: Cookies lose some of their crispness after standing 24 hours. To serve them the second or third day after baking, heat them in a very slow oven (250°) about 10 minutes to restore crispness.

FRENCH APPLE PIE-BARS

Cookies never were better! That's the verdict of men taste-testers

2 c. sifted flour	½ c. sugar
1 tsp. salt	½ c. brown sugar, firmly
¾ c. shortening	packed
4 to 5 tblsp. water	¼ c. flour
4 c. thinly sliced peeled	¼ tsp. ground cinnamon
apples	

To make crust, combine 2 c. flour with salt; cut in shortening until particles are size of small peas. Set aside 1 c. mixture. To the remainder, add water gradually, while stirring with a fork, just until dough is moist enough to hold together. Form into a square. Roll on floured board to a 14 × 10″ rectangle. Fit into ungreased 13 × 9 × 2″ pan.

Combine apples with white sugar. Place in pastry-lined pan.

Combine reserved crumb mixture with brown sugar, ¼ c. flour and cinnamon; sprinkle over apples.

Bake in hot oven (400°) 35 to 40 minutes, or until apples are tender and top is golden brown. Cool in pan on rack. Cut in 2″ (about) squares. Makes 2 dozen.

BROWNIE PIE-BARS

A rich cream cheese crust holds the cake-like chocolate-nut filling

⅓ c. shortening	1 c. sugar
1 (3 oz.) pkg. cream cheese	2 eggs
1¼ c. sifted flour	⅓ c. flour
½ tsp. salt	½ c. chopped nuts
4 to 5 tblsp. water	½ tsp. baking powder
½ c. butter or regular	½ tsp. salt
margarine	½ tsp. vanilla
2 squares unsweetened	¼ c. sifted confectioners
chocolate	sugar (for coating)

To make crust, soften shortening with cream cheese (at room temperature). Add 1¼ c. flour and ½ tsp. salt. Mix just until particles are the size of small peas. Add water gradually, while stirring with a fork, until dough is moist enough to hold together.

Form dough into a square. Roll out on lightly floured surface to 14 × 10″ rectangle. Fit into ungreased 13 × 9 × 2″ pan.

To make filling, melt butter with chocolate in sauce-pan over very low heat. Stir in remaining ingredients, except confectioners sugar; beat to mix well. Pour into pastry-lined pan.

Bake in moderate oven (350°) 40 to 45 minutes. Cool in pan on rack; sprinkle with confectioners sugar. Cut in 2″ (about) squares. Makes 2 dozen.

VARIATION

Frosted Brownie Pie-Bars: Omit sprinkling with confectioners sugar, and spread with this frosting: Melt together 1 (1 oz.) envelope no-melt unsweetened chocolate, or 1 square unsweetened chocolate, 2 tblsp. butter and 1 tblsp. milk. Stir in 1 c. confectioners sugar. Beat until smooth, adding a few drops of milk if necessary to make frosting of spreading consistency. Spread over cooled Brownie Pie-Bars.

DANISH CARAMEL PIE-BARS

We also give a speedy Americanized version of "caramelettes"

1½ c. sifted flour	1 egg
⅓ c. sugar	1 c. sugar
¼ tsp. salt	¾ c. light cream
½ c. butter	¾ c. sliced almonds

Combine flour, ⅓ c. sugar, salt and butter until mixture is crumbly. Blend in egg. Press mixture with fingers into bottom and ½″ up sides of ungreased 9″ square pan.

Melt 1 c. sugar in heavy skillet over medium-low heat, stirring constantly, until it turns a light caramel color. Add cream very slowly, stirring constantly. When mixture is smooth, remove from heat and stir in almonds. Pour into crust-lined pan.

Bake in moderate oven (350°) 30 to 35 minutes, or until edges are golden brown. Cool in pan on rack. Cut in 1½″ squares. Makes 3 dozen.

VARIATIONS

American Caramel Pie-Bars: Make like Danish Caramel Pie-Bars, substituting this speedy filling for the one in which you melt the sugar: Combine ⅔ c. cara-

mel sundae sauce, ¼ c. light cream, 1 tblsp. melted
butter and ¾ c. sliced almonds. Pour into crust-lined
pan and bake as directed.

Danish Caramel Tarts: Press crust for Danish Caramel
Pie-Bars into 18 ungreased 2½″ muffin-pan cups to
cover bottom and ½″ up sides. (Or use small tart pans.)
Place rounded tablespoonfuls caramel filling in each
muffin-pan cup. Bake in moderate oven (350°) about
25 minutes. Cool; loosen carefully and remove from
pans. Makes 1½″ dozen.

CHEESE PIE-BAR COOKIES

Between crisp undercrust and crumb top
there's a velvety, lemon-flavored filling
reminiscent of the best cheese cakes and pies

1¾ c. sifted flour	½ c. dairy sour cream
⅓ c. sugar	2 eggs
¼ tsp. salt	1 tsp. grated lemon peel
⅔ c. butter	⅓ c. sugar
1 (3 oz.) pkg. cream cheese	

Combine flour, ⅓ c. sugar and salt; using electric
mixer on low speed, cut in butter until particles are
fine like cornmeal. Set aside ⅓ of mixture for topping.
Press remaining ⅔ of mixture into bottom of ungreased
9″ square pan. Bake in moderate oven (350°) 15
minutes.

To make filling, soften cream cheese by beating with
sour cream. Blend in eggs, lemon peel and ⅓ c. sugar.
Pour over crust in pan. Sprinkle with reserved crust
mixture.

Bake in moderate oven (350°) 30 to 35 minutes,
or until filling is set. Cool in pan or rack. Cut in 1½″
squares and store in refrigerator until serving time.
Makes 3 dozen.

CHESS PIE-BARS

For dessert cut larger squares;
top with whipped cream or ice cream

1½ c. sifted flour	½ c. sugar
¼ c. brown sugar, firmly packed	½ c. melted butter
	2 tblsp. milk
½ c. butter or regular margarine	1 tblsp. flour
	2 eggs
1 c. brown sugar, firmly packed	½ c. chopped nuts

Combine 1½ c. flour and ¼ c. brown sugar; cut in butter, using mixer on low speed, until particles are fine. Press mixture into bottom of ungreased 13 × 9 × 2" pan. Bake in moderate oven (375°) 10 minutes.

Meanwhile, combine remaining ingredients in mixing bowl; beat well. Pour over crust in pan; bake in moderate oven (375°) 20 to 25 minutes, or until golden brown. Cool in pan on rack; then cut in 2" squares. Makes about 2 dozen.

FRENCH CHOCOLATE PIE-SQUARES

Chocolate creams is a good name
for these specials

1⅔ c. graham cracker crumbs	2 (1 oz.) envelopes no-melt unsweetened chocolate or
¼ c. sugar	2 squares unsweetened
⅓ c. melted butter	chocolate, melted
½ c. butter	2 eggs
1 c. confectioners sugar	1 tsp. vanilla

Combine graham cracker crumbs, sugar and melted butter. Set aside ⅓ of mixture for topping. Press remaining mixture into bottom of ungreased 9" square pan.

Bake in moderate oven (375°) 8 minutes. (Omit baking, if you wish.)

To make filling, cream ½ c. butter with confectioners sugar until very light and fluffy. Blend in chocolate. Add eggs and vanilla; beat well. Spread over crust in pan. Sprinkle with reserved crust mixture. Refrigerate.

To serve, cut in 1½" squares. Makes 3 dozen.

NOTE: Keep cookies in refrigerator. The filling softens at room temperature.

GLAZED JAM PIE-BARS

A cake-like filling bakes in a crust;
spread jam and frosting on top

1⅓ c. sifted flour
½ tsp. salt
¼ c. shortening
¼ c. butter
3 to 4 tblsp. water
½ c. fruit or berry jam, or
    preserves
½ c. butter

⅔ c. sugar
2 eggs
½ tsp. baking powder
½ tsp. salt
1 tsp. vanilla
1 c. sifted flour
Rum Frosting (recipe follows)

Mix 1⅓ c. flour and ½ tsp. salt. Using electric mixer at low speed, cut in shortening and ¼ c. butter until particles are fine. Add water gradually, while stirring with fork, until dough is moist enough to hold together.

Roll out dough on floured surface to a 14 × 10" rectangle. Fit into ungreased 13 × 9 × 2" pan. Spread jam over bottom.

To make filling, cream ½ c. butter and sugar until light and fluffy. Add eggs, baking powder, ½ tsp. salt and vanilla. Beat well. Blend in 1 c. flour. Spread carefully over jam-topped dough in pan.

Bake in moderate oven (375°) 30 to 35 minutes, or until golden brown. While warm spread with Rum Frosting. Cool in pan on rack, then cut in 2" (about) squares. (These cookies are good keepers.) Makes 2 dozen.

Rum Frosting: Blend together until smooth 2 tblsp. soft butter or regular margarine, 1 c. confectioners sugar, 1 tblsp. milk and ½ tsp. rum flavoring.

LEMON FLUFF PIE-BARS

Filling separates to form a creamy layer on bottom,
spongy fluff on top, like lemon sponge pie.
Cookies are light and refreshing

⅓ c. butter
¼ c. confectioners sugar
1 c. sifted flour
¼ c. butter or regular
   margarine
1 c. sugar

¼ c. flour
2 eggs, separated
1 tblsp. grated lemon peel
¼ c. lemon juice
1 c. milk

To make crust, soften ⅓ c. butter with confectioners sugar; blend in 1 c. flour. Press mixture into bottom of ungreased 9" square pan. Bake in moderate oven (350°) 12 minutes.

To make filling, cream together ¼ c. butter, sugar and ¼ c. flour. Beat in egg yolks, lemon peel and juice. Blend in milk.

Beat egg whites until they stand in peaks (stiff, but not dry). Fold into filling mixture and pour into baked crust.

Bake in moderate oven (350°) 35 to 40 minutes, or until deep golden brown. Cool in pan on rack and cut in 2 × 1" bars. Makes 3 dozen.

GOLDEN LEMON PIE-BARS

Crisp crust holds tart-sweet filling—
a treat for lemon pie fans

1⅓ c. sifted flour
½ tsp. salt
½ c. shortening
2 to 3 tblsp. water
⅓ c. butter

1 c. sugar
2 tblsp. flour
2 eggs
1 tblsp. grated lemon peel
¼ c. lemon juice

To make crust, mix 1⅓ c. flour with salt; cut in shortening to form particles the size of small peas. Set aside ⅓ c. mixture for topping. To the remainder add water gradually, while stirring with a fork, until dough is moist enough to hold together.

Roll dough out on floured surface to make a 10" square. Fit into ungreased 9" square pan.

To make filling, cream butter with sugar. Blend in 2 tblsp. flour, eggs, lemon peel and juice. Pour into pastry-lined pan. Sprinkle top with reserved ⅓ c. crust mixture.

Bake in hot oven (400°) 30 to 35 minutes, or until golden. Cool in pan on rack. Cut in 1½" squares. Makes 3 dozen.

MINCEMEAT PIE-BARS

For a holiday dessert cut in 3- or 4-inch bars,
top with ice cream

2½ c. sifted flour	5 to 6 tblsp. water
1 tsp. salt	2 c. prepared mincemeat
1 c. shortening	2 tblsp. sugar (for tops)

Combine flour and salt; cut in shortening until particles are the size of small peas. Gradually add water, while stirring with a fork, until dough is moist enough to hold together.

Divide dough in half. Roll one part on floured surface to make a 14 × 9″ rectangle. Place on ungreased baking sheet. Spread mincemeat to within ½″ of edges.

Roll remaining half of dough to 14 × 9″ rectangle. Place on top of mincemeat; seal edges with a fork. Prick top generously with fork. Sprinkle with sugar.

Bake in hot oven (400°) 25 to 30 minutes, or until golden brown. Serve warm or cold, cut in 2″ (about) squares. Makes 28.

PECAN PIE-BARS

To serve these luscious cookies for dessert,
top with whipped cream

½ c. butter	2 tblsp. flour
1¼ c. sifted flour	3 eggs
¼ c. sugar	1 tsp. vanilla
½ c. brown sugar, firmly packed	¼ tsp. salt
1 c. light or dark corn syrup	½ to 1 c. chopped pecans

To make crust, cut butter with 1¼ c. flour and sugar until particles are fine like cornmeal. Press into bottom of ungreased 9″ square pan. Bake in moderate oven (350°) 15 minutes.

Combine remaining ingredients in mixing bowl, beating until well blended. Pour over partially baked crust in pan.

Bake in moderate oven (350°) 30 to 35 minutes, or until golden brown and knife inserted in center comes out clean. Cool in pan on rack. Cut in 1″ squares. Makes 3 dozen.

Chocolate Pecan Pie-Bars: Make like Pecan Pie-Bars, but in filling use light corn syrup and add 2 (1 oz.) envelopes no-melt unsweetened chocolate, or 2 squares unsweetened chocolate, melted. Bake 35 minutes after pouring filling into crust.

PUMPKIN PIE-SQUARES

Serve these pumpkin squares with coffee for a perfect dessert after a big meal or for evening refreshments that will be talked about

1 c. sifted flour
½ c. quick-cooking rolled oats
½ c. brown sugar, firmly packed
½ c. butter or regular margarine
1 (1 lb.) can pumpkin (2 c.)
1 (13½ oz.) can evaporated milk

2 eggs
¾ c. sugar
½ tsp. salt
1 tsp. ground cinnamon
½ tsp. ground ginger
¼ tsp. ground cloves
½ c. chopped pecans
½ c. brown sugar, firmly packed
2 tblsp. butter

Combine flour, rolled oats, ½ c. brown sugar and ½ c. butter in mixing bowl. Mix until crumbly, using electric mixer on low speed. Press into ungreased 13 × 9 × 2″ pan. Bake in moderate oven (350°) 15 minutes.

Combine pumpkin, evaporated milk, eggs, white sugar, salt and spices in mixing bowl; beat well. Pour into baked crust. Bake in moderate oven (350°) 20 minutes.

Combine pecans, ½ c. brown sugar and 2 tblsp. butter; sprinkle over pumpkin filling. Return to oven and bake 15 to 20 minutes, or until filling is set. Cool in pan on rack and cut in 2″ (about) squares. Makes 2 dozen.

DANISH RAISIN PIE-BAR COOKIES

Cookies have luscious soft filling— serve with a fork, if you like

1 c. butter or regular	2 c. sifted flour
margarine	½ tsp. salt
1½ c. sugar	1 (1 lb. 6 oz.) can raisin pie
3 eggs	filling (2 c.)
1 tsp. vanilla	

Beat butter with sugar until light and fluffy. Beat in eggs and vanilla to mix well.

Sift together flour and salt; add a little at a time to creamed mixture, beating after each addition. Divide dough in half. Spread one half in greased 15½ × 10½ × 1″ jelly roll pan. Carefully spread raisin pie filling evenly over dough.

Drop remaining half of dough over filling with spoon or cake decorator to form a lattice (lattice spreads in the baking.) Bake in moderate oven (350°) 28 to 30 minutes, or until golden. Set pan on rack to cool, then cut in 2½ × 1″ bars. Cookies are best served the same day they are baked, or frozen. Makes 5 dozen.

RAISIN CREAM PIE-BARS

Tasty cookies are rich like raisin cream pie,
so cut into small bars

½ c. butter	¼ tsp. salt
1¼ c. sifted flour	2 c. ground raisins
½ c. quick-cooking rolled	½ c. sugar
oats	1 c. light cream
½ c. brown sugar, firmly	¼ tsp. salt
packed	1 tblsp. lemon juice

To make crust, combine butter, flour, rolled oats, brown sugar and ¼ tsp. salt; mix until crumbly. Press 2 c. mixture into bottom of ungreased 9″ square pan. Set aside remainder of crumb mixture for topping.

To make filling, combine raisins, sugar, cream and ¼ tsp. salt. Cook, stirring, until thick. Remove from heat and stir in lemon juice. Spread over crust in pan. Top with reserved crumb mixture.

Bake in moderate oven (375°) 35 to 40 minutes, or until golden brown. Cool in pan on rack. Cut in 1½″ squares. Makes 3 dozen.

SOUR CREAM/RAISIN PIE-BARS

Praises skyrocket for these cookies
inspired by sour cream raisin pie

1½ c. sifted flour	¾ c. sugar
½ tsp. salt	1 tblsp. flour
⅓ c. shortening	1 tsp. ground cinnamon
¼ c. butter or regular	¼ tsp. ground nutmeg
margarine	⅛ tsp. ground cloves
2 to 3 tblsp. water	½ c. seedless raisins
1 c. dairy sour cream	¼ c. brown sugar, firmly
2 eggs	packed

Mix 1½ c. flour with salt; cut in shortening and butter until particles are the size of small peas. Set aside ⅔ c. mixture for topping.

To remaining mixture, gradually add water, while stirring with a fork, until dough is just moist enough to hold together. Roll out on floured surface to make a 10″ square; fit into ungreased 9″ square pan.

Combine dairy sour cream, eggs, sugar, 1 tblsp. flour, spices and raisins; beat well to blend. Pour into pastry-lined pan.

Blend brown sugar into reserved crumb mixture; sprinkle over filling. Bake in moderate oven (375°) 30 to 35 minutes, or until light golden brown. Cool in pan on rack. Cut in 1½″ squares. Makes 3 dozen.

NOTE: The filling has a custard base. Store cookies in refrigerator if not used soon after baking and cooling.

Ready-Made Cookies

WHEN YOU'RE too busy to bake cookies and the supply in the freezer has vanished, depend on packaged cookies from the supermarket to serve when company comes. Just transform the basic cookies with your own special touches and they will have both a homemade taste and also appearance.

Take Marshmallow Gingersnaps. All you do to glamorize the crisp, spicy cookies is to lay marshmallow halves on them and broil about 5 minutes. Then you spread on a speedy orange confectioners sugar frosting. They're yummy and easy to fix.

Flat oatmeal cookies respond kindly to dress-ups. For our Date Betweens, put the cookies together in pairs with a quickly cooked date filling for pleasing sandwiches.

Another type of store cookie you can personalize speedily is shortbread. For Fudge Shortbread Squares you arrange the square shortbread cookies in a pan, spoon on a fast-fix chocolate frosting and chill in the refrigerator until set. Then you cut them into 2" bars.

You can accomplish so much with vanilla wafers plus imagination in so few minutes. Try Chocolate-Coated Wafers for an adventure in rapid cooking. After a few tries at "dress-ups," you'll be ready to branch out on your own in personalizing the cookies you buy.

Keep a few packages in the cupboard to fix up in a jiffy when you need something delicious to serve with tea, coffee, a fruit drink or ice cream. If friends telephone to say they're coming over, you can have a plate of pretty cookies ready for thoughtful hospitality by the time they arrive. They'll be impressed.

MARSHMALLOW GINGERSNAPS

Gingersnaps taste great topped with
marshmallows, orange icing

15 regular marshmallows, halves	1 tsp. grated orange peel
30 gingersnaps	1 tblsp. butter
1 c. confectioners sugar	1 to 2 tblsp. orange juice

Place a marshmallow half, cut side down, on each gingersnap. Arrange on ungreased baking sheet and put in a very slow oven (200°) 5 minutes. Remove from oven and press marshmallows down slightly.

Combine confectioners sugar, orange peel and butter, and add orange juice until of spreading consistency. Beat until smooth. Spread over marshmallow-topped gingersnaps. Makes 2½ dozen.

ORANGE/COCONUT TOPPERS

Orange/coconut top complements
the spicy flavor of gingersnaps

2 tblsp. butter	2 tsp. grated orange peel
½ c. sugar	1 tblsp. orange juice
½ c. flaked coconut	4 dozen gingersnaps

Melt butter in small saucepan; stir in sugar, coconut, orange peel and juice. Spread a scant teaspoonful on each gingersnap, almost to edges.

Arrange on ungreased baking sheet and bake in very hot oven (450°) 5 minutes, or until topping is bubbly. Remove cookies and cool on racks. Makes 4 dozen.

DATE BETWEENS

Orange/date filling between oatmeal cookies
makes a real treat

½ c. cut-up dates	2 tblsp. sugar
⅓ c. orange juice or water	40 small flat oatmeal cookies
1 tsp. grated orange peel (optional)	

Combine dates, orange juice, orange peel and sugar in small saucepan. Cook over medium heat, stirring constantly, until thick.

Put cookies together in pairs with about 1 tsp. date filling between. Makes 20.

Date-Filled Specials: Substitute small flat butter cookies or vanilla wafers for the oatmeal cookies.

OATMEAL TOSCAS

*Bake these cookies with Swedish
almond topping only 5 minutes*

¼ c. sugar
1 tsp. flour
2 tblsp. light cream or milk
2 tblsp. butter

½ c. sliced almonds
⅛ tsp. almond extract
2 dozen flat oatmeal cookies

In a small saucepan combine sugar and flour; stir to mix. Add cream and butter. Bring to a full boil, stirring constantly. Remove from heat and stir in almond slices and almond extract. Place a teaspoonful on center of each oatmeal cookie. Place cookies on ungreased baking sheet.

Bake in very hot oven (450°) 5 minutes, or until topping is bubbly. Cool cookies on racks. Makes 2 dozen.

FUDGE SHORTBREAD SQUARES

*Quick and easy fudge on shortbread
cookies makes them festive*

16 shortbread square cookies
½ c. sweetened condensed
milk (not evaporated)

1 (6 oz.) pkg. semisweet
chocolate pieces
½ c. chopped nuts
½ tsp. vanilla

Arrange cookies in bottom of lightly greased 8″ square pan.

Cook condensed milk and chocolate pieces over low heat, stirring occasionally, until thick, smooth and shiny. Stir in nuts and vanilla. Spoon over cookies in pan; carefully spread to cover. (You can sprinkle 2 shortbread cookies, crumbled, over top if you wish.) Refrigerate until set.

Cut in 2″ squares to serve. Makes 16.

PEANUT/DATE SHORTIES

Date/peanut filling on shortbread cookies,
topped with chocolate

½ c. peanut butter
2 tblsp. butter
1 c. cut-up dates
1 c. confectioners sugar
36 shortbread cookies

½ c. semisweet chocolate
  pieces
2 tblsp. butter
2 tblsp. milk
½ c. confectioners sugar

Combine peanut butter, 2 tblsp. butter, dates and 1 c. confectioners sugar; add a few drops of milk if necessary to mix. Place 1 teaspoonful of mixture on each cookie.

Melt chocolate pieces and 2 tblsp. butter in milk by heating over hot water. Stir in ½ c. confectioners sugar and beat until smooth and shiny. (Add more milk if necessary.)

Dip tops of cookies in chocolate frosting. Spread on racks until chocolate hardens. Makes 3 dozen.

AUSTRIAN TORTELETTES

Jelly spread between cookies
and frosting is a tasty surprise

¼ c. red jelly or jam (about)
36 shortbread square cookies
  (10 oz. pkg.)
¼ c. sliced filberts
½ c. sugar

2 tblsp. milk
2 tblsp. butter
½ c. semisweet chocolate
  pieces

Spread about ½ tsp. jelly over top of each cookie. Sprinkle with filberts.

Combine sugar, milk and butter in small saucepan. Bring to a boil; boil 1 minute. Remove from heat and stir in chocolate pieces. Continue to stir until smooth and of spreading consistency. If mixture is not smooth and shiny, thin with a few drops of milk. Spread on tops of cookies. Additional sliced filberts may be scattered over tops of cookies before chocolate hardens. Makes 3 dozen.

VARIATION

Peanut Prizes: Omit jelly and filberts. Top each cookie with 1 tsp. peanut butter, then spread on chocolate mixture.

CARAMEL SUNDAY COOKIES

These quick-fix cookies will become favorites at your house

14 caramels (¼ lb.)
2 tblsp. light cream or dairy half-and-half
2 tblsp. butter
½ c. confectioners sugar
¼ c. chopped nuts

⅛ tsp. peppermint extract (optional)
4 dozen vanilla wafers
½ c. milk chocolate pieces
1 tblsp. shortening

Melt together over hot water caramels, cream and butter. Stir in confectioners sugar, nuts and peppermint extract. Place a scant teaspoonful on top each vanilla wafer.

Melt chocolate pieces and shortening over hot water. Stir to mix and spoon a small amount on top of caramel-topped wafers. Makes 4 dozen.

NOTE: Double the recipe for caramel mixture and chocolate topping for 1 (10 to 12 oz.) pkg. vanilla wafers.

VARIATIONS

Chocolate/Caramel Sundae Cookies: Substitute small chocolate cookies for the vanilla wafers.
Shortbread/Caramel Sundae Cookies: Substitute shortbread cookies for the vanilla wafers.
Butter Cookie/Caramel Sundae: Substitute small butter cookies for the vanilla wafers.

CHERRY/CHOCOLATE CREAMS

Maraschino cherries nestle in creamy fondant under the glaze

1 egg white
2 tblsp. maraschino cherry juice
4 c. confectioners sugar
4½ dozen vanilla wafers

27 maraschino cherries, halved and well drained
1 (6 oz.) pkg. milk chocolate pieces
¼ c. maraschino cherry juice
2 tblsp. shortening

Beat together egg white, 2 tblsp. maraschino cherry juice and confectioners sugar. (Add a few drops of milk if too thick.) Place a teaspoonful of this fondant on top each vanilla wafer; press a cherry half, cut side down, on top.

To make glaze, melt together milk chocolate pieces, ¼ c. maraschino cherry juice and shortening in small saucepan. Stir until smooth. Place ½ tsp. glaze on top each cherry half on cookie, allowing it to run down on fondant topping. Makes 4½ dozen.

CHOCOLATE-COATED WAFERS

Fix vanilla wafers this way
when you're having discerning guests

1 (6 oz.) pkg. mint or semisweet chocolate pieces	4 dozen vanilla wafers
2 tblsp. shortening	Cookie coconut or chopped nuts (optional)
2 tblsp. shaved paraffin	

Melt together chocolate pieces, shortening and paraffin over hot water. Stir to blend.

Dip vanilla wafers, one at a time, in chocolate mixture to coat. Lift out with 2 forks, allowing excess chocolate to drip off. Let harden on racks. If desired, decorate tops of wafers before topping hardens with cookie coconut, or with chopped nuts. Makes 4 dozen.

VARIATION

Butterscotch Favorites: Substitute butterscotch pieces for the chocolate pieces.

CHOCOLATE RUM BALLS

Cookies prettied up like this look
and taste like chocolate candy

2 tblsp. butter	4 dozen vanilla wafers
1 c. confectioners sugar	½ c. milk chocolate pieces
1 to 2 tblsp. milk	1 tblsp. shortening
½ to 1 tsp. rum extract	1 tblsp. shaved paraffin

Melt butter in small saucepan over medium heat to a delicate brown. Blend in confectioners sugar. Gradually add milk until of spreading consistency. Stir in rum extract.

Spread mixture generously on bottom sides of half of vanilla wafers. Top with remaining half of cookies, bottom side down.

Melt milk chocolate pieces with shortening and paraffin over hot water; stir to blend. Drop cookie sandwiches into chocolate. Coat on both sides and lift out with 2 forks, letting excess chocolate drop off. Cool on racks. Makes 2 dozen.

MINT STUFFIES

Plain vanilla wafers, dressed up,
become pretty party fare

3 tblsp. butter
2 c. confectioners sugar
2 tblsp. crème de menthe, or
½ tsp. peppermint extract
and a few drops green food
color

1 to 2 tblsp. milk
4 dozen vanilla wafers
½ c. semisweet mint
chocolate pieces
1 tblsp. shortening

Combine butter, confectioners sugar, crème de menthe and enough milk to make frosting of spreading consistency. Put 1 scant teaspoonful of mixture on each vanilla wafer.

Melt mint chocolate pieces and shortening over hot water. Spoon over frosted vanilla wafers. Let cookies cool before serving. Makes 4 dozen.

PARTY-GOERS

Picture-pretty cookies. Gelatin both tints
and flavors coconut

1 (3 oz.) pkg. strawberry
flavor gelatin
⅔ c. sweetened condensed
milk (not evaporated)
2⅓ c. flaked coconut (7 oz.)

2 tblsp. butter
3 tblsp. milk
3 tblsp. sugar
1 c. confectioners sugar
3 dozen vanilla wafers

Reserve 1 tblsp. gelatin for frosting; combine remaining gelatin and sweetened condensed milk. Stir in coconut. Refrigerate 1 to 2 hours.

To make frosting, combine reserved 1 tblsp. gelatin, butter, milk and white sugar; boil 2 minutes. Stir in confectioners sugar.

Shape chilled coconut mixture into ¾" balls; press

one ball firmly down on each vanilla wafer. Spread frosting over topping and cookie. It may be necessary to thin frosting with a few drops of water while spreading on cookies. Makes 3 dozen.

NOTE: You can substitute gelatin of other flavors and colors, such as raspberry, cherry, lime, orange and lemon, for the strawberry flavor gelatin.

BOYS' SPECIAL

You can make one snack cookie sandwich using the ingredients given here—or you can make them by the dozen on short notice

1 tsp. peanut butter	4 or 5 miniature
2 flat unfilled cookies (large	marshmallows
butter cookies, chocolate	6 to 8 semisweet chocolate
chip, etc.)	pieces

Spread a thin layer of peanut butter on bottom side of a flat cookie. Top with marshmallows and chocolate pieces.

Broil until marshmallows are puffy and chocolate pieces appear melted. Top with another cookie, bottom side down. Makes 1 cookie sandwich.

CHILDREN'S SPECIAL

Their favorites combined—marshmallows, chocolate, peanut butter

½ c. peanut butter	1 square semisweet chocolate
24 chocolate chip or chocolate	1 tblsp. butter
cookies	1 tblsp. milk
12 marshmallows, halved	1 c. confectioners sugar

Spread 1 tsp. peanut butter in center of each cookie top. Place a mashmallow half, cut side down, on peanut butter centers.

In small saucepan, melt chocolate and butter with milk over low heat, stirring constantly. Stir in confectioners sugar. Beat until smooth, adding a few drops of milk if necessary for spreading consistency. Spread over marshmallow-topped cookies. Makes 2 dozen.

CHOCOLATE/COCONUT RIBBONS

Ribbons of chocolate decorate coconut bar cookies—really delicious

1 (6 oz.) pkg. semisweet   ½ c. peanut butter
   chocolate pieces   32 coconut bar cookies

Melt together over low heat, stirring constantly, chocolate pieces and peanut butter. Let stand until cool, but not set.

Arrange 4 coconut bars, in a single row with ends touching, on sheet of foil or waxed paper. Spread generously with the chocolate/peanut mixture.

Top with second layer of cookies, using half cookies at each end. Again spread with chocolate/peanut mixture. Repeat with third layer of cookies. Top with frosting, then a fourth layer of cookies.

Repeat procedure, using remaining 16 cookies. Wrap in foil or waxed paper and refrigerate several hours.

To serve, cut in ½″ slices with a sharp knife. Cookies slice easier the day they are made because chocolate hardens more if left longer. If not used, place sliced cookies on plate and slip into a plastic bag. Makes 32.

FROSTED FIG BARS

Glamorize tiny fig-filled cookies this easy way for your tea party

30 fig-filled bar cookies (1 lb.)   1½ tblsp. orange juice
2½ tblsp. butter   1 tsp. grated orange peel
1½ c. sifted confectioners   ½ c. cookie coconut
   sugar

Cut cookie bars lengthwise in halves.

Combine butter, confectioners sugar, orange juice and orange peel. Beat until smooth.

Place coconut in shallow dish.

Hold a half cookie in one hand; spread top with frosting, using a small spatula. Dip cookie top in coconut. Place on waxed paper. Makes 5 dozen.

VARIATION

Snowy Topped Fig Bars: Follow recipe for Frosted Fig

Bars, but omit orange juice and peel and in their place use 1½ tblsp. light cream or milk and ½ tsp. vanilla. (Add enough cream or milk to make frosting of spreading consistency.)

LAZY DAISY SUGAR COOKIES

Good family dessert: these cookies
with broiled tops, and ice cream

2 tblsp. melted butter
½ c. brown sugar, firmly
 packed
1 tblsp. light cream or milk

½ c. cookie coconut or finely
 chopped nuts
12 large sugar cookies

Combine butter, sugar, cream and coconut. Spread a scant tablespoonful on each cookie.

Place cookies on ungreased baking sheet and broil until topping is bubbly. Remove cookies to rack to cool. Makes 1 dozen.

Cookies to Make from a Mix

A COUNTRY cookie custom worthy of a wider adoption than it enjoys today is the use of a homemade cookie mix. Once you make it and have it on hand, it's no trick to bake a hurry-up batch of cookies. We give you recipes for a mix adapted to kitchens located in high country and two mixes for use in locations under 5,000 feet elevation.

Baking Cookies in High Altitudes

One of the easiest, quickest and most successful ways to bake good cookies if you live in a high altitude area is to use a reliable homemade mix. You can buy mixes in packages in mountainous regions that are adapted to high elevations, but it is an economy to make your own. Home economists at the Colorado State University Agricultural Experiment Station have developed a basic mix that is responsible for many of the best cookies that come from home ovens in high country. The recipe for it and for a variety of superior cookies made from it were evolved in the altitude laboratory where the various conditions due to different altitudes are simulated.*

Home economists at the Agricultural Experiment Station and women throughout the Western mountain region have told Farm Journal food editors about the pointers to heed in making the mix. They say it is important to follow the directions with precision because

* From *Cookie Recipes from a Basic Mix for High Altitudes* by Dr. Ferne Bowman and Dr. Edna Page, Colorado State University.

at high altitudes recipes are more sensitive to slight changes than in lower places. Here are some of their suggestions: Measure accurately. Use the ingredients specified; substitutions will disappoint you. Be sure to use hydrogenated shortening, which is available in practically all food markets. It's a good idea to have all the ingredients at room temperature before you start combining them. (You will notice that baking powder is the variable ingredient in the following recipe. The amount for your altitude is given in a table that follows the recipe.)

COLORADO BASIC COOKIE MIX

9 c. sifted flour
3 c. instant nonfat dry milk powder
Baking powder (see table below)

1 tblsp. salt
4 c. hydrogenated shortening
4 c. sugar

Combine flour, dry milk powder, baking powder and salt. Sift together twice.

Soften shortening in 6-qt. (or larger) bowl with electric mixer at medium speed, or with large wooden spoon. Gradually add sugar, beating constantly, until mixture is light and fluffy.

Gradually add dry ingredients, blending them into mixture with electric mixer at low speed, or cut them in with pastry blender as for pie crust. Mixture will resemble coarse cornmeal.

Store in large covered container at room temperature. Mix will keep for several weeks. To use, stir with fork before measuring, then lightly spoon mix into measuring cup and level with straight edge of knife or spatula—do not pack it. Makes about 19 cups.

Amount of Baking Powder to Use

At 5,000 feet—3 tblsp.
At 7,500 feet—2 tblsp. plus ¾ tsp.
At 10,000 feet—1 tblsp. plus 1½ tsp.

If the altitude at which you live is not exactly 5,000, 7,500 or 10,000 feet, use the one nearest to your altitude. For example, if your elevation is 6,000 feet, use the baking powder indicated for 5,000 feet.

Favorite Cookies from the Basic Mix

Here are recipes for some of the best liked cookies made with the Colorado Basic Cookie Mix. Women in high country say they prefer to make comparatively small- or medium-size batches because the cookies are so quick to mix and bake. They like to serve them fresh and fragrant from the oven.

BROWNIES 1

6 squares semisweet chocolate
2 c. Colorado Basic Cookie Mix
2 eggs
¼ c. water
2 tsp. vanilla
½ c. chopped walnuts

Melt chocolate over hot water.

Combine all ingredients and blend thoroughly. Spread in greased and floured 9″ square pan and bake in moderate oven (350°) 25 to 30 minutes. Set pan on rack; when slightly cool, cut in 2 × 1½″ bars. Makes about 2 dozen.

BROWNIES 2

2 squares unsweetened chocolate
2 c. Colorado Basic Cookie Mix
2 eggs
½ c. brown sugar, firmly packed
¼ c. water
2 tsp. vanilla
½ c. chopped walnuts

Melt chocolate over hot water.

Blend all ingredients thoroughly. Spread in greased and floured 9″ square pan and bake in moderate oven (350°) 25 to 30 minutes. Set pan on rack; when slightly cool, cut in 2 × 1½″ bars. Makes about 2 dozen.

CHEWY DATE/NUT BARS

3 c. Colorado Basic Cookie Mix
2 tblsp. water
2 eggs
¼ c. brown sugar, firmly packed
1 tsp. vanilla
1 c. chopped dates
1 c. coarsely chopped walnuts

Blend all ingredients thoroughly. Spread in greased 13 × 9 × 2" pan.

Bake in moderate oven (350°) 35 to 40 minutes. Cool in pan on rack, then cut in 2 × 1" bars. Makes about 4 dozen.

CRISPY BARS

2 c. Colorado Basic Cookie Mix
¼ c. brown sugar, firmly packed
2 eggs
¼ tsp. salt
¾ c. brown sugar, firmly packed
1 tsp. vanilla
1 c. shredded or flaked coconut
1 c. oven-toasted rice cereal
1 c. broken walnuts

Combine cookie mix and ¼ c. brown sugar. Press into greased 9" square pan.

Beat eggs until frothy; add salt. Gradually add ¾ c. brown sugar, beating until thick. Add vanilla, coconut, cereal and nuts. Mix thoroughly. Spread over layer in pan.

Bake in slow oven (325°) 25 to 30 minutes. Cool in pan on rack, then cut in 2 × 1½" bars. Makes about 2 dozen.

DATE LAYER BARS

3 c. Colorado Basic Cookie Mix
1¾ c. quick-cooking rolled oats
1 lb. chopped dates
1 tblsp. lemon juice
1½ c. water
¼ c. brown sugar, firmly packed
2 tblsp. water

Combine cookie mix and rolled oats. Press 2½ c. of mixture into greased 13 × 9 × 2" pan.

Combine dates, lemon juice and 1½" c. water; cook over low heat until mixture is the consistency of thin jam. Spread over crumb layer in pan.

Blend brown sugar and 2 tblsp. water into remaining crumb mixture. Sprinkle over date mixture in pan and press down lightly.

Bake in moderate oven (350°) 30 to 35 minutes. Cool in pan on rack, then cut in 2 × 1" bars. Makes about 4 dozen.

PECAN BARS

2¼ c. Colorado Basic Cookie
  Mix
2 tblsp. water
3 eggs

1 c. brown sugar, firmly
  packed
½ tsp. vanilla
1 c. chopped pecans

Blend 2 c. cookie mix, water and 1 egg thoroughly. Spread in greased 13 × 9 × 2″ pan. Bake in moderate oven (375°) 8 to 10 minutes.

To make topping, beat 2 eggs until foamy. Add brown sugar, ¼ c. cookie mix and vanilla. Blend thoroughly. Stir in nuts. Spread over baked layer.

Return to moderate oven (350°) and bake 20 to 25 minutes. Cool in pan on rack, then cut in 2 × 1″ bars. Makes about 4 dozen.

CHERRY DROPS

3 c. Colorado Basic Cookie
  Mix
2 eggs

½ c. coarsely chopped
  drained maraschino
  cherries
½ c. chopped pecans

Blend cookie mix and eggs. Add cherries and nuts. Drop by teaspoonfuls about 2″ apart onto ungreased baking sheet.

Bake in moderate oven (375°) 10 to 12 minutes. Remove cookies and cool on rack. Makes 3½ to 4 dozen.

CHOCOLATE DROPS

2 c. Colorado Basic Cookie
  Mix
3 tblsp. cocoa
1 egg

2 tblsp. water
1 tsp. vanilla
½ c. chopped walnuts

Blend all ingredients thoroughly. Drop by teaspoonfuls about 2″ apart onto ungreased baking sheet.

Bake in moderate oven (375°) 10 to 14 minutes. Remove cookies and cool on racks. Makes 3 dozen.

CHOCOLATE CHIP COOKIES

4 c. Colorado Basic Cookie
   Mix
1 egg
2 tblsp. water
1½ tsp. vanilla

¼ c. brown sugar, firmly
   packed
1 (6 oz.) pkg. semisweet
   chocolate pieces
1 c. chopped walnuts

Blend all ingredients thoroughly. Drop by teaspoonfuls about 2″ apart onto ungreased baking sheet.

Bake in moderate oven (375°) 10 to 13 minutes. Remove cookies and cool on racks. Makes 5 dozen.

CRISP CHOCOLATE DROPS

4 squares semisweet chocolate
2 c. Colorado Basic Cookie
   Mix

2 tblsp. water
1 tsp. vanilla
½ c. chopped nuts

Melt chocolate over hot water.

Blend all ingredients thoroughly. Drop by teaspoonfuls about 2″ apart onto ungreased baking sheet.

Bake in moderate oven (375°) 10 to 12 minutes. Remove cookies and cool on racks. Makes 3 to 3½ dozen.

COCONUT COOKIES SUPREME

2 c. Colorado Basic Cookie
   Mix
1 egg
2 tblsp. water

1 tsp. vanilla
½ c. shredded coconut
½ c. chopped walnuts

Blend all ingredients thoroughly. Drop by teaspoonfuls about 2″ apart onto lightly greased baking sheet.

Bake in moderate oven (375°) 10 to 12 minutes. Remove cookies and cool on racks. Makes 3 dozen.

LEMON DROPS

2 c. Colorado Basic Cookie
   Mix
1 egg

1 tblsp. lemon juice
1½ tsp. grated lemon peel

Blend all ingredients thoroughly. Drop by teaspoonfuls about 2″ apart onto ungreased baking sheet.

Bake in moderate oven (375°) 10 to 12 minutes. Remove cookies and cool on racks. Makes 2½ dozen.

MINCEMEAT COOKIES

2 c. Colorado Basic Cookie
  Mix
½ c. prepared mincemeat
1 egg

½ tsp. vanilla
1 tblsp. water
½ c. chopped walnuts

Blend all ingredients thoroughly. Drop by teaspoonfuls about 2″ apart onto ungreased baking sheet.

Bake in moderate oven (375°) 10 to 12 minutes. Remove cookies and cool on racks. Makes 3 to 4 dozen.

OATMEAL COOKIES

1 c. raisins
2 c. Colorado Basic Cookie
  Mix
1 c. quick-cooking rolled oats
2 tblsp. brown sugar

½ tsp. ground cinnamon
½ tsp. ground allspice
1 egg
1½ tsp. vanilla
½ c. chopped walnuts

Cover raisins with water and simmer 5 minutes. Drain, reserving ½ c. raisin water.

Blend raisins and reserved ½ c. raisin water with remaining ingredients thoroughly. Drop by teaspoonfuls about 2″ apart onto ungreased baking sheet.

Bake in moderate oven (375°) 13 to 15 minutes. Remove cookies and cool on racks. Makes 3½ to 4 dozen.

CINNAMON COOKIES

2½ c. Colorado Basic Cookie
  Mix
½ c. sugar
1 egg

1 tsp. vanilla
1½ tsp. ground cinnamon
¼ c. finely chopped nuts

Combine cookie mix, sugar, egg and vanilla; blend thoroughly. Combine cinnamon and nuts.

Form dough into small balls, about 1″ in diameter;

roll in cinnamon-nut mixture. Place 2″ apart on un-greased baking sheet.

Bake in moderate oven (375°) 12 to 15 minutes. Remove cookies and cool on racks. Makes 3½ dozen.

MOLASSES COOKIES

4 c. Colorado Basic Cookie Mix	**½ tsp. ground ginger**
¼ tsp. ground cloves	**1 egg**
½ tsp. ground cinnamon	**¼ c. molasses**

Blend all ingredients thoroughly. Refrigerate dough 1 hour.

Form dough into small balls, about 1″ in diameter; place 1 to 2″ apart on lightly greased baking sheet. Flatten cookies with bottom of glass covered with damp cloth.

Bake in moderate oven (375°) 8 to 10 minutes. Remove cookies and cool on racks. Makes 5 to 6 dozen.

PEANUT BUTTER COOKIES

4 c. Colorado Basic Cookie Mix	**1 c. peanut butter**
½ c. brown sugar, firmly packed	**1 egg**
	1½ tsp. vanilla
	1 tblsp. water

Blend all ingredients thoroughly. Form dough into small balls, about 1″ in diameter, and place 1 to 2″ apart on ungreased baking sheet. Flatten cookies with tines of fork.

Bake in moderate oven (375°) 10 to 12 minutes. Remove cookies and cool on racks. Makes 7 dozen.

THUMBPRINTS

1 (3 oz.) pkg. cream cheese	**¾ c. finely chopped nuts**
2 c. Colorado Basic Cookie Mix	**9 drained maraschino cherries, cut in fourths**
¾ tsp. vanilla	**Jelly or tinted frosting (optional)**
1 egg white, slightly beaten	

Soften cream cheese. Add cookie mix and vanilla and blend thoroughly. Form dough into small balls, about 1" in diameter. Dip into egg white, then roll in nuts. Place 1 to 2" apart on greased baking sheet and press top of each cookie with thumb.

Bake in moderate oven (350°) 5 minutes, or until puffy. Remove from oven and quickly press top of each cookie with thumb to make indentation.

Return to oven and bake about 10 minutes longer. Place cookies on racks to cool. Place a maraschino cherry quarter or a bit of jelly or tinted frosting in center of each cookie. Makes 2½ to 3 dozen.

SUGAR COOKIES

3 c. Colorado Basic Cookie Mix	**½ tsp. almond extract, or ¾ tsp. vanilla**
1 egg	**Sugar**

Blend all ingredients thoroughly. Roll dough ⅛ to ¼" thick and cut with a round cookie cutter the size you like, or have. (Chill the dough 2 to 3 hours or overnight before rolling if it is difficult to handle.) Place 1 to 2" apart on ungreased baking sheet.

Bake in moderate oven (375°) 8 to 10 minutes. Place cookies on racks to cool. Sprinkle with sugar, or decorate as desired. Makes 3 dozen.

COOKIE STARTER

This mix is versatile. We give you seven good cookies to make with it

2¼ c. sifted flour	**1 c. butter or regular margarine**
¾ tsp. salt	

Sift flour and salt into bowl.

Cut in butter until mixture resembles coarse bread crumbs.

Store in clean jar with tight-fitting lid. Keep in refrigerator or freezer. Makes 3 to 4 cups.

Tips on using mix

Let the crumbs reach room temperature before adding other ingredients. Loosen with a fork if mix is too compact. Your electric mixer can help you make cookie dough from the mix.

To short-cut cookie making, shape dough into roll; wrap and chill thoroughly. Slice and bake cookies as desired. When dough is cold, allow more time for baking. To get a thicker cookie, shape teaspoonfuls of dough with fingers and roll in palms of hands into balls; stamp with flat-bottomed glass and bake.

When you bake and then freeze, wrap cookies in foil or plastic wrap, or store them in freezer containers.

OLD ENGLISH GINGER CONES

If cookies break in rolling, return them to oven for 1 minute

1 c. Cookie Starter	¼ c. dark brown sugar, firmly
¼ tsp. baking soda	packed
1½ tsp. ground ginger	1 tblsp. dark molasses
¼ tsp. ground nutmeg	1 tblsp. buttermilk
¼ tsp. ground cinnamon	Sifted confectioners sugar

Combine all ingredients, except confectioners sugar, and mix well. Form dough into ball; chill 2 hours.

Shape in 1″ balls. Roll in confectioners sugar, then pat very thin with glass dipped in confectioners sugar. Place 3″ apart on greased baking sheet.

Bake in moderate oven (350°) 4 minutes.

Remove cookies while still hot. Twist over wooden spoon handle and sprinkle with sugar. Cool on racks. Makes 1½ dozen.

BLIND DATES

You shape and bake dough around dates—add charm to cookie tray

1 (3 oz.) pkg. cream cheese	2 tblsp. confectioners sugar
(room temperature)	24 pitted dates
1 c. Cookie Starter	Sifted confectioners sugar
½ tsp. vanilla	

Combine first 4 ingredients. Form into four balls. Chill dough 2 hours.

Work with one ball at a time, and roll ⅛″ thick on board dusted with confectioners sugar.

Cut in rounds with 2½″ cutter.

Place date in center of each round. (Date may be stuffed with nut, or use ½ date and 1 nut.) Fold edges over and pinch ends to points.

Place 1″ apart on lightly greased baking sheet, seam side down. Bake in moderate oven (350°) 10 to 12 minutes.

Sprinkle with confectioners sugar. Remove cookies and cool on racks. Makes 2 dozen.

ICE CREAM WAFERS

Wonderful ice cream accompaniment! Wafers are thin and crisp

1 c. Cookie Starter	⅓ c. sugar
½ tsp. vanilla	½ tsp. baking powder
1 egg yolk	Sifted confectioners sugar

Mix all ingredients, except confectioners sugar. Chill dough thoroughly.

Sprinkle board and rolling pin with confectioners sugar. Roll small amount of dough ⅛″ thick.

Cut with small cookie cutter and place 1″ apart on greased baking sheet. Bake in moderate oven (350°) about 6 minutes, until cookies are lightly browned.

Dust with confectioners sugar. Remove cookies and cool on racks. Makes 3 dozen.

VARIATIONS

Oriental Almond Cookies: Make up Ice Cream Wafers recipe, substituting ½ tsp. almond extract for the vanilla.

Chill dough until firm enough to handle, about 1 hour.

Shape into balls about 1″ in diameter. Flatten with glass dipped in confectioners sugar.

Place cookies 3″ apart on lightly greased baking sheet.

Beat egg white with fork. Brush a little on each cookie.

Decorate each cookie with slivered, blanched almonds to make flower.

Bake in moderate oven (350°) about 12 minutes. Remove cookies and cool on racks. Makes 2 dozen.

Orange and Lemon Wafers: Make up Ice Cream Wafers recipe omitting vanilla and adding grated peel of 1 orange and grated peel of ½ lemon.

Roll out and cut cookies into different shapes. Place 1″ apart on lightly greased baking sheet. (Or roll into balls, using 1 teaspoon dough for each cookie. Dip fork into confectioners sugar and make waffle design by crisscrossing with fork. Don't mash cookies too flat.)

Bake in moderate oven (350°) 10 minutes. Decorate with strips of orange peel. Remove cookies and cool on racks. Makes 1½ dozen.

Sesame Cookies: Make Ice Cream Wafers recipe, substituting ¼ tsp. baking soda and ½ tsp. cream of tartar for baking powder. Add ½ c. toasted coconut and ¼ c. sesame seeds (if unavailable add another ¼ c. toasted coconut).

Mix ingredients well.

Shape dough into roll. Chill 15 minutes.

Slice ⅛″ thick and place 1″ apart on greased baking sheet. Bake in moderate oven (350°) 15 minutes, or until lightly browned. Remove cookies and cool on racks. Makes 2½ dozen.

NOTE: In Charleston, South Carolina, they're called Benne Cookies—benne is the colloquial name for sesame seeds.

Victorian Spice Cookies: Make up Ice Cream Wafers recipe using brown sugar instead of white, and ¼ tsp. baking soda instead of baking powder. Add ½ c. chopped walnuts, 1 tsp. cocoa, ⅛ tsp. ground nutmeg, ½ tsp. ground cinnamon and ¼ tsp. ground allspice.

Mix together all ingredients. Form into balls using 1 tsp. dough for each.

Put 1″ apart on greased baking sheet. Make hole in centers of cookies with fingertip. Place ¼ tsp. firm jelly in each hole.

Bake in moderate oven (350°) about 10 minutes, or until cookies are firm. Remove cookies and cool on racks. Makes 2½ dozen.

EIGHT-IN-ONE SUGAR COOKIES

Many women praised this mix when it appeared in Farm Journal

2 c. butter or regular margarine	4 eggs
2 c. sugar	6½ c. sifted flour
1 c. brown sugar, firmly packed	1 tblsp. cream of tartar
	2 tsp. baking soda
	¼ c. milk

Cream together butter and sugars until smooth and fluffy. Stir in unbeaten eggs, one at a time.

Sift together dry ingredients; add to creamed mixture alternately with milk. Mix thoroughly.

Divide dough in eight 1-cup lots. Wrap each tightly in foil or plastic wrap; freeze. Then place in plastic bag. To use, thaw dough just enough that you can shape or drop it. Place about 2″ apart on greased baking sheet and bake in moderate oven (375°) 10 to 15 minutes. Spread cookies on racks to cool. Mix makes 8 cups dough; each cup makes 2 to 3 dozen cookies, depending on the kind you bake.

NOTE: This dough, tightly wrapped, will keep several days in refrigerator. Freeze as recipe directs for longer storage.

Chocolate Chip Balls: Knead into 1 c. cookie dough, 1 tblsp. cocoa and ⅓ c. semisweet chocolate pieces. Shape into about 24 round balls; flatten slightly with spatula. Bake as directed.

Coconut/Almond Cookies: Knead into 1 c. cookie dough, 1 c. flaked coconut and ¼ tsp. almond extract. Shape into about 24 balls; place on greased baking sheet and press flat with spatula. Top each with a piece of candied cherry. Bake as directed.

Pecan Balls: Knead into 1 c. cookie dough, ½ c. finely chopped pecans and ¼ tsp. vanilla. Shape into 24 round balls. Bake as directed.

Ginger Cookie Balls: Knead into 1 c. cookie dough, 1 tblsp. dark molasses and ¼ to ½ tsp. ground ginger. Shape into about 24 balls (dip fingers occasionally in water so dough doesn't stick to hands). Bake as directed.

Gumdrop Cookie Balls: Mix into 1 c. cookie dough, ½ c. finely cut gumdrops (cut with scissors). Shape into 24 balls; crisscross with a fork. Bake as directed.

Fruit 'n Spice Drop Cookies: Stir into 1 c. cookie dough, ½ c. cooked and drained and chopped dried fruit, 2 tblsp. brown sugar, ¼ tsp. ground cinnamon and ⅛ tsp. ground cloves. Drop by teaspoonfuls 2" apart onto greased baking sheet. Bake as directed. Makes 30.

Orange Wafers: Stir into 1 c. cookie dough, ¼ tsp. grated orange peel and ¼ c. sugar mixed with 4 tsp. orange juice. Drop by teaspoonfuls 2" apart on greased baking sheet. Bake as directed. Makes 24 thin cookies.

Banana/Lemon Drops: Stir into 1 c. cookie dough, ¼ c. mashed ripe banana, ½ tsp. grated lemon peel and ¼ tsp. lemon juice. Drop 1 teaspoonful at a time into finely rolled corn flakes. Coat by turning gently with spoon. (Dough is very soft.) Place 2" apart on greased baking sheet and bake as directed. Watch carefully so cookies do not scorch. Makes 2 dozen.

Cookies Children Will Love to Make

IF YOUR daughter has never baked cookies, you'll find easy-to-follow, step-by-step recipes in this section especially for beginning cooks. It's really *her* cookbook within *your* cookbook. They'll answer the questions she would otherwise have to ask you—will give her a feeling of independence and achievement. Let her use these recipes and she'll not have to bother Mother. What's more, she'll make good cookies.

After your youngster (boys like to bake cookies, too) has made these recipes successfully, she is ready to branch out and try other recipes on the preceding pages. We suggest, in a list preceding the Index, some of the easier ones that will appeal to young people.

The recipes in this section were developed in Farm Journal Countryside Test Kitchens especially for beginners in baking. We have taken them from our book for beginning cooks, *Let's Start to Cook.* These cookie recipes go into much more detail than the others and are easy to read and follow.

Bar Cookies

These are the cookies that are easiest to bake. You spread the dough in a greased pan and bake it the way you bake cakes. Then you cut the cookie into squares or bars.

Here are some recipes for bar cookies almost everybody loves. So get out your measuring cup, mixing bowl and get going.

Do's for bar cookies

1. Do use the pan size the recipe recommends. If your pan is too large, the dough spreads thinner in the pan and it overbakes; the cookies will be tough and dry. If the pan is too small, the dough spreads too thick in it and the cookies may not bake through.

2. Do mix the dough the way the recipe directs. Overmixing gives bar cookies hard, crusty tops.

3. Do spread the dough evenly in the pan with a spatula or spoon so that all of it will bake in the same number of minutes.

4. Do watch the clock. When the time for baking is almost up, make the fingerprint test: When the cookies are lightly browned and a few minutes before the baking time is up, lightly press the top of the cookie with a fingertip. If your finger makes a slight dent or imprint that remains, the cookie is done. Overbaking makes cookies dry and crumbly.

5. Do cool the cookies in the pan at least 10 minutes before cutting. Cutting the bars while they are hot makes the cookies crumble.

FUDGE BROWNIES

For a surprise, frost these brownies with chocolate and white frostings and arrange like a checkerboard

2 (1-ounce) squares unsweetened chocolate	1 cup sugar
⅓ cup soft shortening	2 eggs
¾ cup sifted flour	1 teaspoon vanilla
½ teaspoon baking powder	½ cup chopped or broken nuts
½ teaspoon salt	

Start heating the oven to 350°. Lightly grease an 8 × 8 × 2-inch pan with unsalted shortening or salad oil.

Put the chocolate and shortening in the top of the double boiler and melt them over hot, not boiling, water. Or melt them in a small saucepan over low heat, watching all the time so chocolate won't burn. Cool until lukewarm.

Sift the flour onto a square of waxed paper or into a bowl and then measure. Sift the measured flour with the baking powder and salt. Set aside.

Beat the sugar and eggs together in a large bowl with a spoon, or with an electric mixer on medium speed, until light. If you use an electric mixer, stop the mixer two or three times and scrape sides of bowl with a rubber spatula.

Beat the cooled chocolate-shortening mixture and vanilla into the egg-sugar mixture. Stir in the flour mixture or beat it in with the electric mixer on low speed. Stir in the nuts and mix well. (If you like, you can divide the nuts in half. Stir ¼ cup into the cookie dough and sprinkle the other ¼ cup on top of dough in pan just before baking.)

Spread evenly in the greased pan with the back of a spoon or a spatula. Bake on the rack in the center of the oven 20 to 25 minutes. The crust on top will have a dull look when the cookie is done.

Remove the pan from the oven and set it on a wire rack to cool about 10 minutes, or until completely cooled, before cutting. Cut into 16 (2-inch) bars.

For a change

Before cutting the baked Brownies into squares or bars, sprinkle the top lightly with powdered sugar.

BROWNIES À LA MODE

Here's a dessert that you won't go wrong on if your friends or family are chocolate fans. (That means most Americans!) Bake the Fudge Brownies dough in a greased 9-inch round layer cake pan. Set the pan on a wire rack to cool. To serve, cut the cookie in pie-shaped pieces and top each triangle with vanilla ice cream. Pass a pitcher of chocolate sauce to pour over it. You can buy the sauce in a jar or can, or make it.

MAGIC PARTY SQUARES

The magic of these cookies is the way you frost them with milk chocolate candy bars. And their wonderful taste!

½ cup regular margarine or
butter (¼ pound)
1 cup brown sugar, firmly
packed
¾ cup sifted flour
¾ cup quick-cooking rolled
oats

1 egg
2 tablespoons water
1 teaspoon vanilla
3 (1-ounce) milk chocolate
candy bars
¼ cup chopped nuts

Start heating the oven to 375°.

Put the margarine, brown sugar, flour and rolled oats in a medium bowl and mix well with a pastry blender. Be sure the margarine is evenly distributed. Add the egg, water and vanilla and beat with a spoon to mix thoroughly.

Spread evenly in an ungreased 9 × 9 × 2-inch pan with the back of a spoon or a spatula. Bake on the rack in the center of the oven about 22 to 25 minutes. The crust on top will have a dull look when the cookie is done.

Remove the pan from the oven and top at once with the chocolate candy bars. Let stand about 2 minutes or until the heat softens the candy. Spread the melted chocolate over the top of the cookie to make a frosting. Sprinkle the frosting with chopped nuts. Cool in pan on rack and cut into about 20 bars, or any number you like. (*Double Magic:* You can double this recipe and bake the cookie in a 13 × 9 × 2 inch pan. You'll need to bake it longer, about 35 to 40 minutes in all.)

CANDY BAR COOKIES

The 4-H Club girl who shares this recipe with us says the cookies taste like candy bars. Her friends agree

1 cup brown sugar, firmly
packed
½ cup soft butter
½ cup light corn syrup
3 teaspoons vanilla
1 teaspoon salt

4 cups quick-cooking rolled
oats
½ cup peanut butter
1 cup semisweet chocolate
pieces

Start heating the oven to 350°. Grease a 13 × 9 × 2-inch pan with unsalted shortening or salad oil.

With a spoon or electric mixer on medium speed, mix the brown sugar and butter in a large bowl until light and fluffy. Add the corn syrup, vanilla, salt and rolled oats and beat on low speed to mix ingredients well.

Spread the mixture evenly in the greased pan with the back of a spoon or spatula. Bake on the rack in the center of the oven 15 minutes.

While the mixture bakes, mix the peanut butter and chocolate in a small bowl.

Remove the pan from the oven and at once spread the peanut butter-chocolate mixture evenly over the top to cover until the heat melts the chocolate. Cool in pan on rack, then cut into 27 bars and remove from the pan with a spatula.

RICH BUTTERSCOTCH BARS

If you have a 1-pound box of brown sugar in the cupboard, use it. Then you don't have to measure or roll out lumps

1 pound brown sugar (2¼ to 2⅓ cups, firmly packed)
1 cup soft butter
2 eggs
2 cups unsifted flour

1 teaspoon baking powder
½ teaspoon salt
1 cup coarsely chopped or broken walnuts

Cook the sugar and butter in the top of the double boiler over hot, not boiling, water until the sugar dissolves. Or cook them in a medium saucepan over low heat. Cool until lukewarm.

Start heating the oven to 350°.

Add the eggs, one at a time, to the butter-sugar mixture and beat thoroughly after adding each egg.

Stir together the flour, baking powder and salt to mix well. Add to the butter-sugar mixture and stir in the nuts.

Spread evenly in an ungreased 15½ × 10½ × 1-inch pan (jelly roll pan). Bake on the rack in the center of the oven 25 minutes or until the cookie is a delicate brown; a slight dent is left when you touch the top lightly with a fingertip.

Remove the pan from the oven and set it on a wire rack. Cut while hot into 40 bars, or as many as you like.

DATE LOGS

Chop and measure at the same time—cut the dates fine with scissors and let them drop into the measuring cup

¾ cup sifted flour
1 cup sugar
1 teaspoon baking powder
¼ teaspoon salt

1 cup pitted finely cut-up dates
1 cup chopped walnuts
3 eggs, well beaten
Confectioners sugar

Start heating the oven to 325°. Grease a 9 × 9 × 2-inch pan with unsalted shortening or salad oil.

Sift the flour onto a square of waxed paper or into a bowl and then measure. Sift the measured flour with the sugar, baking powder and salt into a medium bowl. Stir the finely cut dates, walnuts and the well-beaten eggs into the flour mixture.

Spread evenly in the greased pan with the back of a spoon or a spatula. Bake on the rack in the center of the oven 35 to 40 minutes or until the cookie is a delicate brown; a slight dent is left when you touch the top lightly with a fingertip.

Remove the pan from the oven and set it on a wire rack until completely cool. Then, cut cookie into 48 strips or logs, or any number you like, and roll them in confectioners sugar.

Drop Cookies

You don't have to use your imagination to figure out how drop cookies got their name—you drop the soft dough from a spoon onto a baking sheet. They're really push-and-drop cookies because you have to push the dough off the spoon with a teaspoon or a rubber spatula. If you heap the drops of cookie dough up in the center to make little peaks, the cookies will be especially attractive.

To give drop cookies a fancy look in a jiffy, press bits of nuts or candied cherries on the center of each cookie before baking. Or spread the baked and cooled cookies with cake frosting, either a quick-to-fix confectioners sugar frosting or a packaged frosting mix.

CHOCOLATE/NUT DROPS

Use a little showmanship and dress up these cookies—lightly press a nut on each one before baking

½ cup soft butter or regular
   margarine
6 tablespoons brown sugar
6 tablespoons honey
1 egg
1¼ cups sifted flour
½ teaspoon baking soda

½ teaspoon salt
Few drops hot water
½ teaspoon vanilla
1 (6-ounce) package
   semisweet chocolate
   pieces
½ cup chopped walnuts

Start heating the oven to 375°. Grease a baking sheet with unsalted shortening or salad oil.

Beat the butter, brown sugar and honey together until light and fluffy. Add the unbeaten egg and beat well to mix.

Stir the flour onto a square of waxed paper or into a bowl and then measure. Sift the measured flour with the baking soda and salt. Stir into the creamed mixture. Add the hot water and beat to mix. Stir in the vanilla, chocolate pieces and nuts.

Drop 2 inches apart from a teaspoon onto a greased baking sheet. Bake on the rack in the center of the oven 10 to 12 minutes or until the cookies are a delicate brown; a slight dent shows when you touch the top lightly with a fingertip.

Remove the sheet from the oven and set it on a wire rack to cool slightly. Then remove the cookies from the baking sheet with a wide spatula and spread them on a wire rack to finish cooling. Makes about 36 cookies.

MOLASSES LOLLYPOP COOKIES

Wonderful party favors and Christmas gifts for the young fry. You can get skewers at dime stores and meat counters

½ cup soft butter or regular margarine
½ cup sugar
1 egg
½ cup light molasses
2½ cups sifted flour
¼ teaspoon salt
1 teaspoon baking soda
1 teaspoon ground ginger
½ teaspoon ground cinnamon
½ teaspoon ground cloves
½ teaspoon ground nutmeg
2 tablespoons water
Wooden skewers, about 24, 4½ inches long

Start heating the oven to 375°.

Beat the butter and sugar with an electric mixer on medium speed or with a spoon until light and fluffy. Add the egg and molasses and beat to mix well.

Sift the flour onto a square of waxed paper or into a bowl and then measure. Sift the measured flour with the salt, baking soda and spices. Add half of it to the molasses mixture and beat with the electric mixer on low speed to mix. Add the water and stir until smooth. Then mix in the second half of the flour mixture. Stir until smooth.

Drop rounded tablespoonfuls of the dough 4 inches apart onto an ungreased baking sheet. Insert the pointed end of a wooden skewer (popsicle stick) into each cookie with a twisting motion.

Bake on the rack in the center of the oven 10 to 12 minutes or until the cookies are a delicate brown; a slight dent shows when you touch the cookie lightly with a fingertip.

Remove the sheet from the oven and let it stand 1 minute. Then, with a wide spatula, carefully remove the lollypops to a wire rack to cool.

When the cookies are cool, decorate them as you like. One good way is to spread them with confectioners sugar mixed with a little milk until smooth and just thick enough to spread on the cookies. Use candies, raisins, tiny candy red hots, small gumdrops and chocolate pieces to make faces and flaked or shredded coconut for hair. Wonderful for a children's party or gifts to your friends. Makes about 24 large cookies.

ORANGE/COCONUT CRISPS

Use the orange juice as it comes from the can—just thaw

2 eggs
⅔ cup salad oil
1 cup sugar
¼ cup frozen orange juice
  concentrate, thawed

2½ cups sifted flour
2 teaspoons baking powder
½ teaspoon salt
1 cup packaged cookie
  coconut

Start heating the oven to 400°.

Beat the eggs with a fork or a wire whisk in a medium bowl. Stir in the salad oil and sugar and beat until the mixture thickens. Stir in the orange juice (do not dilute).

Sift the flour onto a square of waxed paper or into a bowl and then measure. Sift the measured flour with the baking powder and salt. Add with the coconut to the egg mixture. Stir to mix well.

Drop teaspoons of dough about 2 inches apart onto an ungreased baking sheet. Press each cookie flat with the bottom of a drinking glass, oiled lightly with salad oil and dipped in sugar. Dip the glass in the sugar before flattening each cookie. Bake on the rack in the center of the oven 8 to 10 minutes or until the cookies are a delicate brown; a slight dent shows when you touch the top lightly with a fingertip.

Remove the sheet from the oven and take the cookies from the baking sheet with a wide spatula. Spread them on a wire rack to cool. Makes about 36.

TWICE-AS GOOD COOKIES

Melted chocolate makes these chip cookies different

1 (6-ounce) package
  semisweet chocolate pieces
1 cup sifted flour
½ teaspoon baking soda
½ teaspoon salt
½ cup soft butter or regular
  margarine

½ cup sugar
1 egg
¼ cup warm water
½ cup chopped or broken
  walnuts

Melt ½ cup of the chocolate pieces in the top of the double boiler over hot, not boiling, water or in a small saucepan over low heat. Cool until lukewarm.

Sift the flour onto a square of waxed paper or into a bowl and then measure. Sift the measured flour with the baking soda and salt. Set aside.

Beat the butter, sugar and egg in the large bowl of the electric mixer, on medium speed, until the mixture is light and fluffy, or beat with a spoon.

Beat in the melted chocolate and warm water. Then beat in flour mixture on low speed just enough to mix, or mix in with a spoon.

Stir in the walnuts and the rest of the chocolate pieces with a spoon. Chill in the refrigerator at least 30 minutes.

Start heating the oven to 375°. Lightly grease a baking sheet with unsalted shortening or salad oil.

Drop rounded teaspoons of the dough onto the greased baking sheet about 3 inches apart. Bake on the rack in the center of the oven 10 to 12 minutes or until a slight dent shows when you touch the top lightly with a fingertip.

Remove the sheet from the oven and take the cookies from the baking sheet with a wide spatula. Spread them on a wire rack to cool. Makes 36.

Molded Cookies

If you have ever enjoyed modeling with clay, you'll love to make molded cookies. You shape the stiff dough with your hands, often into balls. To keep the dough from sticking to your hands, chill it thoroughly in the refrigerator. Then rub your hands lightly with flour or a little confectioners sugar before making the balls. You may have to flour or sugar your hands several times while shaping a batch of cookies.

Often recipes direct that you flatten the balls of dough after they are on the baking sheet. Sometimes you use a fork, sometimes the bottom of a glass, dipped in sugar. Then there are thumbprint cookies—you press a hollow in each cookie with your thumb, which you fill with goodies before or after baking. Some of the cookie balls flatten while they bake; some keep their shape. You'll find all kinds among our recipes.

SNACK TIME PEANUT COOKIES

For a snack that satisfies, serve these cookies with
glasses of cold milk, cups of hot cocoa or fruit juice

½ cup soft butter or regular margarine
½ cup peanut butter
½ cup sugar
½ cup brown sugar, firmly packed

1 egg
1¼ cups unsifted flour
½ teaspoon baking powder
¾ teaspoon baking soda
¼ teaspoon salt

In a medium bowl, beat the butter, peanut butter, white and brown sugars and the egg together until the mixture is light and fluffy.

Stir the flour, baking powder, baking soda and salt together in another medium bowl and then stir it into the peanut butter mixture. Chill the dough 1 hour, or until you can handle it easily.

Start heating the oven to 375°. Lightly grease a baking sheet with unsalted shortening or salad oil.

Shape the chilled dough into balls the size of large walnuts. Arrange them on the greased baking sheet about 3 inches apart. Dip a fork into flour and press it first one way and then the other to flatten each cookie and make a crisscross design.

Bake on the rack in the center of the oven until set, but not hard, or about 10 to 12 minutes. Remove from oven and spread cookies on rack to cool. Makes 36.

THUMBPRINT COOKIES

You make a hollow in the cookie balls with your
thumb before baking to fill with treats when the
cookies are cool

½ cup sifted confectioners sugar
1 cup soft butter or regular margarine
½ teaspoon salt

1 tablespoon vanilla
2 cups sifted flour
1 cup finely chopped or broken pecans

Sift the confectioners sugar and measure. Beat it, the butter, salt and vanilla together until fluffy.

Sift the flour onto a square of waxed paper or into a bowl and then measure. Stir the sifted flour and pecans into the confectioners sugar mixture. Mix well. Chill in the refrigerator at least an hour so dough will shape easily.

When you are ready to bake the cookies, start heating the oven to 350°.

Shape the chilled dough into small balls. Place them 3 inches apart on an ungreased baking sheet. Press a small hole in the center of each ball with your thumb tip.

Bake on the rack in the center of the oven about 15 minutes, or until lightly browned and set. Remove from oven and spread cookies on rack to cool. Makes 60 small cookies.

Refrigerator Cookies

Among cookies that were invented in American kitchens are the refrigerator cookies. They contain so much shortening that you have to chill them several hours before baking, which is how they got their name. The shortening makes refrigerator cookies especially crisp.

You shape the cookie dough into long rolls, wrap them in waxed paper, plastic wrap or aluminum foil and chill them in the refrigerator several hours or overnight. Then the shortening hardens and they're easy to slice and bake. If carefully wrapped so they won't dry out, you can keep the rolls of dough in the refrigerator 3 to 5 days. Then you can slice off and bake the cookies when you wish. Serve them warm from the oven—they're so good when freshly baked.

Or you can freeze the wrapped rolls of dough in the freezer and bake them any time within 6 months. When you're ready for some cookies, take the wrapped frozen dough from the freezer and leave it in the refrigerator for an hour, or on the kitchen counter 30 minutes. The rolls of dough will be just right for slicing. You will find many excellent refrigerator cookie dough rolls in the supermarket. All you have to do is slice and bake them.

Refrigerator cookies are thin and crisp. Remember that the thinner you slice them, the crisper they will be.

REFRIGERATOR SCOTCHIES

Shape the roll of refrigerator dough as big around
as you want your cookies—2½ inches is a good size

1 cup soft butter or regular margarine	2 eggs
½ cup white sugar	1½ teaspoons vanilla
½ cup brown sugar, firmly packed	2¾ cups sifted flour
	½ teaspoon baking soda
	1 teaspoon salt

Beat the butter, white and brown sugars, eggs and vanilla until fluffy and well mixed.

Sift the flour onto a square of waxed paper or into a bowl and then measure. Sift the measured flour with the baking soda and salt. Add about half of it to the shortening-sugar mixture and stir to mix well. Gradually add the rest of the flour mixture, working it into the dough with the hands. Mix thoroughly.

Press and shape the dough into a long smooth roll about 2½ inches in diameter. Wrap it tightly in waxed paper or aluminum foil and chill several hours or overnight.

When you are ready to bake some of the cookies, start heating the oven to 400°.

Remove the dough from the refrigerator, unwrap it and cut off thin (⅛-inch) slices—eight slices from an inch of dough! Use a knife with a thin, sharp blade for slicing so the cookie edges will be neat. Rewrap the unused dough and put it back in the refrigerator. The dough will keep 3 to 5 days.

Place the slices a little distance apart on an ungreased baking sheet and bake on the rack in the center of the oven 6 to 8 minutes, or until cookies are lightly browned.

Remove the sheet from the oven, lift the cookies from the baking sheet with a wide spatula and spread them on a wire rack to cool. This recipe will make about 75.

CHOCOLATE REFRIGERATOR COOKIES

Slices of chocolate and nuts—pretty, too, if you add fancy edges

1½ (1-ounce) squares
   unsweetened chocolate
½ cup soft butter or regular
   margarine
1 cup light brown sugar,
   firmly packed
1 egg

½ teaspoon vanilla
2 cups sifted flour
½ teaspoon baking power
¼ teaspoon baking soda
¼ teaspoon salt
3 tablespoons milk
½ cup finely chopped nuts

Put the chocolate in the top of the double boiler and melt over hot, not boiling, water or melt it in a small saucepan over low heat. Cool until lukewarm.

Beat the butter and brown sugar with the electric mixer on medium speed or with a spoon until light and fluffy. Add the egg, chocolate and vanilla. Beat to mix thoroughly.

Sift the flour onto a sheet of waxed paper and then measure. Sift the flour with the baking powder, baking soda and salt into a medium bowl. Add some of it to the chocolate mixture, then add a little of the milk. Beat on mixer's low speed or with a spoon after each addition. Keep on adding the flour mixture and milk, first one and then the other, until all of these ingredients are used.

Stir in the nuts. They must be chopped very fine so the chilled dough can be sliced easily.

Shape the dough in two smooth rolls with your hands —make them about 2½ inches in diameter. Wrap them tightly in aluminum foil or waxed paper, twisting the ends of the paper so they will stay in place. Chill several hours or overnight.

When ready to bake the cookies, start heating the oven to 400°. Unwrap the rolls of dough and cut each into thin slices with a sharp knife. Place the slices a little distance apart on an ungreased baking sheet.

Bake on the rack in the center of the oven 6 to 10 minutes.

Remove the sheet from the oven, lift the cookies from the baking sheet with a wide spatula and spread them on a wire rack to cool. Makes 46 to 48 cookies.

For a change

Fancy Edge Cookies: When you take the roll of dough from the refrigerator, sprinkle a sheet of waxed paper with little candies of many colors (nonpareils), chocolate shot (jimmies) or finely chopped nuts. Unwrap the roll of cookie dough and turn it around in these tiny candies to coat well. Then, slice and bake the cookies.

Rolled Cookies

Get out the rolling pin and cookie cutters before you start to make these cookies. They are a little more difficult to make than other cookies because you have to roll the dough, but this isn't hard if you chill the dough first and use the pastry cloth and stockinet-covered rolling pin. (Rub a little flour into the pastry cloth with your hand. It will disappear into the meshes in the cloth. Brush off any loose flour on the pastry cloth. Then roll the stockinet-covered rolling pin around on the pastry cloth.)

You can dress up rolled cookies in many ways. Just cutting them with various cookie cutters of many shapes gives them a different look. And you can sprinkle the unbaked cookie cutouts with sugar—white or colored —tiny candies or chopped nuts. Also you can spread the cooled, baked cookies with confectioners sugar icing —white or tinted with food color.

Bake these cookies only until they're light brown. Baking them longer will give you a tough, dry cookie.

EXTRA-GOOD SUGAR COOKIES

Sprinkle cookies with sugar before baking—they'll glisten

⅔ cup soft shortening
¾ cup sugar
1 egg
¾ teaspoon vanilla
¼ teaspoon almond extract

2 cups sifted flour
1½ teaspoons baking powder
¼ teaspoon salt
4 teaspoons milk

Beat the shortening and sugar together until light

310

and fluffy. Add the egg and beat to mix well. Add the vanilla and almond extracts. (You can use 1 teaspoon vanilla and omit the almond extract.) Mix thoroughly.

Sift the flour onto a square of waxed paper and then measure. Sift the measured flour with the baking powder and salt. Stir it into the sugar-shortening mixture along with the milk. Divide the dough in half and chill in the refrigerator 1 hour or until the dough is easy to handle.

Start heating the oven to 375°. Grease a baking sheet with unsalted shortening or salad oil.

Roll the dough, half of it at a time, from the center to the edge until it is ⅛ to ¼ inch thick. (The thinner you roll the dough, the crisper the cookies will be.) Cut with a 3- or 4-inch round cookie cutter.

Use a wide spatula to place the cookies ½ inch apart on the greased baking sheet.

Bake on the rack in the center of the oven 8 to 9 minutes, or until the cookies are light brown.

Remove the sheet from the oven at once and use a wide spatula to place the cookies on a wire cooling rack. Makes about 24 cookies.

For a change

Polka Dot Cookies: Dot the tops of cooled Extra-Good Sugar Cookies with dabs of chocolate frosting.

Painted Cookies: Stir ¼ teaspoon cold water into 1 egg yolk. Divide the egg yolk among 3 or 4 small custard cups and tint each part a different bright color with food color of red, green, yellow and pink. Stir to mix the food color and egg yolk. When cookies are ready to bake, paint a design on the top of each with the tinted egg yolk. Use a small, clean, pointed brush for each color. If the egg yolk thickens while standing, add a few drops of cold water and stir.

Cookies on Sticks: Arrange popsicle sticks or wooden skewers with pointed ends on a greased baking sheet and place a round of cookie dough on the pointed end of each skewer. Allow at least ½ inch between each cookie. Bake like Extra-Good Sugar Cookies. Remove the sheet from the oven and at once place a chocolate-coated candy mint on the center of each cookie. The candy will melt enough to stick to the cookie when it is cool. Use a wide spatula to place the cookies on wire racks to cool.

Funny Face Cookies: While Cookies on Sticks are hot, you can decorate them with chocolate pieces instead of mints to make the features of a funny face. Let Funny Face Cookies cool before handling them so that the decorations will stay on. Or frost the tops of the cooled cookies and decorate them with little candies and nuts.

CHOCOLATE PINKS

Flatter everyone by writing his name on the dark chocolate cookies

2 (1-ounce) squares
   unsweetened chocolate
¾ cup soft shortening
1 cup sugar
1 egg
¼ cup light corn syrup

2 cups sifted flour
¼ teaspoon salt
1 teaspoon baking soda
1 teaspoon ground cinnamon
Pink Icing (recipe follows)

Melt the chocolate in the top of the double boiler over hot, not boiling, water or in a saucepan over low heat. Cool until lukewarm.

Beat together the shortening, sugar and egg until light and fluffy. Stir in the chocolate and corn syrup.

Sift the flour onto a square of waxed paper or into a bowl and then measure. Sift the measured flour with the salt, baking soda and cinnamon into the chocolate mixture. Beat to mix well.

Divide the dough into three parts and chill it in the refrigerator at least 1 hour.

When you are ready to bake the cookies, start heating the oven to 350°.

Place ⅓ of the dough on a lightly floured pastry cloth. Keep the rest of the dough in the refrigerator until you are ready to roll it.

Roll the dough from the center to the edge ⅛ inch thick and cut it with a lightly floured cookie cutter. To avoid stretching the cookie cutouts, use a wide spatula to place them ½ inch apart on an ungreased baking sheet.

Bake on the rack in the center of the oven 10 to 12 minutes.

312

Remove the sheet from the oven and take the cookies from the baking sheet with a wide spatula. Spread them on a wire rack to cool.

Roll, cut and bake the remaining two parts of the dough and the scraps, gathered together, in the same way.

When the cookies are cool, spread their tops with a creamy confectioners sugar icing, tinted pink. Makes about 30 to 36.

PINK ICING

1 cup sifted confectioners sugar
¼ teaspoon salt
½ teaspoon vanilla

1 to 1½ tablespoons light cream or water
Red food color

Sift the confectioners sugar onto a square of waxed paper or into a bowl and then measure. Put the measured powdered sugar, salt and vanilla in a small bowl. Add the cream or water and mix well with a spoon or with the electric mixer on low speed to make an icing that you can spread.

Tint the frosting pink with a few drops of red food color.

Spread it on the cookies with a spatula. Or make Pink Icing a little thicker, this way—use only about ¾ tablespoon of cold water or 1 tablespoon cream. Write names on the cookies with a toothpick dipped in the icing. Nice for a party.

GRANDMA'S MOLASSES COOKIES

They taste like molasses cookies Grandma used to make but they're topped with a sweet, shiny Sugar Glaze

4 cups sifted flour
1 teaspoon baking soda
½ teaspoon baking powder
1 teaspoon salt
2 teaspoons ground ginger

½ cup soft shortening
¾ cup sugar
¾ cup light molasses
½ cup buttermilk
Sugar Glaze (recipe follows)

Sift the flour onto a square of waxed paper and then measure. Sift the measured flour with the baking soda, baking powder, salt and ginger into a medium bowl. Set aside.

Beat the shortening in a large bowl with the electric mixer on medium speed or with a spoon until light and fluffy. Gradually add the sugar and beat until very fluffy.

Stir in a little of the flour mixture, then a little molasses and buttermilk. Keep adding the flour and the molasses and milk until you have used all of them. Start and end the mixing by adding some of the flour. Mix well.

Divide the dough into four parts. Cover and chill it at least 4 hours or overnight.

When you are ready to bake the cookies, start heating the oven to 400°. Lightly grease a baking sheet with unsalted shortening or salad oil.

Roll out ¼ of the dough at a time from the center to the edge to ¼-inch thickness if you want fat, soft cookies, or to ⅛-inch thickness if you want thinner, more crisp cookies. Use a floured cutter to make the cutouts. To avoid stretching the cutouts, use a wide spatula to place them about ½ inch apart on the baking sheet.

Bake on the rack in the center of the oven 7 to 10 minutes.

Remove the sheet from the oven and take the cookies from the baking sheet with a wide spatula. Spread them on a wire rack to cool. When partly cooled, spread with Sugar Glaze. Makes about 48 cookies.

SUGAR GLAZE

Put 2 cups sifted confectioners sugar and 2 to 3 tablespoons milk in a medium bowl. Stir until smooth. Spread on tops of Grandma's Molasses Cookies while they are slightly warm.

For a change

Gingerbread Boys: Cut the dough for Grandma's Molasses Cookies, rolled ¼ inch thick, with a floured gingerbread-boy cutter. Lift the cutouts with a wide spatula or pancake turner onto a lightly greased baking sheet. Press raisins into the dough for the eyes, nose, a mouth with a smile and shoe and cuff buttons. Use bits snipped from red or green gumdrops with scissors for coat buttons. Bake like Grandma's Molasses Cookies. You can move the legs and arms of the gingerbread boys on the baking sheet, before baking, to make them look as if they're dancing or running.

GIANT RAISIN COOKIES

Man-sized cookies big enough to satisfy the hungriest cookie eaters. There's a hint of orange flavor

½ cup raisins	4 cups sifted flour
1½ cups soft shortening	2 teaspoons salt
1½ cups sugar	1½ teaspoons baking powder
2 large eggs	⅓ cup milk
2 teaspoons vanilla	Sugar (for tops)
1 teaspoon grated orange peel	Raisins (for tops)

Cut the raisins coarsely with scissors.

Beat the shortening and sugar together in a large bowl with the electric mixer on medium speed or with a spoon until fluffy. Add the eggs, vanilla and orange peel. Beat well.

Sift the flour onto a square of waxed paper and then measure. Sift the measured flour with the salt and baking powder. Stir a little of the flour into the shortening-sugar mixture, then stir in a little milk. Mix well. Do this until all the flour and milk are used.

Stir in the cut-up raisins.

Divide the dough into three parts and chill 1 hour or longer in the refrigerator.

Start heating the oven to 375°. Grease a baking sheet with unsalted shortening or salad oil.

Roll one part of the dough at a time from the center to the edge on a lightly floured surface until a little less than ¼ inch thick.

Cut cookies by cutting around an empty 1-pound coffee can or its lid with a small knife. Place them 1 inch apart on greased baking sheet.

Sprinkle the circles of dough with sugar. Cut the raisins in strips with scissors. Press the raisins into the cookies to make initials or names.

Bake on the rack in the center of the oven 10 to 12 minutes, or until a light brown.

Remove the sheet from the oven and lift the cookies from the baking sheet with a wide spatula. Place them on a wire rack to cool. Store them in a jar with a loose lid. Makes 35.

Cookie Confections

Here are the easiest of all cookies to make. You don't bake them. So get out a saucepan, stirring spoon and your measuring tools and stir up a batch of cookies in a jiffy. We predict you'll have beginner's luck with them—that means *good* luck.

BUTTERSCOTCH CRUNCHIES

You can make these crunchy cookies with any ready-to-eat cereal flakes. So look in your cupboard and take your pick

2 (6-ounce) packages butterscotch pieces

½ cup peanut butter
6 cups corn flakes

In a large saucepan cook and stir butterscotch pieces and peanut butter over medium heat until the mixture melts. Remove from the heat and stir in the corn flakes with a spoon. Mix well.

Drop teaspoonfuls of the mixture onto a sheet of waxed paper. Let set. Makes 36.

NO-BAKE CHOCOLATE COOKIES

Stir these cookies up in a jiffy when something to nibble is in order. Let your guests help you make them

2 cups sugar
½ cup milk
1 stick butter or regular margarine (¼ pound)
3 tablespoons cocoa
1 teaspoon salt

3 cups quick-cooking rolled oats
1 teaspoon vanilla
½ cup broken walnuts
1 cup flaked coconut

Put the sugar, milk, butter, cocoa and salt in a large saucepan and bring to a boil. Remove from the heat and stir in the rolled oats, vanilla, nuts and coconut.

Drop from a teaspoon onto waxed paper to make 48.

SAUCEPAN PEANUT COOKIES

Top favorites of schoolboys, fathers and new cooks.
No wonder—use whatever cereal flakes you have

1 cup light corn syrup   1½ cups peanut butter
1 cup sugar   4 cups cereal flakes

Mix the corn syrup and sugar in a medium saucepan. Bring the mixture to a full boil. Remove from the heat and stir in the peanut butter and cereal flakes. Mix well.

Drop heaping teaspoonfuls onto a buttered baking sheet. Makes 48.

Cookies for Special Occasions

ONCE YOU'VE baked a variety of cookies from recipes in this cookbook, you'll want to choose the kinds you like but for different occasions. We list suggestions for you to consider to help you select a recipe to meet a special need.

Many cookies are exceptionally versatile and suitable for different occasions. For instance, some of those that originated in faraway places frequently are traditionals on the Christmas cookie tray but are also good travelers in lunchboxes. Children, of course, like just about all cookies, although those in our junior cookie section (see Cookies Children Will Love to Make in Index) and some of the cookie confections are probably most popular with them.

We based our selections primarily on the reactions of our taste-testers—men, women and children—and what women who contributed their favorite recipes to this cookbook told us about them. Many superior recipes in this book do not appear on our lists—these are merely suggested "starters."

(See Index for Recipes)
DAINTY HOSTESS COOKIES

Cheesecake Squares
Cheese Pie-Bar Cookies
Chess Pie-Bars
Chocolate Bonbon Cookies
Chocolate Cookie
  Sandwiches
French Chocolate Pie-
  Squares

Grapefruit Sugar Cookies
Holiday Party Kisses
Jam/Cheese Cookie Tarts
Jeweled Meringues
Lemon/Coconut Squares
Meringue-Topped Cookies
Mocha Balls
Molasses/Almond Cookies

318

Nut Butter Cookies
Pumpkin Pie-Squares
Ribbon Cookies
Royal Crowns

Spritz Chocolate Sandwiches
Swirls
Walnut Lace Cookies
Wild Rose Cookies

COMPANY AND COFFEE PARTY SPECIALS

Almond Butterballs
Butter Crispies
Chocolate Meringue Bars
Chocolate/Orange Bars
Date-Filled Oat Cookies
English Tea Squares
French Bars
Frosted Carrot Bars

Frosted Ginger Creams
Hampshire Hermits
Hard-Cooked Egg Cookies
Mom's Fortune Cookies
New Moons
Sesame Wafers
Southern Praline Bars

CHRISTMAS COOKIE FAVORITES

Brazil Nut Bars
Christmas Drop Cookies
Citrus/Nut Drops
Easy Cane Cookies
French Bars
Frosted Yule Logs
Fruitcake Squares
Gingerbread Christmas
    Cookies

Mincemeat/Cheese Cookies
Pretzel Cookies
Rich Anise Cookies
Spiced Christmas Cookies
Star Cookies
White Christmas Cookies

COOKIES FROM FARAWAY PLACES

Chinese Almond Cookies
Danish Raisin Cookies
Finnish Shortbread Cookies
Finnish Star Cookies
Florentines
Golden Coconut Diamonds
Greek Easter Cookies
Lebkuchen
Mexican Fiesta Balls

Orange Wreaths
Pepparkakor
Pepper Nuts
Sandbakelser
Spanish Wedding Cakes
Springerle
Swedish Almond Shortbread
Viennese Crescents

COOKIES FOR LUNCHBOXES

Chocolate Chip Bars
Chocolate Potato Cookies
Cornmeal Cookies
Fruity Gumdrop Cookies
Honeyed Yo-Yos

Indian Bars
Jeweled Oatmeal Drops
Orange/Carrot Cookies
Raisin-Filled Cookies
Rookie Cookies

GOOD SELLERS AT BAZAARS

Candy-Top Brownies
Chocolate Sandwich
  Treasures
Cocoa Bars
Cry Baby Cookies
Date-Filled Oat Cookies
Jumbo Sugar Cookies

Marshmallow/Cherry Bars
Nut and Fruit Bars
Oatmeal/Molasses Cookies
Snickerdoodles
Spicy Apple Bars
Two-Tone Jumbles

COOKIES THAT MAIL WELL

Applesauce Fudgies
Brownies for a Crowd
California Fig Cookies
Circle Ranch Oat Cookies
Fruit Bars
Glazed Apple Cookies
Grandma's Raisin Cookies

Hampshire Hermits
Multi-Fruited Drops
Oatmeal Chocolate Bars
Oregon Date Surprises
Pumpkin Cookies
Raisin/Ketchup Cookies
Two-Tone Jumbles

CHILDREN'S FAVORITES—TO EAT

Chocolate/Coconut Bars
Chocolate Marshmallow
  Cakelets
Chocolate/Peanut
  Crunchers
Date 'Mallow Chews

Double Treat Cookies
Grandma's Soft Sugar
  Cookies
Peanut Candy-Bar Cookies
Potpourri Cookies
Soft Chocolate Chippers

CHILDREN'S FAVORITES—TO MAKE

Butterscotch Crunchies
Candy Bar Cookies
Chocolate/Nut Drops
Chocolate Oatsies
Chocolate/Peanut Clusters
Chocolate/Peanut
  Crunchers
Chocolate Pinks
Chocolate Refrigerator
  Cookies
Date Logs
Date/Nut Macaroons
Extra-Good Sugar Cookies
Fudge Brownies
Giant Raisin Cookies
Grandma's Molasses
  Cookies

Jiffy Candy Cookies
Magic Party Squares
Molasses Lollypop Cookies
No-Bake Chocolate Cookies
Orange/Coconut Crisps
Peanut Butter Drops
Potato Chip Cookies
Refrigerator Scotchies
Rich Butterscotch Bars
Rocky Road Fudge Bars
Saucepan Peanut Cookies
Snack Time Peanut Cookies
Thumbprint Cookies
Twice-as-Good Cookies

Index

321

325